Substance in International Tax Law

Series on International Taxation

VOLUME 83

Series Editors

Prof. Ruth Mason, University of Virginia School of Law
Prof. Dr Ekkehart Reimer, University of Heidelberg

Introduction & Contents

The Series on International Taxation deals with a wide variety of topics in the global tax arena. The authors include many of the field's leading experts as well as talented newcomers. Their expert views and incisive commentary have proven highly useful to practitioners and academics alike.

Objective

The volumes published in this series are aimed at offering high-quality analytical information and practical solutions to international tax practitioners.

Readership

Practitioners, academics and policy makers in international tax law.

Frequency of Publication

2-3 new volumes published each year.

The titles published in this series are listed at the end of this volume.

Substance in International Tax Law

DEMPE Approach, Substantial Activity Requirement and Beneficial Ownership

Florian Navisotschnigg

Wolters Kluwer

Published by:
Kluwer Law International B.V.
PO Box 316
2400 AH Alphen aan den Rijn
The Netherlands
E-mail: lrs-sales@wolterskluwer.com
Website: www.wolterskluwer.com/en/solutions/kluwerlawinternational

Sold and distributed by:
Wolters Kluwer Legal & Regulatory U.S.
7201 McKinney Circle
Frederick, MD 21704
United States of America
E-mail: customer.service@wolterskluwer.com

ISBN 978-94-035-4895-1

e-Book: ISBN 978-94-035-4905-7
web-PDF: ISBN 978-94-035-4915-6

Table of Contents

CHAPTER 1

Setting the Scene

1.1 THE MEANING OF SUBSTANCE IN INTERNATIONAL TAX LAW

The term 'substance' has different dimensions in international tax law.[1] From a countries' perspective, it may refer to the extent a (physical)[2] presence is needed in a jurisdiction so that a jurisdiction is granted a right to tax under the OECD Model Convention (OECD MC) (jurisdiction to tax).[3] This is true for Article 7 OECD MC according to which business profits shall only be taxed in the residence state unless an enterprise carries on business in the other contracting state through a permanent establishment (PE; Article 5 OECD MC) situated therein. Therefore, the source state's taxing right in this case depends on whether there is enough substance in its jurisdiction so that the PE threshold is fulfilled. What is more, the extent of the source state's taxing right is also determined by the substance present in its jurisdiction because it is only granted a right to tax the profits that can be attributed to a PE, and the amount of attributable profits depends on the substance that the PE has.

From the taxpayers' perspective, substance may be seen as the requirements that have to be met for sustaining a chosen tax planning structure. That is, depending on the substance present in a particular structure, specific favourable rules may be applicable or a certain amount of profit may be attributable to a company. However, in the case that a structure lacks the necessary substance, tax administrations may deny tax (treaty) benefits or even disregard certain transactions.[4]

1. *See also Larking*, A Matter of Substance, TNI 2018, 329 (329).
2. The current OECD Model Convention still requires a physical presence in a country in order to tax the business profits of a non-resident company there; however, *see also* the current programme of work to develop new nexus rules in *OECD*, Programme of Work to Develop a Consensus Solution to the Tax Challenges Arising from the Digitalisation of the Economy (2019) Mn 39f.
3. *See also OECD*, Addressing Base Erosion and Profit Shifting (2013) 33ff.
4. *See also Petruzzi/Myzithra*, Substance in Transfer Pricing in a Post-BEPS World and Beyond..., ITPJ 2020, 430 (431).

Furthermore, pressure from the international community narrows the possibilities of individual countries to even offer certain tax benefits in the first place. Accordingly, states may only introduce or maintain certain preferential tax regimes when such regimes require a certain degree of substance on the side of the taxpayer. Otherwise, such regimes would be considered as harmful tax competition, and other countries might adopt effective countermeasures against them.[5]

Keeping that in mind, legislators have to decide how they want to design a specific tax provision. In general, it is usually distinguished between tax provisions that tie to the (legal) form and tax provisions that tie to the (economic) substance of an action.[6] That is, some tax provisions use private law concepts and connect tax consequences to them, whereas others use own tax concepts that are independent from private law. For example, in the case of dual-resident companies, 'the competent authorities of the Contracting States shall endeavour to determine by mutual agreement the Contracting State of which such person shall be deemed to be a resident for the purposes of the Convention, having regard to its place of effective management, [or] the place where it is incorporated' (Article 4 para 3 OECD MC 2017). Therefore, competent authorities should consider a formal (private law) criterion (i.e., the place where the company is incorporated) as well as a substance (tax law) criterion (i.e., the place where the company is effectively managed) when determining the residence state of a company.

In the same vein, it is generally distinguished between legal ownership and economic ownership. While the legal owner is the person who holds the legal title to a good under private law, the economic owner[7] is the person who has the right to the economic benefits (and burdens) associated with the ownership of the asset.

When a provision does not tie to the form but rather to the substance of an action - whether this is the case has to be determined by means of interpretation of the provision in question -[8] there are essentially two different ways how the substance

5. *See* already *OECD*, Harmful Tax Competition: An Emerging Global Issue (1998) Mn 28: 'Countries should remain free to design their own tax systems as long as they abide by internationally accepted standards in doing so.'
6. *See Zimmer*, General Report, in *IFA* (Ed.), Cahiers de droit fiscal international, Vol. 87a Form and substance in tax law (2002) 19 (23f): 'Form (or legal form) refers to the concepts described by terms used in tax statutes, first and foremost terms used to describe the legal conditions of a tax rule. Often these terms are also used in private law statutes to describe private law concepts [...] "Form" also refers to transactions carried out in accordance with the legal conditions set in the tax rule in question. [...] Substance refers to the economic content of the transaction or legal relation (often referred to as economic substance)'; likewise, it is often distinguished between legal substance and economic substance, *see Zimmer* in *IFA* 24f: 'The concept of legal substance most often refers to the characterisation which emerges from a close study of the rights and obligations in a legal relation, for instance whether a transaction should be characterised as a sale or a lease. The main function of the concept of legal substance is to point out that sham or simulation transactions and wrong legal characterisations by the taxpayer will be disregarded for tax purposes.'
7. Based on the definition contained in *OECD*, Transfer Pricing and Intangibles: Scope of the OECD Project (2011) Mn 25 and *OECD*, 2010 Report on the Attribution of Profits to Permanent Establishments (2010) Mn 14 FN 4; *see also* sec. 2.4.3 on economic ownership.
8. *See Gassner*, Austria, in *IFA* (Ed.), Cahiers de droit fiscal international, Vol. 87a Form and substance in tax law (2002) 119 (124).

requirement can be formulated:[9] On the one hand, concrete criteria can be used for which fulfilment can be objectively assessed by a taxpayer (quantitative approach). For example, a provision may require a company to have a certain number of full-time employees to make use of favourable tax treatment. On the other hand, a provision can contain abstract - albeit very detailed - criteria that may only provide indications to assess when the substance requirement is fulfilled (qualitative approach). In this case, the provision would not stipulate a certain number of full-time employees but would state, for example, that the employees of a company have to perform important functions. Indeed, this approach is characterized by the use of words such as 'effective', 'significant', 'important', or 'core'.[10]

Both approaches have their strengths and weaknesses.[11] In general, the quantitative approach provides greater legal certainty and is easier to apply in practice. On the downside, it may not do justice to each individual case. For example, one company may need five full-time employees for a specific activity, whereas another company may only need three full-time employees for the same activity. Let us assume a country has a special tax regime for this activity in place that requires a company to have four full-time employees to benefit from it. In this case, the latter company would have to hire another full-time employee to fulfil the substance requirement although, from a business perspective, it would not need another employee to properly conduct its activity. Therefore, the quantitative approach may even lead to artificial constructions that are only adopted to obtain tax benefits.[12] Conversely, the qualitative approach may be more complex in its practical application but, on the other hand, provide better solutions for each individual case.

The redefinition of substance in international tax law played a major role in the OECD's Base Erosion and Profit Shifting Project (BEPS Project). The OECD approached the issue of substance from the same viewpoints as presented above: What substance is necessary in a jurisdiction for it to be granted a right to tax; what substance is necessary to sustain certain corporate tax planning structures; and what is the necessary substance that preferential tax regimes have to require from taxpayers to prevent harmful tax competition.[13] For these purposes, the OECD used both qualitative and quantitative approaches to define substance requirements. However, the issue of substance in the BEPS Project cannot be dealt with exhaustively without discussing the role of intangibles in this context.

9. *See Monsenego*, The Substance Requirement in the OECD Transfer Pricing Guidelines: What Is the Substance of the Substance Requirement?, ITPJ 2014, 9 (20); *Larking*, TNI 2018, 329.
10. *See Larking*, TNI 2018, 329; *see also* the examples in *Monsenego*, ITPJ 2014, 21.
11. *See also Larking*, TNI 2018, 329.
12. *See also Larking*, TNI 2018, 329f, who provides the old Belgian coordination regime as an example for this phenomenon. This regime required a minimum of ten full-time employees to obtain tax benefits. However, since the rules did not stipulate what kind of employees are necessary, 'you had the absurd scenario [...] [that companies employed] one local manager, a secretary, and eight full-time cleaners'.
13. *See* sec. 1.3.

1.2 CENTRAL IMPORTANCE OF INTANGIBLES IN THE OECD BEPS PROJECT

The significance of intangibles for the business of multinational enterprises (MNEs) has increased dramatically over the last decades.[14] A study found that, in 2015, intangible assets accounted for 87% of the market value of the S&P 500 compared to only 17% back in 1975.[15] Nowadays, intangibles are undoubtedly an important - or even the main - value driver for MNEs.[16] Particularly MNEs with digitalized business models are heavily reliant on intangibles.[17]

Intangibles also play an important role in the area of tax planning due to their high mobility and the (often) high-profit potential attached to them. MNEs may be motivated to transfer intangibles to companies resident in jurisdictions that do not tax received royalties or that offer a preferential tax treatment for received royalties.[18] Rights in the intangibles are then licensed to (associated) operating companies resident in different (high tax) jurisdictions that use them in their operating business. In return, the (associated) operating companies pay royalties that (regularly)[19] reduce their taxable profits and, accordingly, their tax burden. Withholding taxes on such royalties may be avoided by means of double taxation conventions (DTCs).[20] As a result, royalties flow untaxed from the source country to the residence country where they are potentially also not taxed.[21]

All of these above-mentioned planning steps can be observed in the notorious tax avoidance scheme dubbed as 'Double Irish with a Dutch Sandwich'.[22] Extensive media coverage on how MNEs were able to use this scheme to achieve effective corporate tax

14. *See also Dziwiński/Peng*, Introduction to the post-BEPS transfer-pricing aspects of intangibles, in *Lang/Storck/Petruzzi/Risse* (Eds), Transfer Pricing and Intangibles: Current Developments, Relevant Issues and Possible Solutions (2019) 3 (4f).
15. *Ocean Tomo*, Annual Study of Intangible Asset Market Value (available at http://www.oceantomo.com/2015/03/04/2015-intangible-asset-market-value-study/).
16. For more details, *see Bakker/De Baets/Mazio/Szotek*, Increasing Importance of IP Rights, in *Verlinden/Bakker* (Eds), Mastering the IP Life Cycle from a Legal, Tax and Accounting Perspective (2018) 3 (3ff).
17. *OECD*, Addressing the Tax Challenges of the Digital Economy - Action 1: 2015 Final Report (2015) Mn 2 and 151; *OECD*, Tax Challenges Arising from Digitalisation - Interim Report 2018 (2018) Mn 34 and 135ff.
18. *See Fehling/Schmid*, BEPS und die EU: Was ist die 'europäische Dimension' von BEPS? - Das Beispiel grenzüberschreitender Lizenzzahlungen, IStR 2015, 493 (493f).
19. As a countermeasure to excessive royalty payments, some states (e.g., Germany) have introduced royalties barrier rules into their domestic law; *see Kramer*, Germany's New Royalties Barrier Rule: Preventing Tax Evasion By Limiting Deductibility in Specified Cases, TNI 2017, 879 (879ff).
20. According to Art. 12(1) OECD MC, royalties shall only be taxable in the residence state; in the EU, withholding taxes on royalties may be avoided by means of the Interest and Royalties Directive (Council Directive 2003/49/EC of 3 June 2003 on a common system of taxation applicable to interest and royalty payments made between associated companies of different Member States, L 157/49).
21. *OECD*, Addressing Base Erosion and Profit Shifting (2013) 73; *see also Kaul*, Der Nexus-Ansatz: Auswirkungen auf IP-Boxen und Alternativansätze (2018) 1.
22. For more details, *see Pinkernell*, Ein Musterfall zur Internationalen Steuerminimierung durch US-Konzerne, StuW 2012, 369 (369ff); *see also OECD*, Addressing Base Erosion and Profit Shifting (2013) 74ff.

rates in the single digits raised public awareness for this subject matter.[23] This led to a situation 'in which citizens have become more sensitive to tax fairness issues'.[24] As a result, the issue gained momentum on the international level[25] and prompted the OECD to launch the BEPS Project.[26]

Intangibles played the central role in many of the undesired tax planning structures that the OECD wanted to remedy.[27] Against this background, it can be said that '"[i]ntangibles" are the fundament of the "BEPS" project [...] and, in many respects, were the catalyst for it'.[28]

While substance requirements concerning intangibles were one of the top priorities in the BEPS Project, the OECD also dealt with the issue of substance in other fields. However, it is fair to say that, from all of the substance requirements that the BEPS Project brought along, the substance requirements with regard to intangibles are the most advanced. Therefore, this thesis will focus on these substance requirements.

1.3 SUBSTANCE IN THE OECD BEPS PROJECT

1.3.1 Background

In its initial report on the phenomena of BEPS, the OECD acknowledged that the 'current international tax standards may not have kept pace with changes in global business practices, in particular in the area of intangibles [...]'.[29] Accordingly, '[d]omestic rules for international taxation and internationally agreed standards are still grounded in an economic environment characterised by a lower degree of economic integration across borders, rather than today's environment of global taxpayers, characterised by the increasing importance of intellectual property as a value-driver and by constant developments of information and communication technologies'.[30] Consequently, the OECD committed itself to deliver a 'global and comprehensive action plan based on in-depth analysis of the identified pressure areas with a view to provide concrete solutions to realign international standards with the current global

23. *See*, for example, the article in the *New York Times* by *Duhigg/Kocieniewski*, How Apple Sidesteps Billions in Taxes (April 28, 2012); *see also* the media reports mentioned in *OECD*, Addressing Base Erosion and Profit Shifting (2013) 13.
24. *OECD*, Action Plan on Base Erosion and Profit Shifting (2013) 8.
25. *G20*, Leaders Declaration, Los Cabos, Mexico (2012) Mn 48: 'We reiterate the need to prevent base erosion and profit shifting and we will follow with attention the ongoing work of the OECD in this area.'
26. *OECD*, Action Plan on Base Erosion and Profit Shifting (2013) 10f: 'Inaction in this area would likely result in [...] the replacement of the current consensus-based framework by unilateral measures, which could lead to global tax chaos [...].'
27. Two out of three examples provided in the BEPS Action Plan for MNEs' tax planning structures and the issues they raise concern intangibles, *see OECD*, Action Plan on Base Erosion and Profit Shifting (2013) 73ff.
28. *Wilkie*, Transfer Pricing Aspects of Intangibles: The License Model, in *Lang/Storck/Petruzzi* (Eds), Transfer Pricing in a Post-BEPS World (2016) 61 (64).
29. *OECD*, Addressing Base Erosion and Profit Shifting (2013) 7.
30. *OECD*, Addressing Base Erosion and Profit Shifting (2013) 5.

business environment'.[31] Furthermore, the OECD stressed that '[t]he main purpose of that plan would be to provide countries with instruments, domestic and international, aiming at better aligning rights to tax with real economic activity'.[32]

Subsequently, the OECD released its Action Plan on Base Erosion and Profit Shifting (BEPS Action Plan).[33] Therein, the OECD formulated 15 Actions (BEPS Actions) that need to be implemented in order to address the weaknesses in the current tax framework.[34] These actions were based on three fundamental pillars: Coherence, Substance and Transparency.[35] Concerning the substance pillar, the aim was to realign taxation with the relevant substance.[36] The BEPS Actions specifically dedicated to achieve this goal were BEPS Action 6 ('Prevent treaty abuse'), BEPS Action 7 ('Prevent the artificial avoidance of PE status'), and BEPS Actions 8-10 ('Assure that transfer pricing outcomes are in line with value creation').[37] Additionally, some parts of other BEPS Actions may also be of importance in this area, for example, parts of BEPS Action 3 ('Strengthen CFC rules') or parts of BEPS Action 5.[38]

Regarding substance requirements for intangibles, the BEPS Actions that are particularly important are BEPS Action 5 ('Counter harmful tax practices more effectively, taking into account transparency and substance') and BEPS Action 8 ('Intangibles').[39] However, both of these BEPS Actions stipulate substance requirements in different areas: BEPS Action 5 concerns substance in the area of harmful tax practices (i.e., what is the necessary substance to offer certain tax benefits to intangibles), whereas BEPS Action 8 concerns substance in the area of transfer pricing (i.e., what substance is necessary to sustain certain corporate tax planning structures with intangibles).[40] These two BEPS Actions will be discussed in more detail below. Since the substance requirements of BEPS Action 8 have to be applied before the substance requirements of BEPS Action 5, BEPS Action 8 will be discussed first.

1.3.2 Substance in the Area of Transfer Pricing: DEMPE Approach (BEPS Action 8)

In its BEPS Action Plan, the OECD stated that transfer pricing and the enforcement of the arm's-length principle are a major BEPS issue because MNEs 'have been able to use

31. *OECD*, Addressing Base Erosion and Profit Shifting (2013) 9.
32. *OECD*, Addressing Base Erosion and Profit Shifting (2013) 8 and 51.
33. *OECD*, Action Plan on Base Erosion and Profit Shifting (2013); *see also Pinkernell*, OECD-Aktionsplan gegen internationale Gewinnverlagerung und Aushöhlung der Bemessungsgrundlagen (BEPS-Projekt), FR 2013, 737 (737ff).
34. *OECD*, Action Plan on Base Erosion and Profit Shifting (2013) 14ff.
35. *OECD*, Action Plan on Base Erosion and Profit Shifting (2013) 13f.
36. *OECD*, Action Plan on Base Erosion and Profit Shifting (2013) 13.
37. *OECD*, BEPS Frequently Asked Questions (2013) 3; *see also OECD*, Action Plan on Base Erosion and Profit Shifting (2013) 18ff.
38. *See also Danon*, Will nexus based patent boxes be internationally safe?, ASA 2015, 171 (181).
39. *See also Matteotti/Roth*, The OECD's Modified Nexus Approach for Patent Boxes – Is BEPS leading towards coherence or distortion in taxing income from intellectual property?, ASA 2014/2015, 755 (759); *Hinny*, Steuerliche Behandlung von Immaterialgüterrechten gemäss Unternehmenssteuerreform III, IFF 2016, 192 (196 and 214).
40. The classification in 'Transfer Pricing', 'Harmful Tax Practices' and later on 'Tax Treaties' for Beneficial Ownership follows the classification the OECD used in *OECD*, Action Plan on Base Erosion and Profit Shifting (2013) 48.

and/or misapply those rules to separate income from the economic activities that produce that income and to shift it into low-tax environments'.[41] Therefore, 'the rules should be improved in order to put more emphasis on value creation in highly integrated groups, tackling the use of intangibles [BEPS Action 8], risks, capital [BEPS Action 9] and other high-risk transactions [BEPS Action 10] to shift profits'.[42] Furthermore, the OECD even mentioned the possibility of introducing special measures that go beyond the arm's-length principle to address shortcomings in the realm of transfer pricing.[43]

The scope of BEPS Action 8 involved:[44]

(i) adopting a broad and clearly delineated definition of intangibles;
(ii) ensuring that profits associated with the transfer and use of intangibles are appropriately allocated in accordance with (rather than divorced from) value creation;
(iii) developing transfer pricing rules or special measures for transfers of hard-to-value intangibles; and
(iv) updating the guidance on cost contribution arrangements.

From a substance perspective, point (ii) that deals with the allocation of income that results from the exploitation of intangibles (so-called intangible-related returns) is the most relevant. It concerns the issue of how and to whom intangible-related returns should be allocated. The OECD's goal was to align the allocation of intangible-related returns - and, in the end, their taxation - with value creation (value creation as substance).[45] To this end, it introduced a new concept to allocate intangible-related returns between associated enterprises with BEPS Action 8, the so-called DEMPE Approach (acronym for the different stages in the life cycle of an intangible - development, enhancement, maintenance, protection, and exploitation [DEMPE]).[46] Accordingly, members of an MNE have to be compensated 'based on the value they create through functions performed, assets used and risks assumed in the [DEMPE] of intangibles'.[47]

41. *OECD*, Action Plan on Base Erosion and Profit Shifting (2013) 19.
42. *OECD*, Action Plan on Base Erosion and Profit Shifting (2013) 14; other BEPS Actions that have a connection to transfer pricing are BEPS Actions 1, 4, 7, 13, and 14, *see Collier/Andrus*, Transfer Pricing and the Arm's Length Principle After BEPS (2017) Mn 6.02 and *Naumann/Groß*, Verrechnungspreisaspekte immaterieller Werte - der OECD-Bericht zu Maßnahme 8 des BEPS Action Plan, IStR 2014, 906 (906); against this background, it is fair to say that transfer pricing is at the heart of the BEPS Project, *see Kofler*, The BEPS Action Plan and Transfer Pricing: The Arm's Length Standard Under Pressure?, BTR 2013, 646 (649).
43. *OECD*, Action Plan on Base Erosion and Profit Shifting (2013) 20; nevertheless, the OECD wanted to retain the arm's-length principle rather than replace it with an alternative income allocation system (e.g., formulary apportionment) because of the 'practical difficulties associated with agreeing to and implementing the details of a new system consistently across all countries'.
44. *See OECD*, Action Plan on Base Erosion and Profit Shifting (2013) 20.
45. Already recognizable from the title of the BEPS Actions 8-10, *OECD*, Aligning Transfer Pricing Outcomes with Value Creation - Actions 8-10: 2015 Final Reports (2015).
46. *OECD*, Aligning Transfer Pricing Outcomes with Value Creation - Actions 8-10: 2015 Final Reports (2015) 73ff.
47. *OECD*, Aligning Transfer Pricing Outcomes with Value Creation - Actions 8-10: 2015 Final Reports (2015) 63.

Furthermore, BEPS Action 9 ('Risks and capital') also plays a role in the allocation of intangible-related returns as its aim is to 'ensure that inappropriate returns will not accrue to an entity solely because it has contractually assumed risks or has provided capital'.[48] Additionally, BEPS Action 10 ('Other high-risk transactions') may also be important since it clarifies the circumstances when a transaction can be recharacterized and when the profit split method is the most appropriate transfer pricing method (particularly important in the context of global value chains).[49]

In a first step, it has to be determined to whom and to what extent returns from an intangible should be allocated according to the DEMPE Approach (BEPS Action 8). Afterwards, BEPS Action 5 stipulates the requirements under which the allocated returns may be subject to preferential taxation.[50]

1.3.3 Substance in the Area of Harmful Tax Practices: Substantial Activity Requirement (BEPS Action 5)

The increasing number of jurisdictions reducing their corporate tax rates on certain types of mobile income – e.g., offering a preferential tax rate on income from intellectual property (IP) compared to the ordinary corporate income tax rate (preferential IP regime) – to attract foreign investments was a matter of concern for the OECD. There was the fear that, eventually, this may trigger a 'race to the bottom' that 'would ultimately drive applicable tax rates on certain mobile sources of income to zero for all countries, whether or not this was the tax policy a country wished to pursue'.[51] The OECD therefore saw the need to agree to a common set of rules in order to level the playing field and prevent harmful tax competition between jurisdictions.

At the same time, however, the OECD stressed that '[n]o or low taxation is not per se a cause of concern, but it becomes so when it is associated with practices that artificially segregate taxable income from the activities that generate it'.[52] Accordingly, BEPS Action 5 stipulates that preferential regimes must require taxpayers to perform substantial activities to be eligible for tax benefits ('Substantial Activity Requirement'). Conversely, if a preferential regime does not require a substantial activity from a taxpayer for obtaining tax benefits, it will constitute a harmful tax practice.

Regarding preferential IP regimes, the OECD agreed on the 'Modified Nexus Approach' to define the Substantial Activity Requirement.[53] This approach 'allows a taxpayer to benefit from an IP regime only to the extent that the taxpayer itself incurred qualifying research and development (R&D) expenditures that gave rise to the IP

48. *OECD*, Action Plan on Base Erosion and Profit Shifting (2013) 20.
49. *OECD*, Action Plan on Base Erosion and Profit Shifting (2013) 20f.
50. *See also Danon*, General Report, in *IFA* (Ed.), Cahiers de droit fiscal international, Vol. 100a Tax Incentives on Research and Development (R&D) (2015) 17 (51); *Hausmann/Roth/Meyer-Nandi*, Die Patentbox als Steuerplanungsmodell für KMU, Expert Focus 2016, 189 (192).
51. *OECD*, Action Plan on Base Erosion and Profit Shifting (2013) 17.
52. *OECD*, Action Plan on Base Erosion and Profit Shifting (2013) 10.
53. *OECD*, Countering Harmful Tax Practices More Effectively, Taking into Account Transparency and Substance – Action 5: 2015 Final Report (2015) Mn 26ff [abbreviated in this thesis as BEPS Action 5].

income'.[54] That is, it establishes a nexus between the expenditures incurred to develop an IP asset and the preferential taxation of the income generated by that IP.

The same principle shall also apply in the context of other preferential regimes (i.e., non-IP regimes; e.g., a leasing regime that grants preferential tax treatment to income from leasing activities).[55] However, in this case, the OECD uses the concept of 'Core Income Generating Activities' to determine the Substantial Activity Requirement. Accordingly, 'such regimes would only be found to meet the substantial activity requirement if they also granted benefits only to qualifying taxpayers to the extent those taxpayers undertook the Core Income Generating Activities required to produce the type of business income covered by the preferential regime'.[56]

Following the BEPS Project, the OECD extended the application of the Substantial Activity Requirement to no or only nominal tax jurisdictions to 'hold similar mobile business activities to a similar standard, irrespective of whether they are taxed under a preferential regime or a no or nominal tax rate'.[57] For this purpose, the OECD also uses the concept of Core Income Generating Activities to determine the Substantial Activity Requirement.[58] However, peculiar in this case, the OECD also applies the concept of Core Income Generating Activities to determine the Substantial Activity Requirement with regard to IP income - and not the Modified Nexus Approach that applies with regard to IP income under a preferential IP regime.[59]

1.4 SUBSTANCE PRE-BEPS: SUBSTANCE IN THE AREA OF TAX TREATIES - BENEFICIAL OWNERSHIP

The requirement of beneficial ownership is enshrined in the articles on passive income, namely, Article 10 (Dividends), Article 11 (Interest), and Article 12 (Royalties) of the OECD MC. Since this thesis examines substance requirements with regard to intangibles, its focus will be on Article 12 OECD MC and beneficial ownership of royalties. However, the OECD pointed out that '[w]hilst the [...] relevant facts and circumstances might be different in the cases of dividends, interest and royalties, [...] the same principles should apply [...]'.[60] Therefore, considerations concerning beneficial ownership in Article 12 OECD MC are also valid for Articles 10 and 11 OECD MC.

54. BEPS Action 5, 9.
55. BEPS Action 5, Mn 70ff.
56. BEPS Action 5, Mn 71.
57. *OECD*, Resumption of Application of Substantial Activities Factor to No or only Nominal Tax Jurisdictions (2018) Mn 18.
58. *OECD*, Resumption of Application of Substantial Activities Factor to No or only Nominal Tax Jurisdictions (2018) Mn 23ff.
59. *OECD*, Resumption of Application of Substantial Activities Factor to No or only Nominal Tax Jurisdictions (2018) Mn 26ff.
60. *OECD*, OECD Model Tax Convention: Revised Proposals Concerning the Meaning of 'Beneficial Owner' in Articles 10, 11 and 12 (2012) Mn 32; *see also Baker*, The Meaning of 'Beneficial Ownership' as Applied to Dividends under the OECD Model Tax Convention, in *Maisto* (Ed.), Taxation of Intercompany Dividends under Tax Treaties and EU Law (2012) 87 (87):'None of these potential differences [between dividends, interest and royalties] suggest that beneficial ownership in the case of dividends should have in any sense a different meaning from beneficial ownership as it applies to interest, royalties and other income.'

In principle, the residence state has the exclusive right to tax royalties pursuant to Article 12 OECD MC 2017.[61] However, the source state may levy withholding taxes in the case that royalties are not 'beneficially owned by a resident of the other Contracting State' ('Beneficial Ownership Test'). The purpose of the Beneficial Ownership Test is to prevent '[p]ersons not entitled to protection by a particular treaty [...] from obtaining its benefits with the help of interposed persons'.[62]

The beneficial ownership requirement was already introduced into the OECD MC in 1977 and has since been the subject of much discussion.[63] In an effort to provide more clarity, the OECD started a revision of the Beneficial Ownership Test in 2011.[64] In 2013, when the OECD launched the BEPS Project, it also mentioned the Beneficial Ownership Test in its report on addressing BEPS. Therein, the OECD stated that '[t]he current work on the meaning of beneficial owner, which is nearing completion, is also relevant [for BEPS], primarily as it allowed a greater understanding of the limits of this concept in addressing treaty shopping concerns'.[65] Therefore, the OECD did not seize the opportunity to integrate the ongoing revision work into the BEPS Project - as this was done with other current projects -[66] but finished it separately. Eventually, the revision work on the Beneficial Ownership Test resulted in amendments to the OECD MC and Commentary in 2014.[67]

However, whereas the issue of beneficial ownership was not addressed in the BEPS Project, it dealt with other substance requirements in the area of tax treaties (specifically in BEPS Action 6[68] and BEPS Action 7[69]). What is more, in BEPS Action 6, the OECD suggested the introduction of a Principle-Purpose-Test (PPT) into the OECD MC that is intended to prevent treaty shopping cases (conduit company cases) that - as one would usually suspect - should already be tackled by the Beneficial Ownership Test.[70]

61. The justification for the exclusive taxing right of the residence state is that the residence state granted the deduction of the expenses that resulted in an intangible. Therefore, the residence state should be the one to tax the profits that are achieved by exploiting the intangible, *see Ditz/Pinkernell/Quilitzsch*, BEPS-Reformvorschläge zu Lizenzgebühren und Verrechnungspreisen bei immateriellen Wirtschaftsgütern aus Sicht der Beratungspraxis, IStR 2014, 45 (46).
62. *Vogel*, Klaus Vogel on Double Taxation Conventions^3 (1997) Preface to Arts 10-12 Mn 6.
63. *See also du Toit*, The Evolution of the Term 'Beneficial Ownership' in Relation to International Taxation over the Past 45 Years, BIT 2010, 500 (500): 'Beneficial ownership is probably the most well-known undefined treaty term and its international tax meaning is a matter that lends itself to much debate.'
64. *OECD*, Clarification of the meaning of 'Beneficial owner' in the OECD Model Tax Convention – Discussion Draft (2011).
65. *OECD*, Addressing Base Erosion and Profit Shifting (2013) 84.
66. *See OECD*, Action Plan on Base Erosion and Profit Shifting (2013) 84.
67. *See OECD*, 2014 Update to the OECD Model Tax Convention (2014), Mn 5f, 34, 41 and 48.
68. *OECD*, Preventing the Granting of Treaty Benefits in Inappropriate Circumstances - Action 6: 2015 Final Report (2015).
69. *OECD*, Preventing the Artificial Avoidance of Permanent Establishment Status - Action 7: 2015 Final Report (2015).
70. *See also Danon*, Treaty Abuse in the Post-BEPS World: Analysis of the Policy Shift and Impact of the Principle Purpose Test for MNE Groups, BIT 2018, 31 (31ff).

1.5 IP COMPANIES AS TODAY'S BUSINESS REALITY

MNEs often centralize their intangibles in an own legal entity (IP Company).[71] On the one hand, this is done for business reasons. Centralization makes the administration of intangibles easier because, for example, their registration process becomes more streamlined, IP rights infringements can more easily be detected, and complex cross-licensing within the group can be avoided.[72] Additionally, centralization may help to protect the intangibles from creditors' claims in the case that an operating company that uses the intangibles becomes insolvent (because the intangibles are legally owned by the IP Company).[73] What is more, divestments as well as M&A transactions can be carried out easier, and centralization might even facilitate the acquisition of funding in these cases since the intangibles can be used as a collateral.[74] Last but not least, the centralization of intangibles usually goes hand in hand with the centralization of functions and risks associated with the intangibles, and thereby the corporate structure and the respective responsibilities become more efficient and transparent.[75] As a result, changes in the operational structure (e.g., the relocation of a production site to a different country) only have a limited impact on the IP Company.[76]

On the other hand, tax considerations may also play an important role when deciding if and where to establish an IP Company. Of course, when choosing a location for an IP Company, factors such as the proximity to a specific market, existing infrastructure, and availability of a skilled workforce or the political and legal stability in a country can be relevant.[77] However, due to the high-profit potential typically associated with intangibles, MNEs will also pay close attention to the corporate income tax level in a jurisdiction. Therefore, MNEs may decide to establish IP Companies in low or no tax jurisdictions or in jurisdictions that offer a preferential IP regime.[78]

MNEs may assign a wide array of different functions to IP Companies. The spectrum ranges from IP Companies that are in charge of the whole development and exploitation process of intangibles within an MNE (IP Principal), to IP Companies that

71. *See Andree/Liebchen*, Structuring intangibles, in *Lang/Storck/Petruzzi/Risse* (Eds), Transfer Pricing and Intangibles: Current Developments, Relevant Issues and Possible Solutions (2019) 87 (104f); *see also* OECD TPG 2017 Mn 9.2 and 9.57ff.
72. *See Penttilä/Isomaa-Myllymäki*, Centralization of Intangibles and Transfer Pricing under BEPS and Finnish Tax Law, ET 2018, 82 (83); *Kulcsar*, Transfer Pricing Aspects of Licensing Arrangements: The Increasingly Enhanced Engagement between Taxpayers and Tax Auditors, in *Verlinden/Bakker* (Eds), Mastering the IP Life Cycle from a Legal, Tax and Accounting Perspective (2018) 403 (409).
73. *Penttilä/Isomaa-Myllymäki*, ET 2018, 83; *see also Kulcsar* in *Verlinden/Bakker* 409; *Creed*, Steuergestaltungen über Lizenz- bzw. Patentboxen – Ein Auslaufmodell?, GRUR-Prax 2014, 346 (346).
74. *Penttilä/Isomaa-Myllymäki*, ET 2018, 83.
75. *Creed*, GRUR-Prax 2014, 346; *Kulcsar* in *Verlinden/Bakker* 409.
76. *See also Raschle/Borriello/Hämmerle*, Substanz in internationalen Unternehmensstrukturen: Auswirkungen internationaler Entwicklungen auf Verrechnungspreispraxis und Steuerstrategie, ST 2013, 861 (864); *Voje*, Models for Exploiting IP Rights, in *Verlinden/Bakker* (Eds), Mastering the IP Life Cycle from a Legal, Tax and Accounting Perspective (2018) 397 (398).
77. *See also Penttilä/Isomaa-Myllymäki*, ET 2018, 83.
78. *See also Wilkie* in *Lang/Storck/Petruzzi* 66; *Penttilä/Isomaa-Myllymäki*, ET 2018, 83.

only administer intangibles or even to IP Companies that merely hold intangibles without performing any functions themselves.[79]

In the case of a structure with an IP Principal, the IP Company is typically responsible for the management of the R&D process, whereas the operational R&D activities are often performed by related companies[80] on its behalf (contract R&D).[81,82] The IP Company compensates contract researchers for their services and, as a consequence, receives ownership of all of the intangibles that result from the R&D activities. Therefore, '[i]n principle, a separation between the performance of the very research and development activities and the taxation of the return attributable to the intangibles may be achieved'.[83]

In the case that an intangible is successfully developed, IP Companies normally do not directly exploit it themselves (i.e., through manufacturing and selling products that make use of the intangible).[84] Rather, IP Companies license their intangibles to (related) operating companies that use the intangibles in their business activities (so-called licence model).[85] In return, the IP Company receives royalties from the (related) operating companies to which it has granted rights to its intangibles.

This structure is illustrated in Figure 1.1.

Figure 1.1 Licence Model

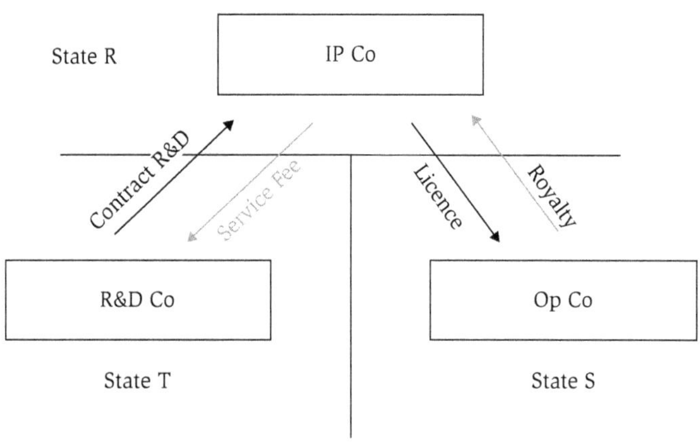

79. *See also Penttilä/Isomaa-Myllymäki*, ET 2018, 84ff.
80. These related companies are usually resident in a different country than the IP Principal to achieve, for example, cost savings by locating them in countries that have lower prevailing labour costs.
81. For more details, *see Monsenego*, Introduction to Transfer Pricing (2015) 70ff.
82. *See also Raschle/Borriello/Hämmerle*, ST 2013, 864.
83. *Monsenego*, Introduction to Transfer Pricing (2015) 72.
84. *Kulcsar* in *Verlinden/Bakker* 409.
85. On the licence model as well as other models that MNEs use for developing and exploiting intangibles, *see Voje* in *Verlinden/Bakker* 397ff; *Storck/Stradinger*, Das Poolkonzept im Bereich Forschung und Entwicklung, in *Bernegger/Rosar/Rosenberger* (Eds), Handbuch Verrechnungspreise (2012) 475 (475ff).

Likewise, it is possible that the companies that perform R&D within an MNE receive ownership of the intangibles they develop. In a next step, the R&D companies license the developed intangibles to the IP Company that on-licenses them to the operating companies (usually, this is the case when an IP Company is only responsible for administering developed intangibles within an MNE).

This structure is illustrated in Figure 1.2.

Figure 1.2 IP On-Licensing

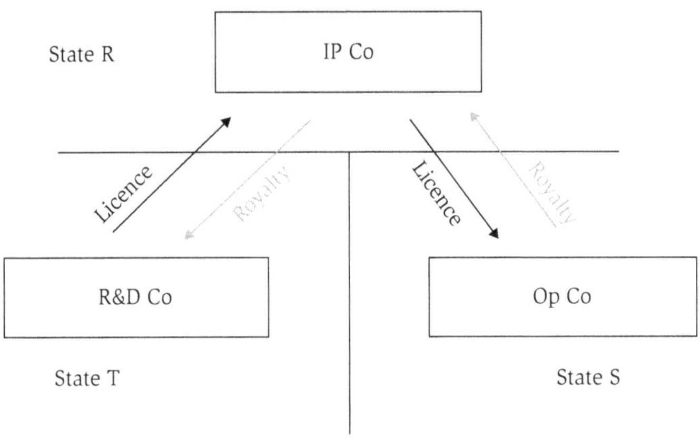

1.6 SCOPE OF THE STUDY

It has to be stressed that 'IP companies might pose tax risks since they separate IP from related activities within a group and strip taxable profit from other jurisdictions (through the transfer of IP to the IP company and payment of corresponding royalties by the operating entities).'[86]

The following substance requirements are vital for sustaining a structure with an IP Company:[87]

1. *Entitlement to the intangible-related returns* (Transfer Pricing):
   The IP Company has to have the necessary substance to be entitled to the intangible-related returns (i.e., the royalties paid by the related operating companies).
   - DEMPE Approach

2. *Preferential taxation/no or only nominal taxation of the income derived from the IP asset* (Harmful Tax Practices):

86. *Kulcsar* in *Verlinden/Bakker* 410; *see also OECD*, Country-by-Country Reporting – Handbook on effective tax risk assessment (2017) Mn 40, 65ff and p. 65, according to which the separation of IP from related activities within a group is a potential tax risk indicator that could be derived from the information contained in a Country-by-Country Report.
87. *See also Zammit*, Centralized Intellectual Property Business Models – Tax Implications of EU Patent Box Regimes, BIT 2015, 540 (542f); *Voje* in *Verlinden/Bakker* 398f; *Kulcsar* in *Verlinden/Bakker* 410ff.

Assuming that the IP Company is resident in a country that offers a preferential IP regime or in a no or only nominal tax jurisdictions, the IP Company has to have the necessary substance to be eligible for this favourable tax treatment.

- Substantial Activity Requirement – Modified Nexus Approach (in case of preferential IP regimes) or Core Income Generating Activities (in case of no or only nominal tax jurisdictions)

3. *Elimination/reduction of withholding taxes on received royalties* (Tax Treaties):
   The IP Company has to have the necessary substance to collect royalties paid by the operating companies to the greatest extent possible, free from withholding taxes.
   - Beneficial Ownership Test

However, 'to date, there does not seem to be a standard internationally accepted definition of the notion of [...] substance'.[88] As a result, MNEs have to consider each of these substance requirements separately when implementing a structure with an IP Company.[89]

Against this background, the purpose of this thesis is to examine the notion of substance in these three different concepts and to contrast them. Furthermore, since the DEMPE Approach originates from Transfer Pricing, the Substantial Activity Requirement from Harmful Tax Practices and the Beneficial Ownership Test from Tax Treaties, this thesis will also analyse how substance requirements are stipulated in different areas of international tax law.

The research will focus on four questions:

- DEMPE Approach vs Substantial Activity Requirement
  1) Like the DEMPE Approach,[90] the Substantial Activity Requirement 'contributes to the second pillar of the BEPS Project, which is to align taxation with substance by ensuring that taxable profits can no longer be artificially shifted away from the countries where value is created'.[91] Thus, the common denominator of both concepts is their aim to align taxation with

88. *Kulcsar* in *Verlinden/Bakker* 411; *see also Pross/Radmanesh*, Seminar A: 'Patentboxen', IStR 2015, 579 (582); in this context, *see* a recent monograph from *Leukefeld*, Das Konzept der Substanz im Steuerrecht: Nationale und multinationale Substanzvorschriften unter besonderer Berücksichtigung der BEPS-Initiativen von OECD und EU, in *Watrin* (Ed.), Münstersche Forschungsbeiträge zu Rechnungslegung und Unternehmensbesteuerung (2018), where the author aims to establish a uniform definition of substance in German tax law *de lege ferenda*.
89. MNEs may also have to consider other substance requirements when establishing an IP Company; for example, tax authorities may challenge its place of effective management (*see also* the decision in the well-known *Indofood* case where a conduit company structure was challenged under both the Beneficial Ownership Test and the Place of Effective Management Test, England and Wales Court of Appeal, 2. 3. 2006, A3/2005/2497, Indofood International Finance Ltd. v. JPMorgan Chase Bank NA, London Branch, Mn 32 and 51ff); furthermore, controlled foreign company (CFC) rules may be applicable or PE issues may arise (*see also Voje* in *Verlinden/Bakker* 398, 400, 402; *Kulcsar* in *Verlinden/Bakker* 411; *Zammit*, BIT 2015, 542f); however, these issues go beyond the scope of this thesis.
90. *See* sec. 1.3.2.
91. BEPS Action 5, Mn 24; *see also OECD*, Harmful Tax Practices – 2017 Progress Report on Preferential Regimes (2017) 9.

value creation (value creation as substance). Against this background, it will be examined whether both concepts share the same understanding of value creation.

2) Additionally, since there are two concepts used to determine the Substantial Activity Requirement, i.e., the Modified Nexus Approach for preferential IP regimes and the Core Income Generating Activities for IP income in no or only nominal tax jurisdictions, it will be analysed whether these concepts are congruent or whether inconsistencies exist between them.

- Beneficial Ownership (Substance pre-BEPS) vs Substance in the BEPS Project

3) As stated above,[92] the OECD did not deal with the issue of beneficial ownership in the BEPS Project. Against this background, this thesis will analyse how substance was defined in the pre-BEPS era (i.e., in the Beneficial Ownership Test) compared to how substance was defined in the BEPS Project (DEMPE Approach and Substantial Activity Requirement).

4) Furthermore, with the BEPS Project, the OECD introduced the PPT that also targets the same structures that the Beneficial Ownership Test does (conduit company cases). Therefore, a comparison will be drawn between the Beneficial Ownership Test and the PPT – two concepts from the same area of international tax law (i.e., tax treaties). The aim is to examine whether both concepts share the same underlying values or whether the BEPS Project changed the perception of substance in this area and, as a consequence, diverging results between them are possible.

As a result, the outcomes of this thesis will not only be relevant from a theoretical perspective but also for practice since they may provide more clarity on how to structure IP Companies within an MNE.

As this thesis is written in the field of law, its focus will naturally be on the interpretation of texts,[93] in this case especially documents issued by the OECD. Regarding international law, principles of interpretation can be found in Articles 31-33 of the Vienna Convention on the Law of Treaties (VCLT).[94] According to Article 31 VCLT, suitable techniques of interpretation are the grammatical interpretation ('ordinary meaning'), the systematic interpretation ('in their context'), and the teleological interpretation ('in the light of its object and purpose'). Even though the historical interpretation is only considered as a 'supplementary means of interpretation' according to Article 32 VCLT, one has to keep in mind that interpretation is not a formalized or schematized process and, therefore, the entire range of the legal methods should be incorporated into it.[95] For this reason, each of these interpretation methods may be useful and will be considered in this thesis.

92. *See* sec. 1.4.
93. *See Torvik*, Transfer pricing and Intangibles: US and OECD Arm's Length Distribution of Operating Profits from IP Value Chains (2019) 16: 'The main object of legal research is text. The main research activity is interpretation.'
94. *See also Vogel/Prokisch*, General Report, in *IFA* (Ed.), Cahiers de droit fiscal international, Vol. 78a Interpretation of double taxation conventions (1993) 55 (56).
95. *Lang*, Austria, in *IFA* (Ed.), Cahiers de droit fiscal international, Vol. 78a Interpretation of double taxation conventions (1993) 197 (206).

It has to be emphasized that, strictly speaking, the object of interpretation is always a specific DTC and not any documents issued by the OECD – like the MC, the Commentary, or the Transfer Pricing Guidelines – as these documents are not legally binding instruments.[96] However, the OECD MC and its Commentary 'are very important in the interpretation of tax treaties'.[97] The same is true with regard to the OECD Transfer Pricing Guidelines.[98] Therefore, a thorough analysis of these documents may yield results that can eventually be used when interpreting and applying a concrete DTC.[99]

96. The OECD MC and its Commentary are merely nonbinding recommendations of the OECD Council, *see Lang/Brugger*, The role of the OECD Commentary in tax treaty interpretation, Australian Tax Forum 2008, 95 (104f); the same is true for the OECD Transfer Pricing Guidelines, *see Langer*, Die Weiterentwicklung der OECD-Verrechnungspreisleitlinien nach dem BEPS-Projekt, TPI 2017, 78 (79f).
97. For more details, *see Lang*, Introduction to the Law of Double Taxation Conventions (2013) Mn 83ff.
98. For more details on the meaning of the OECD Transfer Pricing Guidelines for the interpretation of tax treaties, *see Langer*, TPI 2017, 78ff.
99. For considerations regarding the relevance of the OECD BEPS materials for the interpretation of tax treaties, *see Hattingh*, The Relevance of BEPS Materials for Tax Treaty Interpretation, BIT 2020, 179 (179ff).

CHAPTER 2

Substance in the Area of Transfer Pricing: DEMPE Approach

2.1 BACKGROUND

In 2010, the OECD comprehensively revised its Transfer Pricing Guidelines (OECD TPG).[100] However, the chapter on intangibles (Chapter VI – 'Special Considerations for Intangible Assets') was not subject to this revision but was reproduced unchanged from the OECD TPG 1995.[101] As a consequence, many ambiguities concerning intangibles in the realm of transfer pricing remained. Therefore, the OECD launched a new project in 2011 to clarify open issues.[102] As part of this project, the OECD wanted to address, *inter alia*, definitional issues, i.e., what constitutes an intangible for transfer pricing purposes,[103] and the entitlement to intangible-related returns, i.e., whether an enterprise has a right to share in the return from an intangible that it does not own.[104]

100. For an overview of the supplementations and modifications of the OECD TPG over the course of time, *see* the Foreword in *OECD*, OECD Transfer Pricing Guidelines for Multinational Enterprises and Tax Administrations 2017 (2017); for an overview of the OECD guidance on substance in transfer pricing before the BEPS Project, *see Petruzzi/Myzithra*, ITPJ 2020, 433ff.
101. *See also Haumer*, Brennpunkt immaterielle Wirtschaftsgüter – die eigentliche 'Substanz' jedes Unternehmens, in *Macho/Steiner/Spensberger* (Eds), Verrechnungspreise kompakt (2017) 366 (366).
102. *See OECD*, Transfer Pricing and Intangibles: Scope of the OECD Project (2011); *see also Dawid/Ebering*, Eckpunkte des Scoping Document der OECD vom 25.1.2011, IWB 2011, 490 (490ff).
103. The OECD TPG 2010 did not contain a definition of intangibles for transfer pricing purposes; *see also OECD*, Transfer Pricing and Intangibles: Scope of the OECD Project (2011) Mn 12.
104. For more details on the scope of the project, *see OECD*, Transfer Pricing and Intangibles: Scope of the OECD Project (2011) Mn 11ff; *see also OECD*, Working Party No. 6's Special Session on the Transfer Pricing Aspects of Intangibles: Meeting with Business Representatives on the Transfer Pricing Aspects of Intangibles (2011) 3ff.

In 2012, the OECD presented a first discussion draft.[105] In 2013, the ongoing revision work was integrated into the BEPS Project[106] (BEPS Action 8),[107] and a revised discussion draft[108] was issued. Further work results were delivered in 2014[109] and, in 2015, the final report on BEPS Action 8 was published.[110]

As a result of BEPS Action 8, the previous Chapter VI of the OECD TPG 2010[111] was entirely deleted and replaced by a new one.[112] In 2017, the OECD incorporated these amendments - as well as the outcomes of BEPS Actions 9, 10, and 13[113] - into its revised OECD TPG 2017.[114,115]

105. *OECD*, Discussion Draft: Revision of the special considerations for intangibles in Chapter VI of the OECD Transfer Pricing Guidelines and related provisions (2012); *see also Eigelshoven/Ebering/Schmidtke*, Der OECD Diskussionsentwurf vom 6. 6. 2012, IWB 2012, 487 (487ff); *Shapiro/Mitra/Henshall/Sierra*, The OECD Discussion Draft on Intangibles, TNI 2012, 1245 (1245ff); *Herbert/Luckhaupt*, Bestimmung von Verrechnungspreisen für immaterielle Wirtschaftsgüter - zum Diskussionsentwurf der OECD, Ubg 2012, 672 (672ff); *Rouenhoff*, Erste Analyse des OECD-Diskussionspapiers zur Berücksichtigung von Intangibles bei der Festlegung von Verrechnungspreisen, IStR 2012, 654 (654ff); *Helderman/Sporken*, Revision of the Special Considerations for Intangibles in Chapter VI of the OECD Transfer Pricing Guidelines and Related Provisions, ITPJ 2012, 383 (383ff); *Wittendorff*, 'Shadowlands': The OECD on Intangibles, TNI 2012, 935 (935ff).
106. *OECD*, Addressing Base Erosion and Profit Shifting (2013) 52.
107. On the scope of BEPS Action 8, *see* already sec. 1.3.2.
108. *OECD*, Revised Discussion Draft on Transfer Pricing Aspects of Intangibles (2013); *see also Helderman/Sporken/Okten*, The Revised OECD Discussion Draft on Transfer Pricing Aspects of Intangibles, ITPJ 2014, 3 (3ff); *Bärsch/Luckhaupt/Schulz*, Bestimmung angemessener Verrechnungspreise im Zusammenhang mit immateriellen Vermögenswerten - Eine kritische Analyse der überarbeiteten OECD-Verrechnungspreisleitlinien, Ubg 2014, 37 (37ff); *Schmidtke/Till mann*, Der 2. OECD Diskussionsentwurf immaterielle Wirtschaftsgüter, IWB 2013, 709 (709f); *Wittendorff*, OECD Revised Discussion Draft on Intangibles — A Step in the Right Direction, TNI 2013, 1325 (1325ff).
109. *OECD*, Guidance on Transfer Pricing Aspects of Intangibles - Action 8: 2014 Deliverable (2014); *see also Naumann/Groß*, IStR 2014, 908ff; *Roeder/Fellner*, Base Erosion and Profit Shifting: Immaterielle Vermögenswerte und die OECD - Zusammenfassung des Arbeitsstands des Kapitels VI und erste Analyse aus deutscher Sicht, ISR 2014, 428 (428ff); *Dawid/Schwerdt/Stumpf*, Überblick und Einschätzung des OECD-Papiers zum BEPS-Aktionspunkt 8, IWB 2014, 910 (910ff); *Wittendorff*, More Black Smoke From the OECD's Chimney — Third Draft on Intangibles, TNI 2015, 167 (167ff).
110. *OECD*, Aligning Transfer Pricing Outcomes with Value Creation - Actions 8-10: 2015 Final Reports (2015); *see also Groß*, Anpassung der Ergebnisse von Verrechnungspreisen an die Wertschöpfung - Der G20/OECD-Abschlussbericht zu den Maßnahmen 8-10 des BEPS-Aktionsplans, IStR 2016, 233 (233ff); *Kroppen/Rasch*, Immaterielle Vermögenswerte - Neudefinition des Fremdvergleichsgrundsatzes? - Die finalen Aktionspunkte 8-10 der BEPS-Initiative, IWB 2015, 828 (828ff); *Wittendorff*, BEPS Actions 8-10: Birth of a New Arm's-Length Principle, TNI 2016, 331 (331ff).
111. *OECD*, OECD Transfer Pricing Guidelines for Multinational Enterprises and Tax Administrations 2010 (2010).
112. *OECD*, Aligning Transfer Pricing Outcomes with Value Creation - Actions 8-10: 2015 Final Reports (2015) 63ff.
113. *OECD*, Transfer Pricing Documentation and Country-by-Country Reporting - Action 13: 2015 Final Report (2015).
114. *OECD*, OECD Transfer Pricing Guidelines for Multinational Enterprises and Tax Administrations 2017 (2017).
115. *See* https://www.oecd.org/tax/oecd-council-approves-incorporation-of-beps-amendments-into-the-transfer-pricing-guidelines-for-multinational-enterprises-and-tax-administrations.htm (accessed 24 April 2020).

2.2 ANALYTICAL FRAMEWORK FOR TRANSACTIONS INVOLVING INTANGIBLES

In general, the same principles that are relevant in a transfer pricing analysis for any controlled transaction apply equally to transactions involving intangibles.[116] On top of that, Chapter VI OECD TPG 2017 provides more specific guidance for transactions involving intangibles.[117]

The OECD TPG 2017 provide for the application of a six-step process when analysing transactions involving intangibles.[118] In short, steps 1-3 are concerned with a factual analysis, that is, an identification of:[119]

- the relevant intangible(s) in a transaction;[120]
- the contractual arrangements between the involved parties and an identification of the owner of the intangible(s);[121] and
- the parties performing functions, assuming risks, and using assets in the DEMPE of the intangible(s) (functional analysis).[122]

Subsequently, steps 4-5 require the performance of a deviation analysis. That is, it has to be determined whether the identified contractual agreements are consistent with the conduct of the involved parties (step 4) and, if not, transactions have to be delineated according to the conduct of the involved parties (step 5). Finally, in step 6, arm's-length prices have to be determined for these transactions unless a transaction is to be disregarded.[123]

Ultimately, the aim of a transfer pricing analysis with regard to intangibles is the allocation of the intangible-related returns[124] between associated enterprises (personal scope of Article 9 OECD MC).[125] According to Article 9 OECD MC, associated enterprises 'must be taxed on the basis that they act at arm's length in their transactions with each other' (arm's-length principle).[126] That is, associated enterprises are treated as separate entities for tax purposes (separate entity approach).[127] This entails that, in

116. OECD TPG 2017 Mn 6.3.
117. OECD TPG 2017 Mn 6.2.
118. For more details, *see* OECD TPG 2017 Mn 6.34.
119. *See also* the illustration of the whole six-step procedure in *Koch*, BEPS und Intangibles oder die Grenzen des Fremdvergleichsgrundsatzes, IStR 2016, 881 (882).
120. *See* sec. 2.3.
121. *See* sec. 2.4.
122. *See* sec. 2.5.
123. *See* sec. 2.6.
124. In this regard, it is regrettable that the OECD TPG 2017 do not provide a definition for intangible-related returns; by contrast, a definition was still contained in OECD, Discussion Draft: Revision of the special considerations for intangibles in Chapter VI of the OECD Transfer Pricing Guidelines and related provisions (2012) Mn 28; *see also* the considerations by *Wittendorff*, TNI 2012, 943f.
125. For more details on the notion of associated enterprises, *see Kofler* in *Reimer/Rust*, Klaus Vogel on Double Taxation Conventions[4] (2015) Art. 9 Mn 48ff.
126. OECD TPG 2017 Mn 6.
127. OECD TPG 2017 Mn 5.

a transfer pricing context, the existence of substance has to be assessed on the level of each individual entity.[128]

2.3 INTANGIBLES IN THE CONTEXT OF THE OECD TPG 2017

The OECD TPG 2017 provide its own definition for intangibles. Accordingly, an intangible in a transfer pricing context is:

- something which is not a physical asset or a financial asset,[129]
- which is capable of being owned or controlled for use in commercial activities, and
- whose use or transfer would be compensated had it occurred in a transaction between independent parties in comparable circumstances.[130]

For transfer pricing purposes, it is irrelevant whether an intangible is recognized for accounting purposes.[131] Likewise, the existence of legal protection or separate transferability is not a necessary condition for an item to be characterized as an intangible for transfer pricing purposes.[132] Furthermore, it is made clear that the 'concept of intangibles for transfer pricing purposes and the definition of royalties for purposes of Article 12 of the OECD Model Tax Convention are two different notions that do not need to be aligned' (i.e., a payment may be classified as a royalty according to Article 12(2) OECD MC 2017 but may not be treated as a remuneration for intangibles for transfer pricing purposes and vice versa).[133]

The OECD TPG 2017 provide the following examples for intangibles:

- Patents,[134]
- Know-how and trade secrets,[135]
- Trademarks, trade names and brands,[136]
- Rights under contracts and government licences,[137]

128. *See also Brülisauer,* The substance-based approach in tax law – 'A' Swiss perspective in the context of 'BEPS', ASA 2014/2015, 811 (837).
129. A financial asset is defined as 'any asset that is cash, an equity instrument, a contractual right or obligation to receive cash or another financial asset or to exchange financial assets or liabilities, or a derivative. Examples include bonds, bank deposits, stocks, shares, forward contracts, futures contracts, and swaps', *see* OECD TPG 2017 Mn 6.6 FN 2.
130. OECD TPG 2017 Mn 6.6.
131. OECD TPG 2017 Mn 6.7; critical *Koch,* Die neue OECD-Definition immaterieller Werte für Verrechnungspreiszwecke – hat die OECD ihre selbst gesteckten Ziele erreicht?, IStR 2015, 199 (203f).
132. OECD TPG 2017 Mn 6.8, however, '[t]he availability and extent of legal, contractual, or other forms of protection may affect the value of an item and the returns that should be attributed to it'.
133. OECD TPG 2017 Mn 6.13.
134. For more details, *see* OECD TPG 2017 Mn 6.19.
135. For more details, *see* OECD TPG 2017 Mn 6.20.
136. For more details, *see* OECD TPG 2017 Mn 6.21ff.
137. For more details, *see* OECD TPG 2017 Mn 6.24f.

- Licences and similar limited rights in intangibles,[138] and
- Goodwill and ongoing concern value.[139]

However, this list is not exhaustive; other items that are not included may also constitute intangibles for transfer pricing purposes.[140] In addition, the OECD TPG 2017 give two (much debated)[141] examples for items that are not considered as intangibles for transfer pricing purposes, namely, group synergies[142] and market-specific characteristics.[143] The reason for this is that they are not capable of being owned or controlled by an enterprise. Nevertheless, they have to be considered as comparability factors when performing a comparability analysis.[144]

The OECD TPG 2017 do not attempt to delineate different categories of intangibles and to specify results that are based on such categories.[145] However, to facilitate discussion, a distinction is made between 'marketing intangibles' and 'trade intangibles'.[146]

The term 'marketing intangible' denotes '[a]n intangible [...] that relates to marketing activities, aids in the commercial exploitation of a product or service and/or has an important promotional value for the product concerned. Depending on the context, marketing intangibles may include, for example, trademarks, trade names, customer lists, customer relationships, and proprietary market and customer data that is used or aids in marketing and selling goods or services to customers'.[147]

Conversely, a trade intangible is '[a]n intangible other than a marketing intangible'.[148] The term may comprise patents, for example.[149] The former OECD TPG 2010 did provide a little more information by stating that '[t]rade intangibles often are created through risky and costly [...] R&D activities [...]'[150] and that '[i]ntellectual

138. OECD TPG 2017 Mn 6.26.
139. For more details, *see* OECD TPG 2017 Mn 6.27ff; the fact that goodwill is considered an intangible for transfer pricing purposes received criticism in literature; for more details, *see* *Koch*, IStR 2015, 201f; *Kroppen*, Behandlung immaterieller Wirtschaftsgüter unter BEPS, in *Lüdicke/Schnitger/Spengel* (Eds), Besteuerung Internationaler Unternehmen - Festschrift für Dieter Endres (2016) 199 (200f); *Bärsch/Luckhaupt/Schulz*, Ubg 2014, 38; *Schmidtke/Tillmann*, IWB 2013, 709.
140. OECD TPG 2017 Mn 6.18.
141. For more details, *see Kroppen* in *Lüdicke/Schnitger/Spengel* 205f.
142. OECD TPG 2017 Mn 6.30; *see also* OECD TPG 2017 Mn 1.139ff.
143. OECD TPG 2017 Mn 6.31; *see also* OECD TPG 2017 Mn 1.157ff; examples for market-specific characteristics are a high purchasing power of households in a particular market or low prevailing labour costs in a particular market.
144. For more details, *see Kroppen/Rasch*, IWB 2015, 830f; *see also* OECD TPG 2017 Mn 6.208: 'In particular, comparability adjustments may be required for matters such as differences in markets, locational advantages, business strategies, assembled workforce, corporate synergies and other similar factors. While such factors may not be intangibles [...] they can nevertheless have important effects on arm's length prices in matters involving the use of intangibles.'
145. OECD TPG 2017 Mn 6.15; for example, between soft and hard intangibles or between routine and non-routine intangibles.
146. OECD TPG 2017 Mn 6.16.
147. *See* OECD TPG 2017, Glossary.
148. *See* OECD TPG 2017, Glossary.
149. OECD TPG 2017 Mn 2.144.
150. OECD TPG 2010 Mn 6.3.

property such as know-how and trade secrets can be trade intangibles or marketing intangibles'.[151] Although these statements are not explicitly expressed in the revised OECD TPG 2017, they should still conform to the understanding of trade intangibles contained therein.

Nevertheless, the OECD TPG 2017 stress that 'the use of those terms [does not] suggest that a different approach should be applied in determining arm's length conditions for transactions that involve either marketing intangibles or trade intangibles'.[152]

In light of the abovementioned, it can be said that the intangible definition adopted in the OECD TPG 2017 is very broad.[153]

2.4 CONTRACTUAL ARRANGEMENTS AND INTANGIBLE OWNERSHIP

2.4.1 Relevance of Contractual Arrangements

The former OECD TPG were 'perceived by some as putting too much emphasis on legal structures [...] rather than on the underlying reality of the economically integrated group, which may contribute to BEPS'.[154] Consequently, with their revision in the course of the BEPS Project, the OECD made clear that a 'transfer pricing analysis is based on an accurate delineation of what the associated enterprises actually contribute in the transaction, and not on contractual terms [...] that are not in practice performed'.[155] The contractual arrangements have to be analysed together with the conduct of the relevant parties, and '[t]he conduct will supplement or replace the contractual arrangements if the contracts are incomplete or are not supported by the conduct' (substance-over-form approach).[156,157]

151. OECD TPG 2010 Mn 6.5.
152. OECD TPG 2017 Mn 6.16.
153. *See also Bärsch/Luckhaupt/Schulz*, Ubg 2014, 47; some commentators even criticize the definition as being too wide; for more details, *see Ditz/Pinkernell/Quilitzsch*, BEPS-Reformvorschläge zu Lizenzgebühren und Verrechnungspreisen bei immateriellen Wirtschaftsgütern aus Sicht der Beratungspraxis, IStR 2014, 45 (49); *Koch*, IStR 2016, 882.
154. *OECD*, Addressing Base Erosion and Profit Shifting (2013) 43; *see also OECD*, Aligning Transfer Pricing Outcomes with Value Creation – Actions 8-10: 2015 Final Reports (2015) 9: '[W]ith its perceived emphasis on contractual allocations of functions, assets and risks, the existing guidance on the application of the principle has also proven vulnerable to manipulation.'
155. *OECD*, Aligning Transfer Pricing Outcomes with Value Creation – Actions 8-10: 2015 Final Reports (2015) 14; for more details regarding the accurate delineation of a transaction, *see Prasanna/Petruzzi*, Accurate Delineation and Recognition of Actual Transactions: Comparability Analysis, in *Lang/Cottani/Petruzzi/Storck* (Eds), Fundamentals of Transfer Pricing: A Practical Guide (2018) 35 (35ff).
156. On the substance-over-form approach pre-BEPS, *see Heggmair*, The New Interpretation of the Arm's Length Principle: A Post-BEPS Evaluation, ITPJ 2017, 263 (264).
157. *OECD*, Aligning Transfer Pricing Outcomes with Value Creation – Actions 8-10: 2015 Final Reports (2015) 10.

To emphasize this point, the order of the economically relevant characteristics[158] that 'need to be identified in the commercial or financial relations between associated enterprises to accurately delineate a transaction' was amended.[159] The 'contractual terms of the transaction' were exchanged with the 'characteristics of property transferred or services provided' and are now being ranked first.[160]

This underscores that the contractual arrangements of a transaction form the starting point for any transfer pricing analysis.[161] The same also applies to transactions involving intangibles.[162] Eventually, however, the actual conduct of the parties – determined through the functional analysis – is decisive for the accurate delineation of a transaction.[163] That is, irrespective of the existence of contractual arrangements, the actual conduct of the parties to a transaction has to be examined.[164] As a consequence, the substance expected from a taxpayer is the same notwithstanding whether contractual arrangements exist or are absent.[165]

2.4.2 Relevance of Legal Ownership

Under the OECD TPG 2017, the legal owner of an intangible is considered as the owner of that intangible for transfer pricing purposes.[166] In the case that the legal owner of an intangible cannot be identified,[167] 'the member of the MNE group that [...] controls decisions concerning the exploitation of the intangible and has the practical capacity to restrict others from using the intangible will be considered the legal owner of the intangible for transfer pricing purposes'.[168]

158. The five economically relevant characteristics are the contractual terms of the transaction; the functions performed by each of the parties to the transaction, taking into account assets used and risks assumed; the characteristics of property transferred or services provided; the economic circumstances of the parties and of the market in which the parties operate; and the business strategies pursued by the parties; *see* OECD TPG 2017 Mn 1.36.
159. *See also De Baets/Gao*, Recent Developments on Comparability Analysis in Transfer Pricing, in *Lang/Storck/Petruzzi* (Eds), Transfer Pricing Developments Around the World 2018 (2018) 159 (169f).
160. OECD TPG 2017 Mn 1.36.
161. OECD TPG 2017 Mn 1.42.
162. OECD TPG 2017 Mn 6.35.
163. OECD TPG 2017 Mn 1.45 and 6.36; *see also* the example in OECD TPG 2017 Mn 1.48.
164. OECD TPG 2017 Mn 1.49; *see also* the example in OECD TPG 2017 Mn 1.50.
165. *See also Petruzzi/Myzithra*, ITPJ 2020, 438; *see* already *Monsenego*, ITPJ 2014, 11 concerning the OECD TPG 2010: '[W]hether or not contractual terms exist between the parties, the Guidelines eventually encourage tax administrations to examine the conduct of the parties to ensure that the transfer prices reflect the actual substance of the transaction [...] [and] the same expectations in terms of substance are placed on taxpayers whether or not they have entered into intercompany agreements.'
166. OECD TPG 2017 Mn 6.40.
167. Concerning intangibles that are protected under registration systems (e.g., patents and trademarks; *see* OECD TPG 2017 Mn 6.37), the legal owner can be identified through public records; *see also Peng/Lagarden*, DEMPE Functions and the RACI Concept – More Clarity or Confusion Ahead?, ITPJ 2019, 3 (4); however, concerning intangibles that are not registered for protection (e.g., know-how), the above-mentioned provision can be relevant.
168. OECD TPG 2017 Mn 6.40.

It has to be stressed that an intangible and a licence to it are two different intangibles for transfer pricing purposes.[169] As a consequence, there are different legal owners,[170] and different functional analyses have to be carried out.[171] For example, in the case of an IP Company that licenses and on-licenses developed intangibles within an MNE,[172] a DEMPE analysis concerning the patent and a DEMPE analysis concerning the licence to it have to be conducted.[173]

In the end, however, legal ownership simply serves as a reference point for analysing controlled transactions involving intangibles.[174] Ultimately, legal ownership alone does not grant entitlement to any intangible-related returns.[175] Instead, a mere legal owner is only to be compensated with a service fee.[176]

Contrarily, under the OECD TPG 2010, the general perception was that the legal owner of an intangible is the sole person entitled to its returns (subject to the condition that he provided the necessary funding for the development of the intangible).[177] However, already in the scoping document on the revision of Chapter VI of the TPG in 2011, it was stated that 'it may be that an enterprise that is not the legal owner of an intangible should nevertheless be entitled, at arm's length, to share in any additional return attributable to the development or exploitation of that intangible, e.g. because it has incurred significant risk and expenses related to the development of an intangible or the enhancement of its value'.[178] Consequently, the OECD examined '[u]nder what

169. *See* already sec. 2.3.
170. OECD TPG 2017 Mn 6.41.
171. *See Kulcsar* in *Verlinden/Bakker* 424.
172. *See* sec. 1.5.
173. *See* sec. 5.2 on this issue.
174. OECD TPG 2017 Mn 6.43.
175. OECD TPG 2017 Mn 6.42; *see also OECD*, Aligning Transfer Pricing Outcomes with Value Creation - Actions 8-10: 2015 Final Reports (2015) 64.
176. In this context, *see also* Example 1 in the annex to Chapter VI of the OECD TPG 2017; however, *see also Pankiv*, Post-BEPS Application of the Arm's Length Principle to Intangibles Structures, ITPJ 2016, 463 (471f): '[The] DEMPE rationale could be misinterpreted in a way that the property owner may expect only a zero-return if the management of such property is performed by others. This "zero-valued-ownership" approach to identification of the value of intangibles [denies the essence of ownership]. Such an approach would not be sustainable from the perspective of Adam Smith's labour theory of price (value), which claims that the labour spent on creation of an item should already be accounted for in its acquisition price for the owner, and that it is up to the owner to exploit such item, including intangibles, on its own or to allow the exploitation by others, e.g. via licensing of intangibles. In either of these two scenarios, the owner deserves not a zero-return, but its market equivalent, unless the property owned cannot be commercialized. As a matter of law, ownership should always be remunerated at more than zero. The question of the amount of such remuneration, as a matter of fact, should be addressed in the transfer pricing analysis based on the comparability and/or valuation exercise, as indicated in the supplemental guidance of the Actions 8-10 Final Reports [...] Interpreting the application of the arm's length principle as claiming a zero-return for the property owner would result in treating the principle as an anti-avoidance measure, and would thus be indicative of its clear misinterpretation.'
177. *See Stocker/Schmid*, Entschädigung immaterieller Vermögenswerte: Auswirkungen des Updates 2017 der OECD Verrechnungspreisleitlinien, TPI 2018, 92 (95f).
178. *OECD*, Transfer Pricing and Intangibles: Scope of the OECD Project (2011) Mn 23.

circumstances, if any, should an entity other than the legal title holder be entitled to intangible related returns'.[179]

As a result, the OECD developed the DEMPE Approach.[180] Accordingly, 'allocation of the returns derived by the MNE group from the exploitation of intangibles [...] is accomplished by compensating members of the MNE group for functions performed, assets used, and risks assumed in the [DEMPE] of intangibles [...]'.[181] That is, if members of an MNE other than the legal owner perform functions, assume risks, or use assets in relation to the DEMPE of an intangible, they may be entitled to a share of the intangible-related returns.[182]

In this context, the OECD TPG 2017 are not clear on how the ultimate allocation of intangible-related returns shall be achieved. In principle, two different approaches are conceivable:[183] On the one hand, all intangible-related returns could be attributed to the legal owner of the intangible in a first step. However, since legal ownership alone does not confer any entitlement to intangible-related returns, the legal owner would still have to compensate other associated enterprises corresponding to the value created by them with regard to the DEMPE of the intangible.[184] On the other hand, intangible-related returns could directly be attributed to those associated enterprises that made valuable contributions to the DEMPE of an intangible.[185] Depending on the approach chosen, different DTCs - and thus different withholding tax rates in the case of royalties[186] (if a DTC deviates from the OECD MC) - could be applicable. Furthermore, particularly the first approach - attributing intangible-related returns to the legal owner who has to effectively pass them on to other group companies - may raise the question of the legal owner's status as beneficial owner.[187]

Of course, Article 9 OECD MC - like DTCs in general - does not 'govern issues regarding the proper attribution of income between taxpayers'.[188] Instead, the attribution of income is a prerogative of domestic law.[189] Yet, under the assumption that a

179. *OECD*, Working Party No. 6's Special Session on the Transfer Pricing Aspects of Intangibles: Meeting with Business Representatives on the Transfer Pricing Aspects of Intangibles (2011) 7.
180. *See* OECD TPG 2017 Mn 6.32ff.
181. OECD TPG 2017 Mn 6.32.
182. OECD TPG 2017 Mn 6.71.
183. *See also Jiménez*, Article 12: Royalties, in Vann et al (Eds), Global Tax Treaty Commentaries, sec. 1.1.2.2.2.2.
184. *See Holinski/Schwarz/Stein*, Namensnutzung im Konzern - Implikationen für die Praxis durch die neue BFH-Rechtsprechung, Der Konzern 2016, 316 (320, FN 36); *Koch*, Schaffung und Nutzung immaterieller Vermögenswerte im multinationalen Unternehmen, in *Bischoff/ Kellermann/Sieben/Herzig* (Eds), Steuer, Wirtschaft und Recht; 345 (2014) 76; *Rasch/Maier/ Wenzel* in *Kroppen/Rasch*, Handbuch internationale Verrechnungspreise: Band III[33] (2021) OECD-Kap. VI Mn 244.
185. In this direction *Haumer*, Rechtliches versus wirtschaftliches Eigentum bei immateriellen Wirtschaftsgütern, SWI 2016, 484 (489).
186. Intangible-related returns need not necessarily be royalties in the sense of Art. 12(2) OECD MC; *see* already sec. 2.3.
187. *See* sec. 5.2 on this issue.
188. *See Wittendorff*, Transfer Pricing and the Arm's Length Principle in International Tax Law (2010) 151 with further references.
189. *See also Lang*, CFC Regulations and Double Taxation Treaties, BIT 2003, 51 (53ff).

country adopts the OECD 2017 one-to-one in its domestic law, what would be the preferable solution?

Since the arm's-length principle 'adopts as a benchmark the normal operation of the market',[190] it makes sense to attribute intangible-related returns to the legal owner in a first place. Indeed, this is consistent with the outcome of uncontrolled transactions for which the legal owner of an intangible is regularly the person entitled to its returns.[191] Another advantage of attributing intangible-related returns to the legal owner in the first step is that legal ownership is normally undisputed and easy to identify.[192] Therefore, intangible-related returns should be attributed to the legal owner of an intangible under the DEMPE Approach (who then has to compensate associated enterprises that made valuable contributions to the DEMPE of that intangible).[193]

2.4.3 Economic Ownership and Functional Ownership

In its scoping document on the revision of Chapter VI of the TPG in 2011, the OECD also mentioned other types than legal ownership that are sometimes referred to: 'economic ownership', 'functional ownership' and 'beneficial ownership'.[194]

In the former OECD TPG 2010, the term 'economic ownership' is only used in Mn 6.3 (concerning how R&D can be performed – in someone's own name or on behalf of somebody else – and how this impacts on the ownership of trade intangibles). However, the OECD TPG 2010 did not provide any information about the requirements that have to be fulfilled to claim economic ownership.[195]

The revised OECD TPG 2017 do not mention the term 'economic ownership' at all. This is quite surprising considering that the OECD initially stated at the beginning of the revision project that '[t]here is a need for clarification of this notion [note: economic ownership] and consistent use of the terminology in the context of the TPG'.[196]

Presumably, this was done for the following reasons: First, there is no universal understanding about what constitutes economic ownership.[197] Countries have different understandings about it that may not be reconciled to a uniform understanding, and the parallel existence of them may cause confusion. Second, the OECD 2010 Report on the Attribution of Profits to Permanent Establishments also uses the term 'economic

190. OECD TPG 2017 Mn 1.14.
191. *See also Wittendorff*, TNI 2012, 944.
192. *See also Helderman/Sporken/Okten/Kanter*, A New Era in Determining Arm's Length Compensation for Intangibles? A Comparative Overview of Existing and Possible Future Transfer Pricing Principles, ITPJ 2013, 359 (359).
193. *See also Collier/Andrus*, Transfer Pricing and the Arm's Length Principle After BEPS (2017) Mn 6.64; *Schmidtke*, Maßnahme 8 des BEPS-Aktionsplans – Der Fremdvergleichsgrundsatz und BEPS, IStR 2015, 120 (123).
194. *See OECD*, Transfer Pricing and Intangibles: Scope of the OECD Project (2011) Mn 25.
195. *See also Koch* in *Bischoff/Kellermann/Sieben/Herzig* 71.
196. *OECD*, Transfer Pricing and Intangibles: Scope of the OECD Project (2011) Mn 25.
197. *See Peng/Lagarden*, ITPJ 2019, 3 (4f); *Helderman/Sporken/Okten/Kanter*, ITPJ 2013, 359.

ownership'.[198] In this regard, the OECD already stated in the scoping document that '[i]n an Article 9 context, this is a slightly different notion from the one of "economic ownership" developed under Article 7, although the same phrase is often used for both. This can lead to some confusion between the two notions'.[199] Finally, there is no need to resort to economic ownership under Article 9 OECD MC because associated enterprises can legally own assets, which is different compared to the situation under Article 7 OECD MC between a head office and a PE.[200] For these reasons, the OECD may have decided to not use the term in the revised TPG. For similar reasons,[201] presumably, the OECD may also have chosen to abandon the term 'economic substance'[202] in the revised TPG.[203]

Likewise, the term 'functional ownership' is not used in the OECD TPG 2017. Yet, the term is sometimes used in literature to denote a company's entitlement to intangible-related returns under the DEMPE Approach.[204] Since the ultimate allocation of intangible-related returns is based on the functional involvement of group companies in the DEMPE of an intangible, group companies that performed value-creating activities and are therefore entitled to intangible-related returns are said to have functional ownership of an intangible.

Last but not least, the term 'beneficial ownership' is also not used in the OECD TPG 2017. With regard to the confusion that the application of this term already causes in Articles 10-12 OECD MC,[205] it is understandable that it was not also introduced into the transfer pricing area.

Of course, the fact that the terms 'economic ownership' and 'beneficial ownership' are not used in the OECD TPG 2017 does not mean that there cannot be an overlap between these concepts and the DEMPE Approach. For example, a company that

198. *See OECD*, 2010 Report on the Attribution of Profits to Permanent Establishments (2010) Mn 14 FN 4: '[T]he "economic" ownership of assets in the Article 7 context means the equivalent of ownership for income tax purposes by a separate enterprise, with the attendant benefits and burdens (e.g. the right to the income attributable to the ownership of the asset, such as royalties; the right to depreciate a depreciable asset; and the potential exposure to gains or losses from the appreciation or depreciation of the asset).'

199. *See OECD*, Transfer Pricing and Intangibles: Scope of the OECD Project (2011) Mn 25.

200. *See* OECD, 2010 Report on the Attribution of Profits to Permanent Establishments (2010) Mn 14: 'The factual, legal position in a PE context, on the other hand, is that there is no single part of an enterprise which legally - "owns" the assets, assumes the risks, possesses the capital or contracts with separate enterprises. The legal position is thus unhelpful in a PE context, since Article 7(2) requires the PE to be treated as if it were a separate and independent enterprise, performing its own functions, assuming its own risk and owning or using assets on its own.'

201. Interesting in this context is a statement from *Wilkie*, Substance in International Taxation, ITPJ 2014, 362 (362 FN 7): 'What some speak of in terms of economic substance may, actually, be legal substance - i.e. whether, as an evidentiary matter, the practical realities of a taxpayer's conduct are consistent with the expectations, as a legal matter, of the legal forms and relations, including contracts, adopted by the taxpayer to achieve a certain outcome.'

202. On the terms 'legal substance' and 'economic substance', *see* already FN 6.

203. However, the OECD TPG 2017 use the term 'factual substance'; *see* OECD TPG 2017 Mn 1.46 and 1.120.

204. *See Stein/Schwarz/Holinski*, Funktionales Eigentum und Wertschöpfungsbeitragsanalysen: Steuerliche Erfolgsermittlung bei immateriellen Werten mithilfe betriebswirtschaftlicher Konzepte, DStR 2017, 118 (119) FN 16 with further references.

205. *See* chapter 4 of this thesis.

performs all the value-creating activities in the DEMPE of an intangible may also be considered its economic owner under a country's domestic law.[206] However, when strictly referring to the OECD TPG 2017 and not to a country's domestic law, these terms should be avoided since the OECD deliberately did not use them and otherwise confusion might ensue.[207]

2.5 FUNCTIONAL ANALYSIS AND SUBSTANCE

2.5.1 Introduction

The arm's-length principle operates under the assumption that 'the more extensive the functions/assets/risks of one party to the transaction [are], the greater its expected remuneration will be and vice versa'.[208] Consequently, in order to accurately delineate an intercompany transaction, a functional analysis has to be undertaken where the role of each party with regard to the:

- functions performed;[209]
- risks assumed;[210] and
- assets used[211]

is determined.[212]

For transfer pricing cases involving intangibles, this means that it has to be determined 'which member(s) perform and exercise control over [DEMPE] functions, which member(s) provide funding and other assets, and which member(s) assume the various risks associated with the intangible'.[213] This allows evaluating how each associated enterprise contributed to the creation of intangible value. Thus, in a transfer pricing analysis involving intangibles, 'it is especially important to ground the functional analysis on an understanding of the MNE's global business and the manner in which intangibles are used by the MNE to add or create value across the entire supply chain' (Value Chain Analysis).[214]

---

206. *See Peng/Lagarden*, ITPJ 2019, 5 regarding the DEMPE Approach: 'Though it is not expressly stated by the OECD, this reflects the notion of economic ownership'; on the interplay between the DEMPE Approach and the Beneficial Ownership Test in Art. 12 OECD MC, *see* sec. 5.2; for a differentiation between economic ownership (in Germany) and functional ownership as under the DEMPE Approach, *see Puls/Heravi*, DEMPE-Funktionen und wirtschaftliches Eigentum an immateriellen Werten – Plädoyer für eine differenzierte Betrachtung, IStR 2018, 721 (725ff).
207. *See also Miyatake*, General Report, in *IFA* (Ed.), Cahiers de droit fiscal international, Vol. 92a Transfer Pricing and Intangibles (2007) 17 (26): 'Differences in who the owner of intangible property is could create double taxation, and consistent treatment by the tax authorities concerned is desirable.'
208. *OECD*, Addressing Base Erosion and Profit Shifting (2013) 42.
209. *See* sec. 2.5.2.
210. *See* sec. 2.5.3.
211. *See* sec. 2.5.4.
212. OECD TPG 2017 Mn 1.51.
213. OECD TPG 2017 Mn 6.48.
214. OECD TPG 2017 Mn 6.3; *see also* OECD TPG 2017 Mn 1.36 and 6.12.

However, there is no standardized process applicable to determine what actions create intangible value in every single case.[215] Rather, 'contributions to the creation of intangible value by members of the group in the form of functions performed, assets used and risks assumed will vary depending on the circumstances'.[216] Nonetheless, the OECD TPG 2017 provide certain guidance on which actions contribute to the creation of value (positive source rule)[217] as well as which actions do not (negative source rule).[218] The following sections will focus on this guidance and the expected substance from the legal owner of an intangible to ultimately retain the intangible-related returns from it.

2.5.2 Substance Requirements with Regard to Functions

2.5.2.1 Important Functions

In general, the DEMPE Approach does not require that 'the legal owner physically performs all of the functions related to the [DEMPE] of an intangible through its own personnel'.[219] Therefore, the legal owner can outsource functions to other associated enterprises and, in principle, still be entitled to all of the intangible-related returns.[220] This is consistent with the behaviour in open markets where independent companies regularly outsource functions to other parties without having to share part of the intangible-related returns with them.[221]

However, the DEMPE Approach sets certain limits to the outsourcing of functions. A distinction is made between 'normal functions' and 'important functions'.[222] Whereas 'normal functions' can be outsourced, the DEMPE Approach expects the legal owner to perform the 'important functions' through its own personnel. That is, when 'important functions' are performed by an associated enterprise other than the legal owner, the associated enterprise is entitled to a share of the intangible-related returns corresponding to the intangible value it created – in addition to an arm's-length remuneration for its services. The rationale for this treatment is that 'important functions usually make a significant contribution to intangible value'.[223]

'Important functions' may include 'design and control of research and marketing programmes, direction of and establishing priorities for creative undertakings including determining the course of "blue-sky" research, control over strategic decisions regarding intangible development programmes, and management and control of

215. *See also* OECD TPG 2017 Mn 1.59: 'The relevance of functions, assets and risks in a specific transaction will need to be determined through a detailed functional analysis.'
216. OECD TPG 2017 Mn 6.49.
217. *Jiménez*, Tax Avoidance and Aggressive Tax Planning as an International Standard – BEPS and the 'New' Standards of (Legal and Illegal) Tax Avoidance, in Dourado (Ed.), Tax Avoidance Revisited in the EU BEPS Context (2017) 25 (35).
218. *Wilkie* in *Lang/Storck/Petruzzi* 83ff.
219. OECD TPG 2017 Mn 6.51.
220. *See* sec. 2.5.2.2.
221. *See* OECD TPG 2017 Mn 6.51.
222. *See also Wittendorff*, TNI 2013, 1332.
223. OECD TPG 2017 Mn 6.56.

budgets'. Furthermore, 'important decisions regarding defence and protection of intangibles, and ongoing quality control over functions performed by independent or associated enterprises that may have a material effect on the value of the intangible'.[224]

Although it always depends on the facts and circumstances to determine which functions are 'important functions' in a specific case,[225] it can be concluded from the above-mentioned examples that 'important functions' concern management activities in the DEMPE of an intangible.[226] That is, the focus is on the performance of functions on the strategical and tactical level, whereas functions on the operational level (day-to-day activities) are not necessarily considered as 'important functions'.[227] Consequently, the DEMPE Approach expects a company (or its employees, respectively) to possess certain managerial skills.[228]

2.5.2.2 Outsourcing

As stated above, 'normal functions' can, in principle, be outsourced by the legal owner.[229] If this is the case, the legal owner has to compensate other associated enterprises that performed 'normal functions' at arm's length (e.g., via a service fee).[230] However, unlike in the case of 'important functions', the legal owner regularly does not have to share the intangible-related returns.[231]

This entails, for example, that the operational R&D activity does not necessarily have to be carried out by the legal owner himself in order to be entitled to intangible-related returns.[232] As a result, a structure with an IP Principal[233] is still possible even after the revisions of the BEPS Project.[234]

However, the DEMPE Approach expects the legal owner to control the performance of 'normal functions' that are outsourced.[235] If another associated enterprise controls an outsourced 'normal function', depending on the facts and circumstances, the legal owner has to compensate this associated enterprise either on an arm's-length

224. OECD TPG 2017 Mn 6.56.
225. OECD TPG 2017 Mn 6.56.
226. *See also* OECD TPG 2017 Mn 6.58: 'Because the important functions described in paragraph 6.56 are often instrumental in *managing* the different functions performed, assets used, and risks assumed that are key to the successful [DEMPE] of intangibles, and are therefore essential to the creation of intangible value, it is necessary to carefully evaluate transactions between parties performing these important functions and other associated enterprises' (emphasis added).
227. *See also Helderman/Sporken/Okten/Kanter*, ITPJ 2013, 363.
228. *See also Monsenego*, TPJI 2014, 12f.
229. OECD TPG 2017 Mn 6.51.
230. OECD TPG 2017 Mn 6.52.
231. However, *see also* OECD TPG 2017 Mn 6.79 where it is stated that compensation based on costs plus a modest markup will not reflect an arm's-length price in every contract R&D arrangement.
232. *See* OECD TPG 2017 Mn 1.62, 1.83 and 1.101.
233. *See* already sec. 1.5.
234. *See also Navisotschnigg*, Attribution of intangible-related returns – panel discussion, in Lang/Storck/Petruzzi/Risse (Eds), Transfer Pricing and Intangibles: Current Developments, Relevant Issues and Possible Solutions (2019) 77 (77) (advisor's comment).
235. OECD TPG 2017 Mn 6.53.

basis[236] or even with a share of the intangible-related returns.[237] The latter will usually be the case when the control of an outsourced function is considered as an 'important function' in the DEMPE of an intangible (e.g., control over strategic decisions regarding intangible development programmes).[238]

In assessing whether the legal owner controls the performance of outsourced 'normal functions', the same principles that apply for determining control over risk are relevant.[239] Therefore, the 'control requirement is used [...] to determine which parties assume risks in relation to intangibles, but also for assessing which member of the MNE group in fact controls the performance of outsourced functions in relation to the [DEMPE] of the intangible'.[240] That is, control over the performance of a function and control over risk are congruent concepts (i.e., they require the same substance from a taxpayer). For this reason, the relevant substance requirements will be discussed in the section on control over risk.[241]

2.5.3 Substance Requirements with Regard to Risks

2.5.3.1 New Framework for Risk Allocation

The assumption of risk[242] can significantly affect the transfer prices of transactions between associated enterprises.[243] As it is also usual in uncontrolled transactions, 'the assumption of increased risk would also be compensated by an increase in the expected return, although the actual return may or may not increase depending on the degree to which the risks are actually realized'.[244] According to the OECD, '[t]his economic notion that higher risks warrant higher anticipated returns made MNE groups pursue *tax planning strategies based on contractual re-allocations of risks*, sometimes without any change in the business operations' (emphasis added).[245]

236. OECD TPG 2017 Mn 6.53.
237. OECD TPG 2017 Mn 6.54.
238. On 'important functions' in the DEMPE of an intangible, *see* sec. 2.5.2.1.
239. OECD TPG 2017 Mn 6.53.
240. *OECD*, Aligning Transfer Pricing Outcomes with Value Creation - Actions 8-10: 2015 Final Reports (2015) 63f.
241. *See* sec. 2.5.3.2.
242. Risk is defined as 'the effect of uncertainty on the objectives of the business', *see* OECD TPG 2017 Mn 1.71.
243. *See also OECD*, Aligning Transfer Pricing Outcomes with Value Creation - Actions 8-10: 2015 Final Reports (2015) 14.
244. OECD TPG 2017 Mn 1.56.
245. *OECD*, Aligning Transfer Pricing Outcomes with Value Creation - Actions 8-10: 2015 Final Reports (2015) 10; *see also Collier/Andrus*, Transfer Pricing and the Arm's Length Principle After BEPS (2017) Mn 6.22: 'Given the rules requiring tax administrations to generally respect taxpayers' contractual arrangements, taxpayers often contractually assigned risk, and with it returns arguably attributable to the assumption of risk, to low-function, low-tax members of the MNE group.'

In order to remedy this unwanted situation, the OECD developed a new framework for the allocation of risk in intercompany transactions.[246] In essence, the new guidance provides that risk assumption[247] requires:[248]

- control over risk;[249] and
- financial capacity to assume the risk.[250]

By contrast, the contractual assumption of risk is not determinative.[251]

This new risk framework is also applicable under the DEMPE Approach.[252] That is, in order to retain all of the intangible-related returns, the legal owner has to assume economically significant risks[253] associated with the DEMPE of an intangible. Types of risks that may be particularly important in this context include development risk, risk of product obsolescence, infringement risk, product liability risk, and exploitation risk.[254] The following sections will analyse the two relevant substance requirements for the assumption of risk – i.e., control over risk and the financial capacity to assume the risk – in a transfer pricing context.

2.5.3.2 Control over Risk

Control over risk involves the following two elements:[255]

- the capability to make decisions to take on, lay off, or decline a risk-bearing opportunity, together with the actual performance of that decision-making function and
- the capability to make decisions on whether and how to respond to the risks associated with the opportunity, together with the actual performance of that decision-making function.

In short, control over risk comprises the '*capability* and *authority* to decide to take on the risk, and to decide whether and how to respond to the risk [decision-making functions] [...]' (emphasis added).[256]

246. *See* the six-step process in OECD TPG 2017 Mn 1.60; for criticism on the risk framework, *see Collier/Dykes*, The Virus in the ALP, BIT 2020, 702 (705ff).
247. Risk assumption is defined as 'taking on the upside and downside consequences of the risk with the result that the party assuming a risk will also bear the financial and other consequences if the risk materializes', *see* OECD TPG 2017 Mn 1.63.
248. *OECD*, Aligning Transfer Pricing Outcomes with Value Creation – Actions 8-10: 2015 Final Reports (2015) 14.
249. *See* sec. 2.5.3.2.
250. *See* sec. 2.5.3.3.
251. *See* OECD TPG 2017 Mn 1.98; however, *see also Verlinden/Ledure/Dessy*, The Risky Side of Transfer Pricing: The OECD Base Erosion and Profit Shifting Reports Sharpen the Rules on Risk Allocation under the Arm's Length Standard, ITPJ 2016, 109 (110): '[A] well-considered contractual agreement nevertheless remains paramount, as tax authorities will have to demonstrate that it does not accord with the conduct of the parties.'
252. OECD TPG 2017 Mn 6.67.
253. That is, risks whose impacts on the cost of capital are significant, *see* OECD TPG 2017 Mn 1.74.
254. For more details, *see* OECD TPG 2017 Mn 6.65.
255. OECD TPG 2017 Mn 1.65.
256. OECD TPG 2017 Mn 1.67.

First, the capability to perform decision-making functions requires that decision makers in a company 'possess competence and experience in the area of the particular risk for which the decision is being made and possess an understanding of the impact of their decision on the business'.[257] Their decision-making process should be based 'on a relevant analysis of the information required for assessing the foreseeable downside and upside risk outcomes of such a decision and the consequences for the business of the enterprise'.[258] However, it is not necessary that they gather the relevant information themselves, but this process can be outsourced. If the gathering of information is outsourced, it is expected that decision makers have the 'capability to determine the objectives of the gathering and analysis of the information, to hire the party gathering the information and making the analyses, to assess whether the right information is gathered and the analyses are adequately made, and, where necessary, to decide to adapt or terminate the contract with that provider, together with the performance of such assessment and decision-making'.[259] On the other hand, if decision makers are not capable of performing these functions, it could be claimed that they are merely formally approving decisions that were effectively made by other people (in other locations) which is insufficient to demonstrate control over a risk.[260] Therefore, decision makers should be competent persons in the sense that they have the relevant technical or scientific skills in the field in which a decision is taken.

By contrast, it is not necessary to perform risk mitigation functions - i.e., measures that are expected to affect risk outcomes -[261] to have control over risk.[262] For example, the risk of a product recall may be mitigated by performing quality controls.[263] However, a company is not required to perform such quality controls to have control over risk as the company may simply decide to take the unmitigated product recall risk in order to maximize opportunities (i.e., the company would have lower costs but an increased product recall risk if quality controls are not performed).[264]

Furthermore, a company may also outsource risk mitigation functions (in the above-mentioned example, this would mean that quality controls are performed by a different party). In this case, however, control over risk requires the outsourcing company to have the 'capability to determine the objectives of the outsourced activities, to decide to hire the provider of the risk mitigation functions, to assess whether the objectives are being adequately met, and, where necessary, to decide to adapt or terminate the contract with that provider, together with the performance of

257. OECD TPG 2017 Mn 1.66.
258. OECD TPG 2017 Mn 1.66.
259. OECD TPG 2017 Mn 1.66.
260. OECD TPG 2017 Mn 1.66; for an illustrative example of this issue, *see* the *Canadian Cameco* case discussed in *Navisotschnigg*, Transfer Pricing Adjustments and Re-Characterization: Lessons Learned from the Canadian Tax Court Case Cameco, TPI 2019, 88 (95).
261. *See* OECD TPG 2017 Mn 1.68: 'Such measures may include measures that reduce the uncertainty or measures that reduce the consequences in the event that the downside impact of risk occurs.'
262. OECD TPG 2017 Mn 1.65.
263. OECD TPG 2017 Mn 1.63.
264. OECD TPG 2017 Mn 1.68.

such assessment and decision-making'.[265] Therefore, in line with the evaluations under important functions, control over risk requires a company to perform the strategical and tactical risk management, whereas the operational risk management can be outsourced.[266]

Second, authority to perform decision-making functions relates to the actual performance of a decision-making function.[267] The focus is 'on the decision-making of the parties to the transaction in relation to the specific risk arising from the transaction'.[268] Conversely, the setting of general policies in an MNE with regard to the assumption of risk is not determinative.[269] For example, the parent company in an MNE may, as a general policy, set certain minimum stocking levels in different markets. Nonetheless, the 'inventory risk in a supply transaction between two associated enterprises may be controlled by the party with the capability to determine the production volumes together with the performance of that decision-making' as wider policy-setting 'cannot be regarded as decisions to take on, lay off, decline, or mitigate the specific inventory risk'.[270]

It is important to emphasize that control over risk does not mean that 'the risk itself can be influenced or that the uncertainty can be nullified'.[271] Indeed, MNEs are likely to encounter certain risks that they cannot influence (e.g., commodity price cycles).[272] Rather, control over risk, as elaborated above, focuses on the capability and authority to perform decision-making functions (i.e., to decide whether a risk is taken on and whether and how to respond to the risk). Therefore, it is possible, from a transfer pricing perspective, to have control over a risk that cannot be influenced, for example, 'through the timing of investments, the nature of development programmes, the design of marketing strategies, or the setting of production levels'.[273]

2.5.3.3 Financial Capacity to Assume the Risk

Financial capacity to assume risk is defined as 'access to funding to take on the risk or to lay off the risk, to pay for the risk mitigation functions and to bear the consequences

265. OECD TPG 2017 Mn 1.65; *see also* the example provided in OECD TPG 2017 Mn 1.69.
266. *See also Koch*, IStR 2016, 884.
267. Since the OECD TPG 2017 attach priority to the actual behaviour of the parties, it is determinative which party really makes the decision and not necessarily which party is formally authorized to make a decision (i.e., whose approval is needed for a decision to be made); in this context, *see also* the considerations concerning the OECD TPG 2010 in *Monsenego*, ITPJ 2014, 13ff.
268. OECD TPG 2017 Mn 1.76.
269. *See* OECD TPG 2017 Mn 1.66 and 1.76.
270. *See* OECD TPG 2017 Mn 1.76; however, *see also Verlinden/Ledure/Dessy*, ITPJ 2016, 111 who highlight that a policy that defines certain risk limits also embeds some form of control over risk; depending on how strict the risk limits are defined, it may be difficult to distinguish between actual local decision-making and merely ticking the box.
271. OECD TPG 2017 Mn 1.67.
272. For an illustrative example of this issue, *see* the *Canadian Cameco* case discussed in *Navisotschnigg*, TPI 2019, 94.
273. OECD TPG 2017 Mn 1.67.

of the risk if the risk materializes'.[274] It takes into account the 'available assets and the options realistically available to access additional liquidity, if needed, to cover the costs anticipated to arise should the risk materialize'.[275] Therefore, not the actual capitalization of a company is decisive 'but rather the capitalization to which the company can be assumed to have access [...]'.[276] This should be assessed on the 'basis that the party assuming the risk is operating as an unrelated party in the same circumstances as the associated enterprise [...]'.[277]

However, this does not mean that access to intra-group funding is not sufficient for establishing the financial capacity to assume risk.[278] Consequently, given the fact that funding can easily be transferred between group companies, the hurdle to fulfil this requirement is low.[279] In fact, there is only one example in the OECD TPG 2017 where the financial capacity to assume risk is denied.[280] This example revolves around a transfer of intangibles to a company that is managed by a local trust company. Since the company does not have any employees, the OECD TPG 2017 deny its control over risk and, at the same time, its financial capacity to assume the risk. While it is not clear why the financial capacity to assume the risk is denied, the example seems to indicate that the financial capacity to assume the risk - like control over risk - considers the functionality of a company. The OECD TPG 2017 seem to assume that the higher the functionality of a company, the easier it has access to funding (the prerequisite for financial capacity to assume risk).[281] However, the functionality of a company is also tested under the control over risk-requirement.[282] Therefore, it appears that 'any company with functionality to control risks will have access to capital that will allow it to assume risks'.[283] Against this background, the requirement of financial capacity to assume risk seems to be only a secondary issue compared to control over risk.[284]

2.5.4 Substance Requirements with Regard to Assets

2.5.4.1 Cash Boxes as Targets of the BEPS Project

As in the case of functions and risks, the legal owner has to compensate associated enterprises that provide assets in the DEMPE of an intangible.[285] This may include

274. OECD TPG 2017 Mn 1.64.
275. OECD TPG 2017 Mn 1.64.
276. *Hafkenscheid*, The BEPS Report on Risk Allocation: Not So Functional, ITPJ 2017, 19 (20); *see also Navisotschnigg* in *Lang/Storck/Petruzzi/Risse* 82 (participant's comment).
277. OECD TPG 2017 Mn 1.64.
278. *See* OECD TPG 2017 Mn 1.64: 'Where a party assuming risk receives intra-group funding to meet the funding demands in relation to the risk, the party providing the funding may assume financial risk but does not, merely as a consequence of providing funding, assume the specific risk that gives rise to the need for additional funding.'
279. *See also Collier/Andrus*, Transfer Pricing and the Arm's Length Principle After BEPS (2017) Mn 7.12; *Navisotschnigg* in *Lang/Storck/Petruzzi/Risse* 82 (tax authorities' comment).
280. *See* OECD TPG 2017 Mn 9.123.
281. *See also Navisotschnigg* in *Lang/Storck/Petruzzi/Risse* 82 (participant's comment).
282. *See* sec. 2.5.3.2.
283. *Hafkenscheid*, ITPJ 2017, 20.
284. *See also Navisotschnigg* in *Lang/Storck/Petruzzi/Risse* 82 (participant's comment); *Collier/Dykes*, BIT 2020, 714.
285. OECD TPG 2017 Mn 6.59.

tangible assets (e.g., plant and equipment), other intangibles (e.g., intangibles that are used as a basis for further development), or financial assets (e.g., the provision of funding).[286] Especially the importance of funding for the entitlement to intangible-related returns was subject to discussion in the BEPS Project.[287] So-called cash boxes – '[capital-rich] shell companies with few if any employees and little or no economic activity, which seek to take advantage of low or no-tax jurisdictions' –[288] were a thorn in the side of the OECD.[289] As these companies provided the necessary funding for the development of an intangible (and contractually assumed the associated risks), they could, '[u]nder the old guidance, [...] become the legal owners of intangibles and claim significant amounts of royalties in accordance with the arm's-length principle'.[290]

With the revisions of the BEPS Project, it was clarified that the mere provision of funding does not entitle to any intangible-related returns.[291] In this context, it is distinguished between the following situations:[292]

- provision of funding and control over operational risks;[293]
- provision of funding and control over financial risks;[294] and
- mere provision of funding.[295]

2.5.4.2 *Provision of Funding and Control over Operational Risks*

In order to be entitled to all of the intangible-related returns, the OECD TPG 2017 expect the legal owner to provide the funding for the DEMPE of an intangible and, additionally, exercise control over associated operational risks. Operational risks are risks that 'are linked to the operational activities for which the funding is used'.[296]

For example, in the case of a contract R&D arrangement for which funding is provided for the development of an intangible, the principal is supposed to have

286. OECD TPG 2017 Mn 6.59; *see also* OECD TPG 2017 Mn 1.54.
287. *See* FN 48.
288. *OECD*, Explanatory Statement – 2015 Final Reports (2015) Mn 16.
289. *See also Musselli/Musselli*, Rise of a New Standard: Profit Location in Countries of Important Intangible Functions Managers, ITPJ 2017, 331 (331); *see also Collier/Dykes*, BIT 2020, 705: '[Cases] involving a contractual allocation of profits that was perceived to be at variance with the substantive contribution of the legal entities within the MNE group, were made not just the central target of the transfer pricing work in BEPS but, rather, the central target of the Project as a whole'; on other BEPS Actions that also target cash boxes (besides Action 9), *see OECD*, Aligning Transfer Pricing Outcomes with Value Creation – Actions 8-10: 2015 Final Reports (2015) 11.
290. *Hoor*, The Revised OECD Transfer Pricing Guidance on Intangibles: A Critical Analysis, TNI 2018, 529 (535); *see also Musselli/Musselli*, ITPJ 2017, 332f; on the relevance of legal ownership in the OECD TPG 2017 and the OECD TPG 2010, *see* sec. 2.4.2.
291. *OECD*, Aligning Transfer Pricing Outcomes with Value Creation – Actions 8-10: 2015 Final Reports (2015) 11.
292. *See also Collier/Andrus*, Transfer Pricing and the Arm's Length Principle After BEPS (2017) Mn 6.44ff.
293. *See* sec. 2.5.4.2.
294. *See* sec. 2.5.4.3.
295. *See* sec. 2.5.4.4.
296. OECD TPG 2017 Mn 6.61.

control over the development risk (i.e., the risk that the research project is unsuccessful).[297] The principal may do so 'through exercising its capability and authority in making a number of relevant decisions about whether and how to take on the development risk. These include the decision to perform part of the development work itself, the decision to seek specialist input, the decision to hire the particular researcher, the decision of the type of research that should be carried out and objectives assigned to it, and the decision of the budget allocated to [the contract researcher]'.[298] With respect to the necessary substance requirements, reference can be made to the section on important functions[299] and the section on the control over risk-requirement.[300]

2.5.4.3 Provision of Funding and Control over Financial Risks

Financial risks – in contrast to operational risks[301] – are risks that 'are linked to the funding provided for the investments'.[302] A company that provides funding and exercises control over the respective financial risk but not control over the operational risk is only entitled to a risk-adjusted return on its funding.[303] That is, it is only entitled to the profits associated with the financial risks, whereas the intangible-related returns are allocated to the party that has control over the operational risks.[304]

The substance required for control over financial risks is based on the general guidance for control over risk.[305] Accordingly, 'control over a specific financial risk requires the capability to make the relevant decisions related to [...] the provision of the funding, together with the actual performance of these decision making functions'.[306] This includes *inter alia* 'the capability to make decisions to take on or decline the financing opportunity, or the capability to make decisions on whether and how to respond to the risks associated with the financing opportunity'.[307] More precisely, it is expected that a taxpayer can and actually does evaluate a potential project for which funding is provided from a financial perspective (like an investor who determines the likelihood and amount of cash flows that a potential project could generate if successful

297. OECD TPG 2017 Mn 6.65; *see also Stein/Schwarz/Holinski*, DStR 2017, 121.
298. OECD TPG 2017 Mn 1.83.
299. *See* sec. 2.5.2.1.
300. *See* sec. 2.5.3.2.
301. *See* sec. 2.5.4.2.
302. OECD TPG 2017 Mn 6.61.
303. OECD TPG 2017 Mn 6.61; *see also* Example 6 in the annex to Chapter VI of the OECD TPG 2017; for more details on how to determine a risk-adjusted rate of return, *see OECD*, Transfer Pricing Guidance on Financial Transactions (2020) 43f.
304. However, *see also Musselli*, Anti-Abuse Notion of 'Control over Intangible- Related Functions' Is Beyond the Arm's Length Principle, ET 2018, 191 (193ff) and *Schmidtke*, IStR 2015, 119f according to whom a properly calculated risk-adjusted return may have the result that the funder is entitled to a significant return.
305. *See* sec. 2.5.3.2.
306. OECD TPG 2017 Mn 6.63.
307. OECD TPG 2017 Mn 1.103; *see also* OECD TPG 2017 Mn 6.64: 'Depending on the facts and circumstances, such decisions may depend on an assessment of the creditworthiness of the party receiving the funds and an assessment of how the risks related to the development project may impact the expectations in relation to the returns on funding provided or additional funding required.'

and hence the appropriate risk premium that should be earned).[308] That is, unlike control over operational risk, control over financial risk does generally not require active involvement in the development of the intangible.[309]

As a consequence, control over the operational risk (in particular, the development risk) requires knowledge in the field for which funding is provided (focus on technical or scientific skills),[310] whereas control over the financial risk requires knowledge about the funding itself (focus on financial skills). However, control over financial risk may also require certain technical or scientific knowledge since operational risks often have an influence on financial risks.[311] For example, in order to accurately project future cash flows from a potentially funded project (and hence the borrower's ability to repay the funding), it may be important to assess the current state of the project and the probability of its success which requires an understanding in the field of the project.[312] In such a situation, the question may arise whether a taxpayer is already entitled to a share of the intangible-related returns.[313]

---

308. *Bilaney*, Understanding Risk in the Era of the OECD/G20 Base Erosion and Profit Shifting Initiative, BIT 2016, 576 (577); *see also* the example in OECD TPG 2017 Mn 1.85 and 1.103; with regard to the outsourcing of information gathering and the outsourcing of risk mitigation functions in such a case, the same considerations apply as in sec. 2.5.3.2, *see* OECD TPG 2017 Mn 6.63.

309. In this direction, *OECD*, Aligning Transfer Pricing Outcomes with Value Creation – Actions 8-10: 2015 Final Reports (2015) 65: 'An associated enterprise providing funding and assuming the related financial risks, *but not performing any functions relating to the intangible*, could generally only expect a risk-adjusted return on its funding' (emphasis added); *see also Collier/Andrus*, Transfer Pricing and the Arm's Length Principle After BEPS (2017) Mn 6.45: '[A]n entity might make independent decisions about whether to fund investments in research and development, and review those decisions from time to time, without also controlling the course of the research itself. Such an investor would be deemed to bear investment risk but not development risk.'

310. *See* sec. 2.5.3.2.

311. *See also Polonska*, Cost Contribution Arrangements and Funding Activities, ITPJ 2018, 92 (107).

312. *See also* OECD TPG 2017 Mn 6.64: 'The higher the development risk and the closer the financial risk is related to the development risk, *the more the funder will need to have the capability to assess the progress of the development of the intangible* and the consequences of this progress for achieving its expected funding return, and the more closely the funder may link the continued provision of funding to key operational developments that may impact its financial risk' (emphasis added).

313. In this context, *see also Collier/Andrus*, Transfer Pricing and the Arm's Length Principle After BEPS (2017) Mn 6.46: 'Virtually no guidance is given on what it means for an individual member of an MNE group to bear and control investment risk. Presumably there is some requirement that the entity have an independent say in how its excess cash will be invested and an ability to evaluate and choose between alternative investments. How such a requirement fits in the centralized management and decision making structures of modern MNE groups is, however, quite mysterious. Whether a local low-tax group member must have the ability to defy the group's senior global management on investment decisions in order to control its investment risk is unclear at best, as is the evidence of independence that might be required for a single group member to establish control over its investment risks. The typical corporate decision making process might involve collaborative decision making and efforts to find consensus, but whether such practices will prevent or enable a finding of control in a particular local, tax-advantaged affiliate is not clear.'

2.5.4.4 *Mere Provision of Funding*

A company that merely provides funding but has no control over the operational risk or even the financial risk is only entitled to a risk-free return on its funding.[314] This would be the case, for example, if a company 'just provides the money when it is asked to do so, without any assessment of whether the party receiving the money is creditworthy'.[315] Moreover, in this case, the commercial rationality of the transaction has to be assessed which could lead to its non-recognition, and thus the company may not even receive a risk-free return.[316]

Therefore, according to the OECD TPG 2017,[317] funding alone does not create any value; i.e., it does not constitute relevant substance with regard to the entitlement to intangible-related returns.[318] Nonetheless, this does not mean that funding is irrelevant since the OECD TPG 2017 expect the legal owner to provide 'all assets, including funding, necessary to the [DEMPE] of the intangibles' to be entitled to all of the corresponding intangible-related returns.[319] However, funding always has to be undertaken together with other relevant economic activities (i.e., the performance of important functions or the control over operational risks) to have an impact on the allocation of intangible-related returns.[320] Effectively, the OECD TPG 2017 prioritize the production factor labour over capital.[321]

2.5.5 Synopsis

In order to be entitled to all of the intangible-related returns, the legal owner must:[322]

- perform the important DEMPE functions through its own personnel;[323]
- have control over risks related to the DEMPE of the intangible;[324]

314. OECD TPG 2017 Mn 1.103; *OECD*, Aligning Transfer Pricing Outcomes with Value Creation - Actions 8-10: 2015 Final Reports (2015) 65; *see also* Example 16 in the annex to Chapter VI of the OECD TPG 2017; for more details on how to determine a risk-free rate of return, *see OECD*, Transfer Pricing Guidance on Financial Transactions (2020) 42f.
315. *OECD*, Aligning Transfer Pricing Outcomes with Value Creation - Actions 8-10: 2015 Final Reports (2015) 11.
316. OECD TPG 2017 Mn 1.103; OECD, Aligning Transfer Pricing Outcomes with Value Creation - Actions 8-10: 2015 Final Reports (2015) 11; on the non-recognition of accurately delineated transactions, *see also* sec. 2.6.
317. For criticism on this general assumption, *see* sec. 2.7.
318. *See also OECD*, Aligning Transfer Pricing Outcomes with Value Creation - Actions 8-10: 2015 Final Reports (2015) 13: '*[C]apital without functionality* will generate no more than a risk-free return, assuring that no premium returns will be allocated to *cash boxes without relevant substance*' (emphasis added).
319. OECD TPG 2017 Mn 6.71.
320. *See also OECD*, Aligning Transfer Pricing Outcomes with Value Creation - Actions 8-10: 2015 Final Reports (2015) 11: '[T]his guidance will ensure that capital-rich entities without any other relevant economic activities ("cash boxes") will not be entitled to any excess profits.'
321. Critical *Hoor*, TNI 2018, 535; *Musselli/Musselli*, ITPJ 2017, 339; *Pankiv*, ITPJ 2016, 471; *Sim/Rigo/Agrawal*, Treatment of Funding Risk and Capital - Financial Services versus Non-Financial Services: Never the Twain Shall Meet?, ITPJ 2020, 229 (233); *see also* sec. 2.7.
322. *See also* OECD TPG 2017 Mn 6.71.
323. *See* sec. 2.5.2.1.
324. *See* sec. 2.5.3.2; this is equivalent to having control over an outsourced normal function; *see* sec. 2.5.2.2.

- have the financial capacity to assume risks related to the DEMPE of the intangible;[325] and
- provide the necessary funding for the DEMPE of the intangible.[326]

The DEMPE Approach is an activity-based concept because 'operational profits [are] allocated to the economic activities which generate them' (link between activity and income).[327] A company performs such economic activities through its personnel who should be competent in the relevant technical or scientific field and actually make decisions with regard to the DEMPE of an intangible.[328] Therefore, the DEMPE Approach focuses on functions - more precisely, important functions and decision-making functions - that people perform.[329] Such an approach is not new in itself but is already applied under the authorized OECD approach[330] ('significant people functions') for the allocation of income between a head office and a PE.[331] However, in contrast to the situation between a head office and a PE where an income allocation based on legal obligations (more specifically, the contractual assumption of risk) is not possible since the head office and the PE are one and the same legal entity,[332] this would very well be possible in the context of Article 9 OECD MC which concerns the allocation of income between two separate legal entities.[333] In fact, the intended purpose of emphasizing the importance of people functions under Article 9 OECD MC is 'to prevent tax planning based on separation of functions from risks and assets'.[334] Cash box companies that only contractually assume risks and provide funding are unwanted.[335] In this context, the control over risk-requirement plays a central role.[336]

325. *See* sec. 2.5.3.3; however, *see also* the comments made there that a party that has control over risk regularly will have the financial capacity to assume the risk.
326. *See* sec. 2.5.4.2.
327. *OECD*, Aligning Transfer Pricing Outcomes with Value Creation - Actions 8-10: 2015 Final Reports (2015) 10; *see also Chand/Malek*, The relevant economic activity test and its impact on the international corporate tax policy framework, BTR 2019, 394 (398ff).
328. *See* secs 2.5.2.1 and 2.5.3.2.
329. *See also Kroppen* in *Lüdicke/Schnitger/Spengel* 205.
330. *See OECD*, 2010 Report on the Attribution of Profits to Permanent Establishments (2010) Mn 15ff.
331. *See also Kroppen* in *Lüdicke/Schnitger/Spengel* 205; *Andresen*, Comments on Professor Schoueri's Lecture 'Arm's Length: Beyond the Guidelines of the OECD', BIT 2015, 717 (717); *Stein/Schwarz/Holinski*, DStR 2017, 120 FN 24; *Wittendorff*, TNI 2016, 338; for a comparison on risk assumption under the Authorised OECD Approach and the 2017 OECD Transfer Pricing Guidelines, *see De Baets*, Risk Assumption under the Authorised OECD Approach and the 2017 OECD Transfer Pricing Guidelines, TPI 2018, 243 (243ff).
332. *See also OECD*, 2010 Report on the Attribution of Profits to Permanent Establishments (2010) Mn 14f.
333. *See also Kroppen* in *Lüdicke/Schnitger/Spengel* 205; *Wittendorff*, TNI 2012, 946.
334. *Wittendorff*, TNI 2016, 338.
335. *See* sec. 2.5.4.1; *see also OECD*, Guidance on Transfer Pricing Aspects of Intangibles - Action 8: 2014 Deliverable (2014) 11 where the OECD explicitly states that it would consider '[r]equiring application of rules analogous to those applied under Article 7 and the Authorised OECD Approach to certain situations involving excessive capitalisation of low function entities'.
336. *See* secs 2.5.4.2 and 2.5.4.3; *see also Collier/Andrus*, Transfer Pricing and the Arm's Length Principle After BEPS (2017) Mn 6.65: 'The notions regarding risk, the difference between financing risk and development risk, the control of risk, and the control of functions, including important development and intangible protection functions play a central role in the discussion

Value creation under the DEMPE Approach concerns people functions on the strategical and tactical level (management activities) as opposed to people functions on the operational level (day-to-day activities).[337] A company is expected to have the internal competencies to perform important functions and decision-making functions and to actually perform these functions, meaning they must not be outsourced (otherwise, it will not be solely entitled to all of the intangible-related returns if such functions are performed by associated enterprises).[338] By contrast, external factors (e.g., market-specific characteristics)[339] are not considered as value-creating factors under the DEMPE Approach.[340] Therefore, they are also not considered as substance of a company. Nevertheless, they have to be considered as comparability factors when performing a comparability analysis.[341] As a result, it is possible that associated enterprises resident in different countries may receive a different remuneration even though they have the same level of substance.

The DEMPE Approach is a qualitative approach for defining substance as it only provides abstract criteria ('important functions') to assess whether the relevant substance requirements are met.[342] That is, although the DEMPE Approach provides an illustrative list of important functions, it always has to be assessed based on the facts and circumstances which functions are 'important functions'.[343] As is generally the case in a functional analysis, it is not relevant which party performs more functions (quantitative) but which party performs the more valuable functions (qualitative).[344] Therefore, it cannot be deduced that one company contributed more to the creation of value than another company simply because it has deployed more personnel.[345] Vividly speaking, 'a handful of IT programmers in one jurisdiction may generate more value than hundreds of people assembling a product in another jurisdiction'.[346]

---

of intangible ownership and the entitlement to returns from the exploitation of intangibles. These notions are intended to keep economic activity and income from intangibles aligned so as to avoid the separation of income from value creation.'

337. *See* secs 2.5.2.1 and 2.5.3.2.
338. *See also Monsenego*, ITPJ 2014, 12.
339. *See* FN 144.
340. I.e., the analysis is focused on the supply side, *see Becker/Englisch*, Taxing Where Value Is Created: What's 'User Involvement' Got to Do with It?, Intertax 2019, 161 (165); *Jiménez*, Value Creation: A Guiding Light for the Interpretation of Tax Treaties?, BIT 2020, 197 (207); however, *see also* the considerations in *Das*, The Concept of Value Creation: Is It Relevant for the Allocation of Taxing Rights?, BIT 2020, 134 (136ff) with regard to value creation and demand side factors.
341. *See* sec. 2.3.
342. *See* sec. 1.1.
343. *See* sec. 2.5.2.1.
344. *See also* OECD TPG 2017 Mn 1.51: 'While one party may provide a large number of functions relative to that of the other party to the transaction, it is the economic significance of those functions in terms of their frequency, nature, and value to the respective parties to the transactions that is important.'
345. *See also Hey*, 'Taxation Where Value is Created' and the OECD/G20 Base Erosion and Profit Shifting Initiative, BIT 2018, 203 (203).
346. *Petruzzi/Navisotschnigg*, BEPS and EU requirements for Country-by-Country Reporting, in *Lang/Haunold* (Eds), Transparenz und Informationsaustausch: Der gläserne Steuerpflichtige (2016) 51 (64), who, for this reason, question the informative value of reporting the number of employees under the Country-by-Country Report.

The DEMPE Approach does not prohibit MNEs from establishing or maintaining IP Companies in low or no tax jurisdictions or in jurisdictions that offer a patent box regime.[347] However, with its focus on people functions – and where these functions are performed –[348] MNEs have to locate competent personnel with decision-making authority in the jurisdiction of an IP Company in order to sustain such a structure.[349] IP Companies that are only responsible for administrating intangibles will not be entitled to any intangible-related returns.[350] The DEMPE Approach may therefore have the unintended consequence that MNEs will shift not only profits (based on shifting contracts and capital as before the BEPS Project) but also people – and the profit potential attached with them – from high-tax jurisdictions to low-tax jurisdictions.[351] Such a transfer is not considered in conflict with the DEMPE Approach.

2.6 RECOGNITION OF THE ACCURATELY DELINEATED TRANSACTION

The functional analysis ensures that the parties' contracts are consistent with their conduct, that is, that the form and the substance of a transaction are aligned. This enables the accurate delineation of the transaction. In the next step, an accurately delineated transaction should be priced at arm's length.[352] In exceptional circumstances, however, the OECD TPG 2017 provide the possibility to disregard an accurately delineated transaction.[353]

In general, it is acknowledged that 'MNEs are free to organize their business operations as they see fit' and that '[t]ax administrations do not have the right to dictate to an MNE how to design its structure or where to locate its business operations'.[354] Consequently, when a controlled transaction can also be found between independent parties in comparable circumstances, it must not be disregarded.[355] On top of that, 'the

347. *See also Screpante,* Rethinking the Arm's Length Principle and Its Impact on the IP Licence Model after OECD/G20 BEPS Actions 8-10: Nothing Changed But the Change?, WTJ 2019, 425 (475ff).
348. *Screpante,* WTJ 2019, 467; critical in this regard *Kroppen* in *Lüdicke/Schnitger/Spengel* 206; in this context, *see also* the practical tips on the physical presence of an IP Company's management team provided in *Huibregtse/Peeters/Verdoner/Carey,* IP companies and substance: no-fly zones? TPIJ 2011, 4 (8).
349. *See also Wittendorff,* TNI 2016, 332f.
350. *Penttilä/Isomaa-Myllymäki,* ET 2018, 86; *see also* Example 1 in the annex to Chapter VI of the OECD TPG 2017.
351. *Screpante,* WTJ 2019, 475ff; *Wittendorff,* TNI 2016, 332f; *Hoor,* TNI 2018, 537.
352. *See also OECD,* Aligning Transfer Pricing Outcomes with Value Creation – Actions 8-10: 2015 Final Reports (2015) 14.
353. *See* OECD TPG 2017 Mn 1.121ff; likewise, the OECD TPG 2010 also addressed the recognition of transactions, *see* OECD TPG 2010 Mn 1.64ff; however, this section was revised with the BEPS Project, *see OECD,* Aligning Transfer Pricing Outcomes with Value Creation – Actions 8-10: 2015 Final Reports (2015) 38ff; *see also OECD,* BEPS Actions 8, 9 and 10: Discussion Draft on Revisions to Chapter I of the Transfer Pricing Guidelines (Including Risk, Recharacterisation, and Special Measures) (2014) Mn 85ff on why – according to the OECD – there is a need for the non-recognition of arrangements under the TPG.
354. OECD TPG 2017 Mn 9.34.
355. OECD TPG 2017 Mn 1.122.

mere fact that the transaction may not be seen between independent parties does not mean that it should not be recognized'.[356] Indeed, '[a]ssociated enterprises may have the ability to enter into a much greater variety of arrangements than can independent enterprises, and may conclude transactions of a specific nature that are not encountered, or are only very rarely encountered, between independent parties [like IP Companies[357]], and may do so for sound business reasons'.[358]

In order to disregard a transaction, the key question that has to be answered is whether the transaction 'possesses the commercial rationality of arrangements that would be agreed between unrelated parties under comparable economic circumstances' (commercial rationality test).[359] More precisely, a transaction 'may be disregarded, and if appropriate, replaced by an alternative transaction, where the arrangements made in relation to the transaction, viewed in their totality, differ from those which would have been adopted by independent enterprises behaving in a commercially rational manner in comparable circumstances, thereby preventing determination of a price that would be acceptable to both of the parties taking into account their respective perspectives and the options realistically available to each of them at the time of entering into the transaction'.[360] By contrast, it is not required that a transaction was primarily undertaken to obtain a tax benefit.[361] At the same time, however, the OECD TPG 2017 mention that it is relevant to consider 'whether the MNE group as a whole is left worse off on a pre-tax basis since this may be an indicator that the transaction viewed in its entirety lacks the commercial rationality of arrangements between unrelated parties'.[362]

If a transaction is disregarded, it should be replaced with an alternative transaction that comports 'as closely as possible with the facts of the actual transaction undertaken whilst achieving a commercially rational expected result that would have enabled the parties to come to a price acceptable to both of them at the time the arrangement was entered into'.[363]

All in all, the guidance on the recognition of an accurately delineated transaction is far from clear.[364] In particular, 'it remains difficult to determine what independent enterprises behaving in a commercially rational manner would have done'.[365] Moreover, there is the risk that tax administrations, with the benefit of hindsight, judge the

356. OECD TPG 2017 Mn 1.122.
357. *See also Pankiv*, Contemporary application of the Arm's Length Principle in Transfer Pricing (2017) 89.
358. OECD TPG 2017 Mn 1.122; *see also* OECD TPG 2017 Mn 9.35.
359. OECD TPG 2017 Mn 1.123.
360. OECD TPG 2017 Mn 1.122; *see also* the similar wording in OECD TPG 2010 Mn 1.65; for a detailed analysis of this provision, *see Bullen*, Arm's Length Transaction Structures: Recognizing and restructuring controlled transactions in transfer pricing (2011) 511ff.
361. *See also* OECD TPG 2017 Mn 9.38.
362. OECD TPG 2017 Mn 1.122.
363. OECD TPG 2017 Mn 1.124; *see also* OECD TPG 2017 Mn 9.35.
364. *Wittendorff*, TNI 2016, 340.
365. *Wittendorff*, TNI 2016, 340; furthermore, the two examples provided in OECD TPG 2017 Mn 1.126ff are not particularly instructive, *see also Collier/Andrus*, Transfer Pricing and the Arm's Length Principle After BEPS (2017) Mn 6.12; what is more, *de Lange/Lankhorst/Hafkenscheid*,

commercial rationality of a transaction differently when knowing that an originally expected financial benefit eventually did not materialize.[366]

In the context of IP Companies, the OECD TPG 2017 state that when a sale of an intangible 'is part of a broader restructuring involving changes to the arrangements relating to the development and use of the intangible, then the commercial rationality of the intangible sale should not be examined in isolation of these changes'.[367] That is, the commercial rationality of the restructuring as a whole (i.e., the centralization of the ownership of valuable intangibles) has to be assessed. However, since IP Companies are (typically) established for sound business reasons,[368] and 'the fact that a business restructuring arrangement is motivated by a purpose of obtaining tax benefits does not of itself warrant a conclusion that it is a non-arm's length arrangement',[369] IP Companies should regularly not be challenged by the commercial rationality test unless there is no apparent business reason for their existence. The focus should primarily be on the pricing of the relevant transactions (i.e., establishing an arm's-length price for the sale of intangibles or for corresponding royalties or for outsourced activities).[370]

2.7 COMPATIBILITY OF THE NEW REQUIREMENTS WITH THE ARM'S-LENGTH PRINCIPLE

In its BEPS Action Plan, the OECD stated that '*special measures*, either within or *beyond the arm's length principle, may be required* with respect to intangible assets, risk and

(Non-)Recognition of Transactions between Associated Enterprises: On Behaving in a Commercially Rational Manner, Decision-Making Traps and BEPS, ITPJ 2015, 85 (90ff) highlight that independent enterprises do not always behave in a commercially rational manner; therefore, it would not be appropriate to assume a level of rationality for associated enterprises that does not apply to independent enterprises.

366. *See also Heggmair*, ITPJ 2017, 266.

367. OECD TPG 2017 Mn 9.36.

368. *See* sec. 1.5; admittedly, this section deals with reasons to establish an IP Company from the perspective of an MNE as a whole and not from the perspective of one of its constituting entities; however, based on the separate entity approach, the OECD TPG 2017 Mn 9.37 state that 'it is not sufficient from a transfer pricing perspective that a restructuring arrangement makes commercial sense for the group as a whole: the arrangement must be arm's length at the level of each individual taxpayer, taking account of its rights and other assets, expected benefits from the arrangement (i.e. any consideration of the post-restructuring arrangement plus, if applicable, any compensation payments for the restructuring itself), and realistically available options'; however, it is also stated that when 'a restructuring makes commercial sense for the group as a whole on a pre-tax basis, it is expected that an appropriate transfer price (that is, any compensation for the post-restructuring arrangement plus, if applicable, any compensation payments for the restructuring itself) would generally be available to provide arm's length compensation for each accurately delineated transaction comprising the business restructuring for each individual group member participating in it' [i.e., the transaction has to be recognized]; therefore, the reasons provided in sec. 1.5 may be used to establish that a restructuring makes commercial sense for the group as a whole on a pre-tax basis.

369. *See also* OECD TPG 2017 Mn 9.38.

370. *See also* the considerations in *Bullen*, Arm's Length Transaction Structures: Recognizing and restructuring controlled transactions in transfer pricing (2011) 651ff; furthermore, interesting in this context, although not particularly enlightening, the example provided in OECD TPG 2017 Mn 9.122ff.

over-capitalisation to address [flaws in the current system]' (emphasis added).[371] In the final reports on BEPS Actions 8-10, however, it is claimed that 'the goals set by the BEPS Action Plan in relation to the development of transfer pricing rules have been achieved *without the need to develop special measures outside the arm's length principle*' (emphasis added).[372]

By contrast, criticism is voiced in literature that certain presumptions - control over risk and the insignificance of the provision of funding - are no longer in line with the arm's-length principle.

With regard to control over risk, *Schön* expresses the following concerns:[373]

> In most cases, independent parties hire service providers simply because they trust them and rely on contractual and legal remedies if they fail to deliver. Nobody would hire a doctor, a lawyer or an architect if he were supposed to possess superior knowledge enabling him to 'control' the activities of the agent. Against this background, it seems that the notion of 'control' is dangerous and misleading in so far as it goes beyond the basic contractual limitations for opportunistic behaviour of agents. *The arm's length standard does not require full and substantial control of the agent's activities* (emphasis added).

Furthermore, the insignificance of the provision of funding for an entitlement to intangible-related returns is heavily criticized.[374] Indeed, in arm's-length situations, it is regularly the case that a person who merely puts funds at disposal is also entitled to a bulk of the returns generated by them irrespective of any active involvement in the funded activity.[375]

Of course, the reason behind these requirements is that, within an MNE, capital as well as the contractual assumption of risk can easily be transferred to a company in a low-tax country.[376] According to the OECD, '[s]uch arrangements may result in or contribute to BEPS'.[377] Therefore, the OECD saw the need to '[d]evelop rules to prevent

371. *OECD*, Action Plan on Base Erosion and Profit Shifting (2013) 20; *see* already sec. 1.3.2.
372. *OECD*, Aligning Transfer Pricing Outcomes with Value Creation - Actions 8-10: 2015 Final Reports (2015) 12.
373. *Schön*, International Taxation of Risk, BIT 2014, 280 (289); similar criticism is expressed by Musselli, ET 2018, 204; *Heggmair*, ITPJ 2017, 264; *Kroppen's* comment in *Kroppen/Eigelshoven*, Verrechnungspreise im Wandel, TPI 2019, 2 (2f).
374. *See* already the references in FN 321; particularly critical *Kroppen* in *Lüdicke/Schnitger/Spengel* 205.
375. *See Boidman/Kandev*, BEPS: A Spent Force or Radical Change?, TNI 2015, 837 (842), with reference to the standard '2/20' fee arrangement in the private equity industry; *Bärsch/Luckhaupt/Schulz*, Ubg 2014, 44, with reference to common contract R&D arrangements between unrelated parties in the mechanical engineering industry and the software industry; for an analysis based on contract theory, *see also Musselli*, Intangible Revenues Assigned to the Developer and Not to the Funder Lacking 'Development Monitoring Staff': OECD Transfer Pricing Anti-Abuse Rule Clashes with Economics of Contracts, International Tax Journal 2017, 37 (37ff).
376. *See OECD*, Addressing Base Erosion and Profit Shifting (2013) 42: 'While it may be difficult to shift underlying functions, the risks and ownership of tangible and intangible assets may, by their very nature, be easier to shift'; *see also* sec. 2.5.5.
377. *OECD*, Addressing Base Erosion and Profit Shifting (2013) 42.

BEPS by transferring risks among, or allocating excessive capital to, group members'.[378] As a result, the new requirements as mentioned above were primarily introduced to remedy perceived abusive arrangements, whereas the 'problem of matching "conditions that independent parties would have agreed upon in similar circumstances" is clearly a secondary target [...]'.[379]

However, the arm's-length principle as such is a neutral concept that seeks to 'put related parties on an equal footing with unrelated parties [...]'.[380] The above-mentioned requirements, on the other hand, understand the arm's-length principle as an anti-abuse rule.[381] Effectively, this means that the DEMPE Approach may require more substance from a taxpayer for an entitlement to intangible-related returns in related party transactions than what can be found in transactions between unrelated parties under comparable circumstances.[382] For this reason, critics opine that the OECD should have addressed the undesirable arrangements with tools other than the arm's-length principle (e.g., CFC rules) as the arm's-length principle - if applied properly - cannot be used to tackle them.[383]

In this context, the OECD TPG 2017 state the following with regard to control over risk:[384]

> In light of the potential complexity that may arise in some circumstances when determining whether an associated enterprise assuming a risk controls that risk, *the test of control should be regarded as being met where comparable risk assumptions can be identified in a comparable uncontrolled transaction.* To be comparable those risk assumptions require that the economically relevant characteristics of the transactions are comparable. If such a comparison is made, it is particularly relevant to establish that the enterprise assuming comparable risk in the uncontrolled transaction performs comparable risk management functions relating to control of that risk to those performed by the associated enterprise assuming risk in the controlled transaction. The purpose of the comparison is to establish that an independent party assuming a comparable risk to that assumed by the associated enterprise also performs comparable risk management functions to those performed by the associated enterprise (emphasis added).

378. *OECD*, Action Plan on Base Erosion and Profit Shifting (2013) 20.
379. *Musselli/Musselli*, ITPJ 2017, 333.
380. *Pankiv*, ITPJ 2016, 463.
381. *See also Hoor*, TNI 2018, 536; *Musselli*, International Tax Journal 2017, 42; expressly, the two leading figures of the BEPS Project, *Saint-Amans/Russo*, The BEPS Package: Promise Kept, BIT 2016, 236 (238): 'In the area of transfer pricing, the guidance on the arm's length principle has been updated to ensure that what dictates results is the economic rather than the purely legal reality. What is, in effect, an anti-avoidance principle cannot and should not be applied to achieve the very results it is intended to prevent.'
382. *Hoor*, TNI 2018, 536; *Musselli/Musselli*, ITPJ 2017, 332f; *Heggmair*, ITPJ 2017, 265; *Kroppen's* comment in *Kroppen/Eigelshoven*, TPI 2019, 2f; *see also* the example provided in *L. Schoueri*, Arm' s Length: Beyond the Guidelines of the OECD, BIT 2015, 690 (714f).
383. *See Kroppen's* comment in *Kroppen/Eigelshoven*, TPI 2019, 3; *Wittendorff*, TNI 2013, 1333; *see also L. Schoueri*, BIT 2015, 716: '[I]f the problem faced by the BEPS initiative is the allocation of profits to low-tax jurisdictions, discrimination against such jurisdictions could be an alternative to the BEPS solution to intangibles. This solution cannot be derived from a correct application of the [arm's length principle] and can, therefore, hardly be justified under the principle of equality.'
384. OECD TPG 2017 Mn 1.97.

Likewise, concerning the provision of funding, the following is stated:[385]

> The nature and amount of compensation attributable to an entity that bears intangible-related costs, without more, must be determined on the basis of all the relevant facts, and *should be consistent with similar funding arrangements among independent entities where such arrangements can be identified* (emphasis added).

Therefore, a company that has no control over risk and merely provides funding should, in theory,[386] still be able to claim intangible-related returns when it can establish that an independent company under similar circumstances would be entitled to these returns (i.e., empirical evidence can disprove the hypothetical assumptions).[387] This would be consistent with the original intent of the arm's-length principle to cater for 'the need for equality between related and unrelated firms'.[388] At the same time, however, this would undermine the effectiveness of the new rules.[389]

2.8 NEW APPLICATION OF THE ARM'S-LENGTH PRINCIPLE

On a similar note, criticism is voiced that the changes introduced with BEPS Actions 8-10 have led to the 'birth of a new arm's-length principle'.[390] Generally, the OECD TPG 2010 stressed that an examination of transfer prices 'should be based on the transaction actually undertaken by the associated enterprises as it has been structured by them [...]' (as-structured principle).[391,392] That is, save for exceptional circumstances,[393] a controlled transaction must be recognized and priced at arm's length. If the set transfer prices are not at arm's length, a price adjustment can be made.

The OECD TPG 2017, on the other hand, apply a two-step approach:[394] First, it is examined whether the conduct of the parties is at arm's length. Specifically, the contractual allocation of risk is only accepted when a party that contractually assumes the risk has control over risk and the financial capacity to bear the risk.[395] If not, the risk is allocated to the party that has control over risk and the financial capacity to bear the risk based on the hypothetical assumption that independent companies in comparable

385. OECD TPG 2017 Mn 6.59.
386. However, *Collier/Andrus*, Transfer Pricing and the Arm's Length Principle After BEPS (2017) Mn 7.20 point out that OECD TPG 2017 Mn 1.97 (*see* wording above) requires strict comparability between the tested transaction and the comparable transaction. This could thus prevent an independent transaction being considered comparable.
387. Same opinion *Polonska*, ITPJ 2018, 92 (108).
388. *L. Schoueri*, BIT 2015, 695.
389. *See also Collier/Andrus*, Transfer Pricing and the Arm's Length Principle After BEPS (2017) Mn 7.21.
390. *Wittendorff*, TNI 2016, 331.
391. *See Bullen*, Arm's Length Transaction Structures: Recognizing and restructuring controlled transactions in transfer pricing (2011) 83ff.
392. OECD TPG 2010 Mn 1.64.
393. *See* OECD TPG 2010 Mn 1.65ff; on the recognition of the accurately delineated transaction in the OECD TPG 2017, *see* sec. 2.6.
394. *Kroppen* in *Lüdicke/Schnitger/Spengel* 203.
395. *See* sec. 2.5.3.

circumstances would have agreed to this type of risk allocation.[396] Effectively, this is a partial recharacterization of the transaction as structured by the taxpayer (i.e., a structural adjustment is made).[397] Only in a second step is the (adjusted) transaction priced at arm's length and, if priced incorrectly, a price adjustment can be made by tax administrations. Therefore, 'now both the transfer price and certain aspects of the controlled transaction itself must be arm's length'.[398]

In light of the above,[399] it is clear that the updates of the BEPS Project (more specifically, the DEMPE Approach) are not mere clarifications but an introduction of new concepts.[400] Admittedly, it is true that the requirements of control over risk and financial capacity to assume the risk can already be found in Chapter IX of the OECD TPG 2010.[401] However, unlike in the OECD TPG 2017, they were only considered as relevant but not determinative factors for the allocation of risk.[402] Therefore, the transfer pricing updates of the BEPS Project 'cannot be applied under existing tax treaties'.[403]

What is more, in order to become effective, the new requirements must also be translated into domestic law.[404] Article 9(1) OECD MC itself is not a suitable legal basis to perform adjustments of intra-group transactions.[405] Article 9(1) OECD MC only

396. However, empirical evidence of the risk allocation between independent parties in comparable circumstances may disprove this hypothetical assumption, *see* already sec. 2.7.
397. *Wittendorff*, TNI 2016, 334; this partial recharacterization is unconditional to the existence of exceptional circumstances, *see Wittendorff*, TNI 2016, 335.
398. *Wittendorff*, TNI 2016, 332.
399. *See also* the considerations in sec. 2.7.
400. The OECD probably has the opposite opinion, *see OECD*, Aligning Transfer Pricing Outcomes with Value Creation - Actions 8-10: 2015 Final Reports (2015) 10.
401. *See* OECD TPG 2010 Mn 9.20ff.
402. *See also De Baets/Gao* in *Lang/Storck/Petruzzi* 174; furthermore, the new guidelines are also stricter than before; for more details, *see Broemel*, Konzerninterne Auftragsforschungsverhältnisse im Spannungsfeld aktueller Entwicklungen bei der Zurechnung von immateriellen Wirtschaftsgütern, IStR 2013, 249 (251ff).
403. *Wittendorff*, TNI 2016, 333; *see also Kroppen* in *Lüdicke/Schnitger/Spengel* 204; *Langer*, TPI 2017, 85f; in general, a tax treaty should be interpreted on the basis of the OECD TPG that were available to the parties upon conclusion of the relevant tax treaty; this is because updates to the OECD TPG that were published after the conclusion of the relevant tax treaty 'cannot offer any clues as to what had then been the parties' intentions', *see Lang*, Later Commentaries of the OECD Committee on Fiscal Affairs, Not to Affect the Interpretation of Previously Concluded Tax Treaties, Intertax 1997, 7 (7) concerning updates of the OECD Commentary but the same is also true with regard to updates of the OECD TPG; for considerations on when OECD Commentaries that were published after the conclusion of a tax treaty - and again, the same is true with regard to later published OECD TPG - might be used in the interpretation thereof as a subsequent practice within the meaning of Art. 31(3)(b) VCLT, *see Lang*, Wer hat das Sagen im Steuerrecht?, ÖStZ 2006, 203 (208f); in practice, however, the opposite can be observed as tax authorities sometimes apply the DEMPE Approach even when auditing fiscal years prior to the update of the OECD TPG in 2017, *see Colling Russo/Karnath*, Intercompany Licensing of Intangibles - A Comparative Global Outlook, ITPJ 2019, 381 (384).
404. For more details, *see Wittendorff*, TNI 2012, 936ff.
405. As an example, *see* the case law in Finland, *Penttilä/Isomaa-Myllymäki*, ET 2018, 90ff; in general, 'DTC rules patterned after Art. 9 OECD Model are not an independent legal basis for the adjustment of profits between affiliated companies. Like every other DTC provision, these rules do not create tax liability. The legal basis can therefore only be found in domestic law. If there is no domestic law allowing for the adjustment of profits, there can be no profit

provides that 'domestic rules that provide for profit adjustments between affiliated companies must apply the arm's length principle'.[406] This entails that Article 9(1) OECD MC prohibits contracting states from increasing profits beyond the arm's-length principle under domestic law.[407]

At the same time, however, it has to be emphasized that the OECD TPG 2017 can only be used for the interpretation of Article 9(1) OECD MC insofar as they do not exceed its wording.[408] In this regard, it is questioned whether the wording of Article 9(1) OECD MC, which was left unchanged during the BEPS Project, even allows for structural adjustments as envisaged in the OECD TPG 2017.[409] If this is not the case, this would entail that the respective amendments of the OECD TPG 2017 could not become effective.[410] That is, even if a contracting state had translated the OECD TPG 2017 into its domestic law, Article 9(1) OECD MC would limit its taxing rights to mere price adjustments under this line of argumentation (i.e., structural adjustments that are possible under domestic law would be barred by Article 9(1) OECD MC).[411] This view was also confirmed, for example, in some decisions of the German Fiscal Federal Court.[412] This would mean that the OECD would have needed to change the wording of Article 9(1) so that structural adjustments as provided in the OECD TPG 2017 can successfully be performed.[413] However, there are also convincing arguments that the current wording of Article 9(1) OECD MC already covers structural adjustments.[414] In

adjustment pursuant to Art. 9 OECD Model', *see Lang*, Introduction to the Law of Double Taxation Conventions (2013) Mn 475.

406. *Lang*, Introduction to the Law of Double Taxation Conventions (2013) Mn 474; on the limiting effects of DTCs in general, *see Lang*, Introduction to the Law of Double Taxation Conventions (2013) Mn 44ff.
407. *See Kofler*, Die 'Sperrwirkung' des Art. 9 OECD-MA, TPI 2017, 70 (71f).
408. *See Vetter*, Zur rechtlichen Bedeutung der OECD Verrechnungspreisgrundsätze, SWI 1997, 547 (548).
409. An argument often brought forward in this regard is that Art. 9(1) OECD MC refers to 'their' (i.e., the 'associated enterprises') commercial or financial relations which is interpreted in the sense that the transaction as structured by the associated enterprises has to be respected, *see Wittendorff*, Transfer Pricing and the Arm's Length Principle in International Tax Law (2010) 152; therefore, 'only the "made or imposed" price or other types of valuation conditions - but not the underlying transactions themselves (i.e., the commercial and financial relations) - should be the object of an adjustment', *Kofler* in *Reimer/Rust*, Klaus Vogel on Double Taxation Conventions[4] (2015) Art. 9 Mn 96; *see also* the arguments mentioned in *Collier/Andrus*, Transfer Pricing and the Arm's Length Principle After BEPS (2017) Mn 4.100 FN 63.
410. *See also Collier/Andrus*, Transfer Pricing and the Arm's Length Principle After BEPS (2017) Mn 4.100.
411. *See Gosch*, Sperrwirkungen - Nationales Recht und Abkommensrecht, allgemeines und spezielles Recht im Widerstreit, ISR 2018, 289 (289ff) with further references.
412. *See Kroppen* in *Lüdicke/Schnitger/Spengel* 203f.
413. *See Wittendorff*, TNI 2012, 938.
414. For an extensive analysis, *see Bullen*, Arm's Length Transaction Structures: Recognizing and restructuring controlled transactions in transfer pricing (2011) 109ff; concerning the argument that Art. 9(1) OECD MC only allows the adjustment of 'made or imposed conditions' but not the adjustment of 'commercial or financial relations' (*see* FN 409), the author highlights that an adjustment of the 'conditions' would regularly involve an adjustment of the 'relations' since conditions and relations are interdependent; therefore, 'if Art. 9(1) is interpreted as only authorizing the adjustment of "conditions" but not of "relations", domestic tax administrations would be unable to do what they are authorized to do (i.e. adjust "conditions") without simultaneously doing what they are not authorized to do (i.e. adjust "relations")'; furthermore,

the same vein, the German Fiscal Federal Court eventually departed from its prior case law.[415] Still, a possible way to achieve more certainty in this context would have been if the OECD had redrafted Article 9(1) OECD MC in the BEPS Project and 'if [this] amendment had been implemented in tax treaties through the multilateral instrument under BEPS action 15'.[416]

2.9 APPROACHES TO DETERMINE SUBSTANCE IN PRACTICE: VALUE CONTRIBUTION ANALYSIS AND RACI ANALYSIS

With BEPS Action 8, the OECD aims at aligning transfer pricing outcomes with value creation.[417] However, while the OECD provides demonstrative examples for important functions that contribute significantly to the value creation of an intangible,[418] a concrete definition of what is to be understood by value creation itself is missing.[419] Criticism is voiced that the assessment of the relative importance of a group company's contribution to the overall value creation always contains an element of subjectivity.[420] There is a concern that tax authorities could assess the individual contributions to the creation of value differently which would eventually lead to double taxation.[421] For example, one country's tax administration may be biased to overestimate the value created by the functions performed in its jurisdiction, whereas an opposing tax administration may opine that the very same functions performed are not as important or even only of a routine character.[422]

Bullen points out that 'price conditions – the adjustment of which is clearly not prevented by the wording of Art. 9(1) – are also part of a commercial or financial relation', *see Bullen*, Arm's Length Transaction Structures: Recognizing and restructuring controlled transactions in transfer pricing (2011) 115; in this context *see also Kofler/Verlinden*, Unlimited Adjustments: Some Reflections on Transfer Pricing, General Anti-Avoidance and Controlled Foreign Company Rules, and the 'Saving Clause', BIT 2020, 269 (279f) who state that 'the practical effect of the restrictive force of article 9 of the OECD Model should not be overstated, as – despite the static language of the provision since 1963 – the ALP has evolved dramatically and increasingly become standard-based over the past few decades, specifically following the OECD/G20 BEPS Project. The ALP is frequently viewed as more "result-oriented, thereby meaning that the objective is parity in taxable income rather than parity in the method of allocation itself"; i.e., it is not limited to comparable transactions. Accordingly, the relevant standard focuses less on finding comparable transactions than on testing if "the actual transaction possesses the commercial rationality of arrangements that would be agreed between unrelated parties under comparable economic circumstances", i.e., arm's length behaviour' (footnotes removed by the author).

415. *See Rasch*, Sperrwirkung reloaded, TPI 2019, 201 (201ff).
416. *Wittendorff*, TNI 2016, 333.
417. *See* already sec. 1.3.2.
418. *See* sec. 2.5.2.1.
419. *See Mansori/Sanschagrin*, Assessing Value Creation for Transfer Pricing, TNI 2016, 1123 (1123ff); *Morse*, Value Creation: A Standard in Search of a Process, BIT 2018, 196 (196ff); *Navisotschnigg* in *Lang/Storck/Petruzzi/Risse* 77 (advisor's comment).
420. *Hoor*, TNI 2018, 532 and 536; *Musselli/Musselli*, ITPJ 2017, 340.
421. *See also Stein/Schwarz/Holinski*, DStR 2017, 125; Hey, BIT 2018, 207.
422. *See also Mansori/Sanschagrin*, TNI 2016, 1123, who see the possibility that tax authorities may revert to the closely related and more familiar concept of value added (i.e., 'comparing the value of inputs with the value of outputs'); yet, the concepts of value added and value created are different, since 'the value created within an MNE may involve far more than what is

To remedy this unwanted situation, various business concepts are adopted in practice to determine the value created by individual group companies. Their goal is to limit the above-mentioned discretion by putting the analysis on a more objective basis.[423] In the following, two of such concepts, namely, a Value Contribution Analysis (VCA) and a RACI Analysis, are briefly outlined.

A VCA assesses the value drivers (e.g., brand equity) of a business at the level of an MNE group.[424] That is, it aims to answer which features allow an MNE to stay competitive and to price margins.[425] Furthermore, the key business processes that underlie the identified value drivers (e.g., marketing) are evaluated to analyse which activities within an MNE drive value.[426] Together, this provides a qualitative overview of how value is created within an MNE (qualitative VCA). However, it has to be kept in mind that a VCA per se 'is not meant to determine the profit allocation nor an arm's length remuneration for controlled transactions involving intangibles [...], as it is not focused on individual transactions'.[427] Nevertheless, in combination with other tools, a quantification of the contributions from different group companies to the creation of value may be achieved (quantitative VCA).[428]

The performance of a RACI Analysis, which is used to identify the roles and responsibilities of different entities in various business process, may be instructive in such cases.[429] RACI is an acronym that denotes four different roles that an entity can have in an identified business process: Responsible, Accountable, Consulted, and Informed.[430] 'Responsible' refers to the entity/entities that are in charge of the execution of a process.[431] An entity that is 'Accountable' provides the necessary information to undertake a process, releases and controls the budget, and approves

happening at any given stage in the value chain, especially for many of today's companies whose outputs may be services, information, technologies, know-how, brand awareness, and ideas. MNEs amass and put at risk large quantities of capital, set strategic objectives, assemble unique teams of personnel with highly specialized abilities from across the globe, and develop market and bargaining power far beyond the reach of most individuals. These attributes of modern MNEs are often tremendously important profit drivers, even though there may be no stage in the value chain where they are directly measurable'.

423. *See Stein/Schwarz/Holinski*, DStR 2017, 118 and 121.
424. *See Lagarden*, Attribution of intangible-related returns – case study, in *Lang/Storck/Petruzzi /Risse* (Eds), Transfer Pricing and Intangibles: Current Developments, Relevant Issues and Possible Solutions (2019) 51 (55ff).
425. *See Navisotschnigg* in *Lang/Storck/Petruzzi/Risse* 84 (advisor's comment).
426. *See Lagarden* in *Lang/Storck/Petruzzi/Risse* 58f; such key business processes may also be further subdivided, for example, in long-term and short-term marketing strategy.
427. *See Lagarden* in *Lang/Storck/Petruzzi/Risse* 55.
428. *See also Stein/Schwarz/Holinski*, DStR 2017, 124ff on the transition from a qualitative to a quantitative analysis.
429. *See also Lagarden* in *Lang/Storck/Petruzzi/Risse* 59ff; *Peng/Lagarden*, ITPJ 2019, 7ff; *Stein/Schwarz/Holinski*, DStR 2017, 122; *Raschle/Borriello/Hämmerle*, ST 2013, 863ff; furthermore, *OECD*, BEPS Action 10: Discussion Draft on the use of Profit Splits in the Context of Global Value Chains (2014) Mn 38ff where the OECD elaborates on the use of a RACI Analysis to weight individual contributions to value creation.
430. Occasionally, the analysis also includes a support role which is then referred to as a RASCI-analysis.
431. On the content of the different roles, *see also Meyer/Reher*, Projektmanagement: Von der Definition über die Projektplanung zum erfolgreichen Abschluss (2016) 87.

achieved results (hence, it should have the necessary competence and decision-making authority). For a given process, only one entity can be accountable, whereas one or more entities can be responsible.[432] For example, when an entity commissions two other entities with the performance of R&D activities on its behalf, the principal is accountable for the R&D process, whereas the contractors are responsible for the performance of the operational R&D activities. 'Consulted' denotes entities that have expert knowledge concerning a specific process and are therefore asked for their expertise in the course of a process. 'Informed' refers to entities that are informed about the status of a process but do not have any active involvement in it; hence, they do not create any value as regards to it.[433]

In order to quantify the value contribution of a legal entity, it is assessed which entity has what role in the identified processes, that is, who is responsible for the performance of a process and who is accountable, consulted, or informed.[434] A weight is assigned to the different roles based on their importance for an identified process, for example, 30% for Responsible, 50% for Accountable, 20% for Consulted, and 0% for Informed.[435] Afterwards, the value assigned to an entity is multiplied with the value that a process has with regard to an identified value driver.[436]

To provide a very simplified example:[437] The performance of a VCA reveals that brand equity is an important value driver in an MNE's business; i.e., 50% of the value creation in the MNE is attributed to it. The identified key business process that generates brand equity is marketing. In the respective MNE, the parent company is accountable for the marketing process; that is, it creates marketing concepts that are then implemented by other group companies. A RACI Analysis reveals that this accountable-role contributes to 50% to the performance of the marketing process. Next, these two values are multiplied in order to assess the entity's contribution to the overall value creation. In this case, the parent company's contribution to the overall value creation in the respective MNE accounts for at least 25% (50% [brand equity] x 50% [accountable for the marketing process]).[438]

In the end, the results of a quantitative VCA may provide an indication regarding the profitability of different group companies and, therefore, the ultimate entitlement to intangible-related returns.[439] However, as already mentioned above, a VCA cannot directly be used to price individual intra-group transactions.[440]

432. *See Peng/Lagarden*, ITPJ 2019, 8.
433. *See Lagarden* in *Lang/Storck/Petruzzi/Risse* 60.
434. *See also Peng/Lagarden*, ITPJ 2019, 8f.
435. *See Lagarden* in *Lang/Storck/Petruzzi/Risse* 60 on the percentages that are usually attributed to the different roles.
436. *See Lagarden* in *Lang/Storck/Petruzzi/Risse* 61.
437. For a detailed case study, *see Lagarden* in *Lang/Storck/Petruzzi/Risse* 51ff; *see also Vallat*, Application of the DEMPE Concept in the Pharmaceutical Industry, ITPJ 2020, 168 (173ff).
438. The number might be higher depending on the parent company's contribution to other value drivers, which were left out in this example for simplicity reasons.
439. *See Lagarden* in *Lang/Storck/Petruzzi/Risse* 61.
440. On the linkages between VCA, RACI Analysis and DEMPE Approach, *see Lagarden* in *Lang/Storck/Petruzzi/Risse* 67f; *see also Lagarden* in *Lang/Storck/Petruzzi/Risse* 62ff on how to derive a royalty rate via the use of the residual profit split method.

While a VCA may certainly be insightful, the time and resources it takes to gather the necessary information must not be underestimated.[441] Furthermore, while the DEMPE Approach requires an understanding of how value is created within an MNE, a specific documentation requirement for the performance of a VCA cannot be found in the OECD TPG 2017.[442]

It has to be emphasized that the new focus on value creation in a transfer pricing analysis impacts not only MNEs but also tax administrations. That is, tax administrations have to build the necessary knowledge and capacity to understand and timely process the often complex way of how value is created in a specific business.[443]

2.10 PRELIMINARY CONCLUSIONS

- The DEMPE Approach is concerned with the allocation of intangible-related returns between associated enterprises.
- To this end, the OECD TPG 2017 contain their own – very broad – definition of an intangible.
- Contractual arrangements form the starting point of the transfer pricing analysis.
- The identification of the legal owner of an intangible is important because income should be attributed to the legal owner in a first step.
- Ultimately, however, the allocation of intangible-related returns depends on the actual conduct (respectively, the relevant substance) of the associated enterprises in the DEMPE of an intangible.
- The DEMPE Approach is a qualitative approach to define substance.
- It expects the legal owner of an intangible to have personnel with the relevant technical or scientific skills that performs important functions and decision-making functions with regard to the DEMPE of an intangible (i.e., these functions must not be outsourced for the ultimate retention of intangible-related returns).
- According to the DEMPE Approach, value is created by the performance of functions on the strategical and tactical level (management activities).
- By contrast, the provision of funding without any functionality does not entitle to any intangible-related returns (cash box companies as targets of the BEPS Project).
- Therefore, the DEMPE Approach is an activity-based concept (link between activity and income).

441. *Lagarden* in *Lang/Storck/Petruzzi/Risse* 66; *see also Navisotschnigg* in *Lang/Storck/Petruzzi /Risse* 80 (MNE's comment); the necessary information is usually gathered via interviews conducted with managers in the MNE under consideration, *see Lagarden* in *Lang/Storck /Petruzzi/Risse* 56 and 58; as a result, the subjectivity of a VCA may also be criticized, *see* the discussion in *Navisotschnigg* in *Lang/Storck/Petruzzi/Risse* 79f.
442. *See also* the discussion in *Navisotschnigg* in *Lang/Storck/Petruzzi/Risse* 81.
443. *Heggmair*, ITPJ 2017, 265f.

- When establishing an IP Company, MNEs have to make sure that they locate competent personnel with decision-making authority in the jurisdiction of the IP Company; administration of intangibles alone does not entitle to any intangible-related returns.
- IP Companies that are established without a business reason might be challenged based on their commercial rationality; primarily, however, the transfer pricing analysis should focus on the pricing of the corresponding transactions.
- The presumptions of control over risk and the insignificance of the provision of funding may strain the arm's-length principle beyond its limits; yet, empirical evidence of third-party behaviour should always be able to disprove these hypothetical assumptions (i.e., related parties need not have more substance than unrelated parties in the same or similar circumstances).
- The DEMPE Approach is not a mere clarification but a new concept for the allocation of intangible-related returns between associated enterprises; therefore, it cannot be applied under existing tax treaties.
- In practice, various business concepts (e.g., a VCA or RACI Analysis) are used to objectify the assessment of value creation by individual group companies.

CHAPTER 3

Substance in the Area of Harmful Tax Practices: Substantial Activity Requirement

3.1 R&D INCENTIVES AND HARMFUL TAX COMPETITION

R&D and the innovation that comes with it contribute significantly to a country's economic growth.[444] Therefore, countries have a high interest in promoting R&D activities within their territory.[445] From a tax policy perspective, there are numerous possibilities for a country to incentivize R&D for which a distinction is generally made between 'input incentives' and 'output incentives'.[446]

Input incentives are already granted with the start of an R&D activity.[447] They are based on the resources used during the R&D process, and they are granted independently of the success of an R&D project (i.e., also when an R&D project does not yield any results or when the results cannot be commercially exploited).[448] Typical examples are 'tax credits, enhanced allowances (super-deductions) and accelerated depreciation'.[449]

Output incentives, on the other hand, are only granted when an R&D activity produced results, and these results are commercially exploited. This is done by treating the income generated by a developed intangible preferentially either by applying a

444. *See also Schwarz*, Rationale, design and effectiveness of R&D tax measures, ASA 2014/2015, 711 (712) with further references.
445. *See also EC*, Europe 2020: A strategy for smart, sustainable and inclusive growth (2010) 5, according to which 3 % of the EU's GDP should be invested in R&D by 2020.
446. *Danon* in *IFA* 19; *see also Raab*, Patent-, Lizenz- und IP-Boxen – Übersicht und aktuelle Entwicklungen, SWI 2018, 125 (125).
447. *See also Dziurdź/Huisman/Kollmann/Spies/Turić*, Tagungsbericht zum IFA-Kongress 2015 in Basel, ÖStZ 2016, 32 (32).
448. *See also Pross/Radmanesh*, IStR 2015, 579f.
449. *Danon* in *IFA* 19; *see also Raab*, SWI 2018, 125.

lower tax rate to it than the general income tax rate or by exempting parts of it from the tax base.[450] Such preferential IP regimes are commonly referred to as patent boxes.[451]

Since patent boxes come only into play when R&D activities have already been successful (and income is generated), critics deny their ability to effectively promote R&D.[452] Certainly, this criticism is all the more justified when a country's patent box regime does not require the actual performance of R&D activities within its territory in order to benefit from it.[453] In such a case, patent boxes rather contribute to the shifting of existing patents - and thus profits and tax revenues - between countries than to the promotion of R&D activities which is generally regarded as harmful tax competition.[454]

Against the background that many countries introduced or contemplated introducing patent box regimes,[455] the OECD decided to address this issue in the BEPS Project.[456] Input incentives, however, were not considered in the BEPS Project since they '[p]resumably [...] have been regarded as less problematic than patent boxes from the perspective of harmful tax competition'.[457]

With BEPS Action 5, the OECD embarked on a mission to '[r]evamp the work on harmful tax practices with a priority [...] on requiring substantial activity for any preferential regime' (Substantial Activity Requirement).[458] However, the Substantial Activity Requirement itself is not an innovation of the BEPS Project.[459] It was already included in the 1998 Report on Harmful Tax Competition and served as a factor to identify tax havens and harmful preferential tax regimes.[460] Nevertheless, it was not

450. *See also Monteith*, Steuergestaltung mit Lizenzboxen: Mögliche Gegenmaßnahmen des deutschen Gesetzgebers, StuB 2014, 883 (883).
451. *Danon* in *IFA* 19.
452. For a differentiated consideration, *see Matteotti*, Fairness im Steuerrecht: Schlaglichter auf Anspruch und Wirklichkeit in laufenden Steuervorhaben, ASA 2015/2016, 51 (66f).
453. *See also Danon* in *IFA* 38.
454. *See also Pross/Radmanesh*, IStR 2015, 580; *Danon* in *IFA* 41f.
455. *See* already sec. 1.3.3.
456. For an overview of existing patent box regimes in European countries in 2013 as well as their features, *see Evers/Miller/Spengel*, Intellectual Property Box Regimes: Effective Tax Rates and Tax Policy Considerations, ZEW Discussion Paper No. 13-070, 8 (available at http://ftp.zew.de/pub/zew-docs/dp/dp13070.pdf).
457. *See Danon* in *IFA* 28; *see also* BEPS Action 5, Mn 26: 'Regimes that provide for a tax preference on income relating to IP raise the base-eroding concerns [...].'
458. *OECD*, Action Plan on Base Erosion and Profit Shifting (2013) 18.
459. BEPS Action 5, Mn 14.
460. *See OECD*, Harmful Tax Competition: An Emerging Global Issue (1998) Mn 52 for tax havens and 79 for preferential tax regimes; however, whereas the Substantial Activity Requirement was a key factor in identifying tax havens, it only served as one of eight other factors that could assist in identifying harmful preferential tax regimes; the overarching rationale provided for the use of the Substantial Activity Requirement was that 'the absence of a requirement that the activity be substantial [suggests] that a jurisdiction may be attempting to attract investment or transactions that are purely tax driven (transactions may be booked there *without the requirement of adding value* so that there is little real activity, i.e. these jurisdictions are essentially "booking centres")' (emphasis added), *see OECD*, Harmful Tax Competition: An Emerging Global Issue (1998) Mn 52; furthermore, '[i]t may also indicate that a jurisdiction does not (or cannot) provide a legal or commercial environment or offer any economic advantages that would attract substantive business activities in the absence of the tax minimising opportunities it provides', *see OECD*, Harmful Tax Competition: An Emerging Global Issue (1998) Mn 55.

applied until the BEPS Project[461] because of 'technical challenges in applying the criteria, and the fact that at the time the jurisdictions affected by it [note: tax havens according to the 1998 report] were not participants in the work'.[462] BEPS Action 5 renewed the focus on the Substantial Activity Requirement and formulated it concretely.[463] Furthermore, the Substantial Activity Requirement gained additional importance within the framework that the OECD's Forum on Harmful Tax Practices (FHTP)[464] uses to assess the harmfulness of preferential regimes (elevation from an 'other factor' to a 'key factor').[465]

To define the Substantial Activity Requirement, the OECD established:

- the Modified Nexus Approach for preferential IP regimes;[466] and
- the concept of Core Income Generating Activities for preferential non-IP regimes and for no or only nominal tax jurisdictions.[467]

461. *OECD*, Resumption of Application of Substantial Activities Factor or No or only Nominal Tax Jurisdictions (2018) Mn 12 and 14; the 1998 Report on Harmful Tax Competition already stated that the 'determination of when and whether an activity is substantial can be difficult', *see OECD*, Harmful Tax Competition: An Emerging Global Issue (1998) Mn 55.
462. *See OECD*, Resumption of Application of Substantial Activities Factor or No or only Nominal Tax Jurisdictions (2018) 20 FN 5; the reason why the Substantial Activity Requirement was eventually dropped is because tax havens successfully argued that they would otherwise be worse off compared to OECD members with preferential regimes because the Substantial Activity Requirement is a key factor in identifying tax havens but only an other factor for identifying harmful preferential tax regimes (*see* already FN 460); for more details, *see Becker/Hoeck*, Aktionspunkt 5: Bekämpfung von schädlichem Steuerwettbewerb durch mehr Substanz und Transparenz, in *Kofler/Schnitger* (Eds), BEPS-Handbuch: Maßnahmen gegen Gewinnverlagerung und Gewinnverkürzung internationaler Konzerne (2019) 309 (315f); *see also OECD*, The OECD's Project on Harmful Tax Practices: The 2001 Progress Report (2001) Mn 27: 'In the light of the discussions with the jurisdictions, the Committee concluded that it should not use this method to determine whether or not a tax haven is uncooperative.'
463. *See* BEPS Action 5, Mn 23ff.
464. The FHTP was created as a result of the 1998 Report on Harmful Tax Competition, *see OECD*, Harmful Tax Competition: An Emerging Global Issue (1998) Mn 139. It is *inter alia* responsible for reviewing whether jurisdictions comply with the standards on harmful tax practices, *see OECD*, Harmful Tax Competition: An Emerging Global Issue (1998) Mn 145; for more details on the review process, *see Larking*, Navigating the EU-OECD Harmful Tax Competition Jungle, TNI 2019, 501 (502f and 505f).
465. BEPS Action 5, Mn 25; *see also OECD*, Harmful Tax Practices - 2018 Progress Report on Preferential Regimes (2019) Annex A, 40 Mn 15; for the further revisions of the factors that were initially used in the Report on Harmful Tax Competition (*see OECD*, Harmful Tax Competition: An Emerging Global Issue (1998) Mn 60ff) to assess preferential regimes, *see OECD*, Harmful Tax Practices - 2018 Progress Report on Preferential Regimes (2019) Annex A, 39 Mn 13ff.
466. *See* sec. 3.2.
467. *See* sec. 3.3.

3.2 THE SUBSTANTIAL ACTIVITY REQUIREMENT WITH REGARD TO PREFERENTIAL IP REGIMES: MODIFIED NEXUS APPROACH

3.2.1 Background

Initially, the OECD examined three different approaches to determine the Substantial Activity Requirement with regard to preferential IP regimes, namely, a Value Creation Approach, a Transfer Pricing Approach, and the Nexus Approach.[468]

The Value Creation Approach would have required 'taxpayers to undertake a set number of significant development activities' to benefit from a patent box regime.[469]

The Transfer Pricing Approach would have allowed a 'regime to provide benefits to all the income generated by the IP if the taxpayer had located a set level of important functions in the jurisdiction providing the regime, if the taxpayer is the legal owner of the assets giving rise to the tax benefits and uses the assets giving rise to the tax benefits, and if the taxpayer bears the economic risks of the assets giving rise to the tax benefits'.[470] That is, the entitlement to intangible-related returns according to the DEMPE Approach would have also been relevant for the preferential treatment of the respective income (e.g., entitlement to 80% of the intangible-related returns according to the DEMPE Approach would, at the same time, allow the same amount of income to be taxed preferentially). On a side note, the understanding of substance under the Transfer Pricing Approach ('important functions', i.e., functions that 'usually make a significant contribution to intangible value')[471] and under the Value Creation Approach ('significant development activities') appears to be 'similar or at least overlapping'.[472]

Finally, the Nexus Approach is based on the same principle that underlies input incentives.[473] Under input incentives, there is a direct link between expenditures incurred by a taxpayer and the benefits that may be claimed. The Nexus Approach extends this principle to patent box regimes by making the preferential treatment of IP income conditional on the R&D expenditures incurred by a taxpayer. However, unlike in the case of input incentives, it is not the amount of expenditures that determines the extent of benefits. Instead, the Nexus Approach differentiates between expenditures incurred for a substantial R&D activity of the taxpayer itself (qualifying expenditures) and expenditures incurred for a substantial R&D activity of other parties (overall expenditures), and the ratio of these determines the proportion of income that may be treated preferentially.[474]

468. *OECD*, Countering Harmful Tax Practices More Effectively, Taking into Account Transparency and Substance - Action 5: 2014 Deliverable (2014) 28f.
469. *OECD*, Countering Harmful Tax Practices More Effectively, Taking into Account Transparency and Substance - Action 5: 2014 Deliverable (2014) 28.
470. *OECD*, Countering Harmful Tax Practices More Effectively, Taking into Account Transparency and Substance - Action 5: 2014 Deliverable (2014) 28f.
471. OECD TPG 2017 Mn 6.56; *see* already sec. 2.5.2.1.
472. *Matteotti/Roth*, ASA 2014/2015, 763.
473. BEPS Action 5, Mn 28.
474. *OECD*, Countering Harmful Tax Practices More Effectively, Taking into Account Transparency and Substance - Action 5: 2014 Deliverable (2014) 29.

Whereas the Value Creation Approach did not find any support, the Transfer Pricing Approach would have been the preferred choice for some countries.[475] They pointed out that the Transfer Pricing Approach would be consistent with international tax principles[476] (i.e., the arm's-length principle) and expressed concerns about the compatibility of the Nexus Approach with EU law.[477]

The majority of countries, however, was sceptical about the Transfer Pricing Approach,[478] particularly because it would not have imposed any additional substance requirements compared to those that are already stipulated by the arm's-length principle (more precisely, the DEMPE Approach).[479]

Eventually, an agreement could be reached,[480] after the initial proposal of the Nexus Approach was - based on a joint proposal by Germany and the United Kingdom -[481] modified (hence the title Modified Nexus Approach).[482] In 2015, the OECD published its final report on BEPS Action 5 in which a few remaining issues[483] were clarified.

---

475. *OECD*, Countering Harmful Tax Practices More Effectively, Taking into Account Transparency and Substance - Action 5: 2014 Deliverable (2014) 28f; for more details, *see Gupta*, Modifying the Modified Nexus Approach—Behind Closed Doors, TNI 2015, 1128 (1129ff); *Felder /Giezendanner*, Liechtenstein, in *IFA* (Ed.), Cahiers de droit fiscal international, Vol. 100a Tax Incentives on Research and Development (R&D) (2015) 425 (445f).
476. For this reason, preferring the Transfer Pricing Approach, *Matteotti/Roth*, ASA 2014/2015, 765; *Gentsch/Matteotti/Roth*, Aufwandseitige Förderung von Forschung und Entwicklung: Vorschlag für eine verfassungskonforme und standortfördernde Ausgestaltung von Art. 25a Abs. 2 E-StHG, Expert Focus 2015, 1058 (1062 FN 8).
477. Literature on the compatibility of patent boxes with EU law (primary law, state aid, and the code of conduct) is extensive; *see*, for example, *Schwarz Martínez*, IP Box Regime im Europäischen Steuerrecht (2017); *Shi*, IP Boxes in Light of the BEPS Project and EU Law - Part II, ET 2016, 371 (371ff); *Shi*, IP Boxes in Light of the BEPS Project and EU Law - Part I, ET 2016, 334 (334ff); *Thiede*, Besitzen Patentboxregime eine Zukunft? - Eine beihilferechtliche Untersuchung, IStR 2016, 283 (283ff); *Sanz-Gómez*, The OECD's Nexus Approach to IP Boxes: A European Union Law Perspective, WU International Taxation Research Paper Series No. 2015 - 12 (available at https://papers.ssrn.com/sol3/Delivery.cfm/SSRN_ID2589065_code1908122.pdf?abstractid=2589065&mirid=1); *Luts*, Compatibility of IP Box Regimes with EU State Aid Rules and Code of Conduct, EC Tax Review 2014, 258 (258ff); *Mang*, The (In)Compatibility of IP Box Regimes with EU Law, the Code of Conduct and the BEPS Initiatives, ET 2015, 78 (78ff); *Matteotti/Roth*, ASA 2014/2015, 768ff.
478. *OECD*, Countering Harmful Tax Practices More Effectively, Taking into Account Transparency and Substance - Action 5: 2014 Deliverable (2014) 29.
479. *See Becker*, Der OECD-Bericht zu Maßnahme 5 des BEPS-Aktionsplans, IStR 2014, 704 (708); *Pross/Radmanesh*, IStR 2015, 582.
480. *OECD*, Action 5: Agreement on Modified Nexus Approach for IP Regimes (2015).
481. *Germany/UK*, Joint Statement: Proposals for New Rules for Preferential IP Regimes (2014) (available at https://assets.publishing.service.gov.uk/government/uploads/system/uploads/attachment_data/file/373135/GERMANY_UK_STATEMENT.pdf).
482. Although Ireland, for example, still expressed concerns about the Nexus Approach in its modified version claiming it would put smaller countries at a disadvantage compared to larger countries, *see* Irish finance minister says German/UK patent box proposal may disadvantage small countries, worries BEPS will target US MNEs (available at https://mnetax.com/irish-finance-minister-says-germanuk-patent-box-proposal-may-disadvantage-small-countries-worries-beps-targets-us-mnes-5483); *see also Vlasceanu*, Intellectual Property Structuring in the Context of the OECD BEPS Action Plan, in *Cotrut* (Ed.), International Tax Structures in the BEPS Era: An Analysis of Anti-Abuse Measures (2015) 220 (242).
483. *See OECD*, Action 5: Agreement on Modified Nexus Approach for IP Regimes (2015) 5.

BEPS Action 5 is a 'minimum standard'; that is, countries committed themselves to adhere to it.[484] The Modified Nexus Approach 'describe[s] the outer limits of an IP regime that grants benefits to R&D but does not have harmful effects on other countries'.[485] However, it is left at the discretion of countries whether they want to fully exhaust these limits or be more restrictive in the implementation (or whether they want to introduce a patent box regime at all).[486] The FHTP will monitor the compliance of countries' preferential IP regimes with the Modified Nexus Approach.[487]

The following sections will elaborate on the limitations set by the Modified Nexus Approach as outlined in the final report of BEPS Action 5.[488]

3.2.2 Analytical Framework: The Nexus Formula

The Modified Nexus Approach is concerned with the preferential treatment of income that:

- a qualifying taxpayer;[489] receives from
- a qualifying IP asset.[490]

In order to determine the income that may be taxed preferentially, the following formula – the nexus formula – shall be applied:[491]

$$\frac{\text{Qualifying expenditures incurred to develop IP asset}}{\text{Overall expenditures incurred to develop IP asset}} \times \text{Overall income from IP asset} = \text{Income receiving tax benefits}$$

That is, the relevant factors that have to be identified at the level of a qualifying taxpayer are:

- The ratio of qualifying expenditures to overall expenditures (nexus ratio) incurred to develop a qualifying IP asset;[492] and

484. *OECD*, Explanatory Statement (2015), Mn 11; on the binding character of the Modified Nexus Approach, *see P. Schoueri*, The OECD's Approach to IP-Boxes as a Norm: Hard, Soft or Half-Baked?, BTR 2017, 438 (438ff).
485. BEPS Action 5, Mn 26.
486. It was also agreed that new entries to existing IP regimes that are not in line with the Modified Nexus Approach are only allowed until 30 June 2016; by 30 June 2021 at the latest, all existing preferential regimes not compliant with the Modified Nexus Approach have to be abolished, *see* BEPS Action 5, Mn 63 and 65.
487. BEPS Action 5, Mn 153; *see also OECD*, Harmful Tax Practices – 2017 Progress Report on Preferential Regimes (2017) 15ff and *OECD*, Harmful Tax Practices – 2018 Progress Report on Preferential Regimes (2019) 17ff.
488. *See* BEPS Action 5, Mn 26ff.
489. *See* sec. 3.2.3.
490. *See* sec. 3.2.4.
491. BEPS Action 5, Mn 30.
492. *See* sec. 3.2.6.

- the overall income generated by a qualifying IP asset.[493]

These two factors are multiplied in order to calculate the amount of income that may receive tax benefits. However, in the first place, the amount of intangible-related returns allocable to a qualifying taxpayer must be determined through the DEMPE Approach. Only in a second step does the Modified Nexus Approach stipulate to what extent the allocated income under the DEMPE Approach may be taxed preferentially.[494] It has to be highlighted that the Modified Nexus Approach is only concerned with the amount of income that may receive preferential treatment.[495] By contrast, the extent of the benefits granted to eligible income, e.g., the applicable tax rate, is at a country's discretion.[496]

3.2.3 Qualifying Taxpayers

Under the Modified Nexus Approach, taxpayers that may apply for a patent box regime include:[497]

- resident companies;
- domestic PEs of foreign companies; and
- foreign PEs of resident companies that are subject to tax in the jurisdiction providing benefits.

'Resident' indicates that persons subject to full tax liability in a country may claim preferential treatment (Article 4(1) OECD MC 2017), whereby the factors giving rise to full tax liability are determined by the individual countries' domestic law.[498]

The use of the term 'company' seems to suggest that only legal entities and, hence, corporate tax subjects[499] may qualify if one was to follow the definition contained in Article 3(1) lit b OECD MC 2017.[500] Of course, BEPS Action 5 is a different OECD document than the OECD MC and concerns harmful tax competition compared to tax treaties. Nevertheless, one would assume that the OECD is careful to ensure consistency between its publications in tax law, especially when intentional deviations

493. *See* sec. 3.2.7.
494. *See* already sec. 1.3.2.
495. *See* BEPS Action 5, Mn 32: 'Where the amount of income receiving benefits under an IP regime does not exceed the amount determined by the nexus approach, the regime has met the substantial activity requirement.'
496. BEPS Action 5, Mn 54; *see also Hinny*, IFF 2016, 214.
497. BEPS Action 5, Mn 33.
498. *See Kaul*, Der Nexus-Ansatz: Auswirkungen auf IP-Boxen und Alternativansätze (2018) 12f; *see also* OECD MC 2017 Art. 4 Mn 4: '[DTCs] do not lay down standards which the provisions of the domestic laws on "residence" have to fulfil in order that claims for full tax liability can be accepted between the Contracting States. In this respect the States take their stand entirely on the domestic laws.'
499. For example, in the UK, only corporate tax subjects are eligible, *see* https://www.gov.uk/guidance/corporation-tax-the-patent-box#who-can-benefit (accessed 7 May 2020).
500. '[T]he term "company" means any body corporate or any entity that is treated as a body corporate for tax purposes.'

are not readily apparent (e.g., by providing a different definition for a term). Interestingly, in the German version of BEPS Action 5, the term 'Unternehmen' is used[501] which would correspond to the term 'enterprise' as used in Article 3(1) lit c OECD MC 2017. Accordingly, also individuals 'carrying on [...] any business' and subject to income tax should be qualifying taxpayers.[502] Their inclusion would also not create any additional risks from the perspective of harmful tax competition and, at the same time, would contribute to neutrality in terms of legal forms. Therefore, individuals may also apply for patent box regimes.[503]

Furthermore, there are two instances when a PE may be a qualifying taxpayer. First is a domestic PE of a foreign company. Second is a foreign PE of a resident company that is subject to tax in the country offering benefits, i.e., when the credit method applies.[504] This means that when 'qualifying income stems from an intangible asset allocated to a foreign permanent establishment, such income, to the extent that it is taxable in the state of residence, may benefit from the patent box'.[505] In the end, this results in a different treatment of foreign PEs depending on whether the credit method or the exemption method is applicable. A foreign PE may qualify only in the case of the credit method.[506]

3.2.4 IP Assets in the Context of the Modified Nexus Approach

Contrary to the DEMPE Approach, the Modified Nexus Approach does not use the term 'intangibles' but uses the term 'IP assets' to define its substantive scope. Qualifying IP assets under the Modified Nexus Approach are:[507]

- patents; and
- IP assets that are functionally equivalent to patents; these are subdivided into:
  - patents in the broad sense,
  - copyrighted software, and
  - certain IP assets of SMEs.

501. *See OECD*, Wirksamere Bekämpfung schädlicher Steuerpraktiken unter Berücksichtigung von Transparenz und Substanz: Aktionspunkt 5 – Abschlussbericht 2015 (2016) Mn 33.
502. For example, in Switzerland, also sole proprietorships and partnerships may qualify, *see Hausmann*, Die Patentbox und zusätzliche F&E-Abzüge im Rahmen der Steuervorlage 17, Expert Focus 2018, 506 (506); likewise, the patent box regime in Luxembourg is also open to individuals, *see Vukovic/Mermet*, An Overview of the Future Luxembourg Intellectual Property Tax Regime, ITPJ 2018, 39 (40).
503. *See also Danon* in *IFA* 47 who attributes the non-mentioning of taxpayers other than legal entities to the scope of the OECD's mandate in the BEPS Project.
504. *See also Matteotti/Roth*, ASA 2014/2015, 765.
505. *Danon* in *IFA* 46.
506. This differentiation is criticized by some as being a potential infringement of EU law; furthermore, critics lament that it makes countries that resort to the exemption method unjustifiably less attractive; on top of that, this differentiation leads to an unequal treatment of foreign permanent establishments and foreign subsidiaries as foreign subsidiaries are never eligible; for these reasons, it was suggested to delete foreign PEs from the personal scope, *see Kaul*, Der Nexus-Ansatz: Auswirkungen auf IP-Boxen und Alternativansätze (2018) 13 with further references.
507. BEPS Action 5, Mn 34ff.

A patent is characterized by being novel, non-obvious, and useful.[508] BEPS Action 5 neither stipulates a certain process of granting patents that has to be followed nor explicitly requires that only domestically registered patents are eligible. Consequently, also patents granted in other countries than the taxpayer's residence state may qualify.[509]

Functionally equivalent IP assets are eligible under the Modified Nexus Approach, provided they are legally protected[510] and subject to similar approval and registration processes as are patents (when such processes are relevant).[511] As mentioned above, they are subdivided into patents in the broad sense, copyrighted software, and certain IP assets of SMEs.

Patents in the broad sense comprise 'utility models, IP assets that grant protection to plants and genetic material, orphan drug designations, and extensions of patent protection'.[512]

Software, in general, may have the same characteristics as patents - novelty, non-obviousness, and usefulness.[513] For this reason, it is patentable in some countries. Other countries, however, provide copyright protection instead of patent protection for developed software. To ensure that 'the different treatment of software under the patent laws of different jurisdictions does not affect whether or not income from software could benefit from IP regimes', copyrighted software is also included in the definition of functionally equivalent IP assets.[514] However, 'other copyrighted assets are not included [...] because they do not arise out of the same type of R&D activities as software'.[515]

What is more, certain assets of SMEs are eligible for benefits under a nexus-compliant patent box regime regardless of any patent protection.[516] Taxpayers that have less than EUR 50 million in global group-wide turnover (group view) and earn less than EUR 7.5 million per year in gross revenues from all of their IP assets (individual view) may qualify under this category.[517] Accordingly, this category comprises IP assets that share the characteristics of patents (i.e., novelty, non-obviousness, and

508. BEPS Action 5, Mn 36.
509. *See also Hinny*, IFF 2016, 212; *Koch*, Patentbox und steuerliche Förderung von Forschung und Entwicklung, Expert Focus 2016, 828 (829).
510. '[L]egal protection includes exclusive rights to use the IP asset, legal remedies against infringement, trade secret law, and contractual and criminal protections against use of the IP asset or unauthorised disclosure of information related to the IP asset', *see* BEPS Action 5, 41 FN 5; in this context, *see also* OECD TPG 2017 Mn 6.37: 'Generally, the registered legal owner of such intangibles has the exclusive legal and commercial right to use the intangible, as well as the right to prevent others from using or otherwise infringing the intangible.'
511. BEPS Action 5, Mn 34.
512. On the precise understanding of these terms, *see* BEPS Action 5, Mn 35.
513. BEPS Action 5, Mn 36.
514. BEPS Action 5, 41 FN 6.
515. BEPS Action 5, Mn 36.
516. *See also Hausmann/Roth/Meyer-Nandi*, Expert Focus 2016, 189ff.
517. BEPS Action 5, Mn 37; both thresholds have to be calculated on an annual basis and by using a five-year average that changes every year, *see* BEPS Action 5, 41 FN 7; *see also Kaul*, Der Nexus-Ansatz: Auswirkungen auf IP-Boxen und Alternativansätze (2018) 14, who points out that BEPS Action 5 does not provide a definition of a group and does not stipulate the applicable accounting standard; hence, the calculation of the two thresholds may provide difficulties.

usefulness) that are substantially similar to the IP assets of the two categories mentioned above (i.e., patents in the broad sense and copyrighted software) and that 'are certified as such in a transparent certification process by a competent government agency that is independent from the tax administration'.[518] Therefore, compared to the general rule, this exception has a limited personal scope because only SMEs may benefit from it but, at the same time, a wider substantive scope because unpatented assets may also qualify.

However, BEPS Action 5 is vague about the concrete assets that fall under this category.[519] Primarily, this category will consist of assets that would, in principle, be patentable but are not patented for certain reasons (e.g., know-how).[520] Particularly, SMEs abstain from patenting innovations because of, for example, confidentiality reasons[521] and the high costs associated with the patenting process but sometimes also because of the simple unawareness of the effects of patents.[522] Against this background, this special provision for SMEs appears reasonable.[523]

At the same time, however, the fact that generally only patents are granted preferential treatment under the Modified Nexus Approach is criticized.[524] Since a patent already enjoys legal protection and provides a temporary monopoly to its holder,[525] it is - according to critics - incomprehensible why it should also be more worthy in terms of favourable tax treatment compared to innovations that are not patented or not patentable.[526] Still, BEPS Action 5 does not account for this criticism.

518. BEPS Action 5, Mn 37; that means that countries that implement this category into their domestic laws may have to establish a certification body; furthermore, countries that implement this category have to provide certain information about it to the OECD, and the OECD will generally review this category no later than 2020, *see* BEPS Action 5, Mn 37; the reason for this additional information requirement is presumably a potential misuse that may arise because of the use of this category, *see Kaul*, Der Nexus-Ansatz: Auswirkungen auf IP-Boxen und Alternativansätze (2018) 14.
519. *See also Kaul*, Der Nexus-Ansatz: Auswirkungen auf IP-Boxen und Alternativansätze (2018) 14.
520. *Hinny*, IFF 2016, 212.
521. *See* in this regard also the remarks in OECD TPG 2017 Mn 6.20: 'The value of know-how and trade secrets is often dependent on the ability of the enterprise to preserve the confidentiality of the know-how or trade secret. In certain industries the disclosure of information necessary to obtain patent protection could assist competitors in developing alternative solutions. Accordingly, an enterprise may, for sound business reasons, choose not to register patentable knowhow, which may nonetheless contribute substantially to the success of the enterprise.'
522. *See Boivin/Vollenweider*, Patentbox und KMU - Bloss eine gute Absicht?, Expert Focus 2016, 841 (844); *Koch*, Expert Focus 2016, 831.
523. In the same vein, *Boivin/Vollenweider*, Expert Focus 2016, 844; *Koch*, Expert Focus 2016, 831.
524. *See EC*, A Study on R&D Tax Incentives: Final Report (2014) 45: 'It is not clear why especially innovations for which clear property rights are defined should receive a tax incentive. By subsidizing inventions that do not need a subsidy, patent boxes would induce inventions that are difficult to patent (and therefore might have high spillovers) relatively less attractive.'
525. *See Schwarz*, ASA 2014/2015, 714.
526. *Matteotti*, ASA 2015/2016, 67f; *Matteotti/Roth*, ASA 2014/2015, 773; *see also Danon* in *IFA* 48 who proposes that 'the scope of qualifying intangible assets should rather be settled in the light of the definition of qualifying R&D expenditure. Specifically, the issue should not be whether or not an intangible asset is patented (or even patentable) but rather whether this asset is linked to qualifying R&D substantial activity and corresponding expenditure in the relevant jurisdiction'.

Marketing intangibles[527] can never qualify for benefits under the Modified Nexus Approach.[528] The reason for this is that 'the policy rationale of an IP regime is to encourage and reward scientific innovation rather than marketing activity'.[529] Additionally, it is very difficult to establish a link between activities and return in the case of marketing intangibles (i.e., to determine which returns are generated because of the marketing activities).[530]

In a nutshell, the substantive scope of the Modified Nexus Approach is rather narrow.[531] Compared to the definition of intangibles under the OECD TPG 2017,[532] only trade intangibles that are legally protected – legal protection according to intellectual property laws[533] – are encompassed. By contrast, trade intangibles, like know-how that may enjoy legal protection, for example, according to competition law,[534] are generally not included.[535] Only in the case of SMEs is the criterion of legal protection waived so that also other trade intangibles that are relevant in a transfer pricing analysis may be eligible.[536] Nonetheless, the criterion of legal protection is of great importance under the Modified Nexus Approach which is diametrically opposed to the value it has under the OECD TPG 2017 for which the 'existence of such protection is not [...] a necessary condition for an item to be characterised as an intangible'.[537]

3.2.5 Relevance of Legal Ownership

BEPS Action 5 does not specify whether a qualifying taxpayer always has to be the legal owner of a qualifying IP asset (i.e., the person that is registered as the patent holder) in order to be eligible for preferential treatment.[538] In this regard, an interesting statement can be found in the agreement document on the Modified Nexus Approach:

> Under the currently proposed Modified Nexus Approach, businesses using already existing Patent Box regimes might see a reduction in income receiving preferential treatment, as R&D expenditure to develop the patent must be undertaken in a more

527. On marketing intangibles and their distinction to trade intangibles, *see* sec. 2.3.
528. BEPS Action 5, Mn 38.
529. *OECD*, Resumption of Application of Substantial Activities Factor or No or only Nominal Tax Jurisdictions (2018) Mn 31.
530. *OECD*, Addressing the Tax Challenges of the Digitalisation of the Economy (2019), Mn 36; *see also Pross/Radmanesh*, IStR 2015, 581 and 583.
531. *See also Matteotti/Roth*, ASA 2014/2015, 772f.
532. *See* sec. 2.3.
533. On the relevant degree of legal protection for functionally equivalent IP assets, *see* FN 510.
534. *See also* OECD TPG 2017 Mn 6.20.
535. Furthermore, the inclusion of such trade intangibles under the Modified Nexus Approach would usually also fail because they are not subject to a similar registration process as are patents.
536. Still, the relevant IP assets have to undergo a certification process in this case in order to be considered under the Modified Nexus Approach which is not the case under the OECD TPG 2017.
537. OECD TPG 2017 Mn 6.8; *see also* sec. 2.3.
538. *See also Hinny*, IFF 2016, 212.

limited number of entities, *including the company holding the relevant patent*, to qualify (emphasis added).[539]

This indicates that a qualifying taxpayer should also be the legal owner of a qualifying IP asset. Of course, countries may choose to require a qualifying taxpayer to have the economic ownership and not necessarily the legal ownership of a qualifying asset when implementing a patent box regime into their domestic laws.[540] *That is, not the legal owner but only the economic owner of a qualifying asset may be eligible for benefits in such cases.*[541] *However, for the same reasons as under the OECD TPG 2017,*[542] *it makes sense to refer to legal ownership only when discussing BEPS Action 5 in order to ensure a common understanding.*

What is more, also in countries that focus on economic ownership, legal ownership is relevant to a certain extent. A positive patent prosecution normally ends with the entry of the patent applicant into the patent register whereby the patent applicant becomes the legal owner of a patent. That is, only with this registration does the patent come legally into existence and economic ownership to it can be claimed.[543] *This also entails that preferential treatment – albeit by the economic owner – can only be claimed once legal ownership has been established.*

In the same vein, legal ownership is relevant for the beginning and duration of preferential treatment. Generally, BEPS Action 5 is silent about from what point in time preferential treatment may first be obtained and for how long. It seems obvious *that the preferential period may span from the granting of the patent for as long as patent protection exists (i.e., from the emergence until the extinction of the legal ownership of a patent).*[544]

Likewise, a question that is not directly addressed under BEPS Action 5 is whether only the patent holder may apply for a patent box regime or whether – as under the OECD TPG 2017[545] – a patent and a licence to it are two distinct assets. If this is the case, then a patent holder and an exclusive licensee *may both claim preferential*

539. *OECD*, Action 5: Agreement on Modified Nexus Approach for IP Regimes (2015) 3.
540. This is the case, for example, in Switzerland, *see Koch/Küttel/Trüssel*, Die Schweizer Patentbox, TPI 2018, 154 (155).
541. A reference to economic ownership will also be necessary if a PE is the qualifying taxpayer; on this point, *see* already FN 200.
542. *See* sec. 2.4.3.
543. *See also Schwarz*, Are legal rights irrelevant for transfer pricing after BEPS Actions 8, 9 and 10?, Kluwer International Tax Blog (2015) (available at http://kluwertaxblog.com/2015/11/15/are-legal-rights-irrelevant-for-transfer-pricing-after-beps-actions-8-9-and-10/): 'Unlike tangible property which has a physical existence, intangibles only exist because the law says they exist. Thus intangibles themselves are bundles of rights and obligations. One consequence of this is that ownership (the legal relationship between the asset [and] a person) in the case of intangibles, is inherently tied up with the existence of the asset.'
544. *See also Hinny*, IFF 2016, 212, according to whom preferential treatment may be obtained retroactively from the date of the patent application; while acknowledging that this approach is covered by BEPS Action 5, *Koch*, Expert Focus 2016, 830, advises against it because of the complexity this approach entails (e.g., complex recalculation of the nexus ratio); a related issue concerns the question of how to proceed when an initially granted patent is revoked later; BEPS Action 5 leaves this unanswered; for considerations in this regard, *see Hinny*, IFF 2016, 212f; *Koch*, Expert Focus 2016, 830.
545. *See* secs 2.3 and 2.4.2.

treatment. This question is not merely theoretically of interest but may also have great relevance in practice. For example, two group companies, A and B, may enter into a cost contribution arrangement (CCA) to jointly develop a patent.[546] *Their endeavour is successful, and the developed patent is registered in the name of Company A (i.e., Company A becomes the legal owner of the patent). To account for Company B's involvement in the development process, Company A as the patent holder grants an exclusive licence (i.e., the exclusive right to use the patent in the geographic area in which Company B operates) to Company B free of charge.*[547] *Under the assumption that both companies are resident in different jurisdictions that both offer a nexus-compliant patent box regime, is it possible that also Company B as a licensee only may receive preferential treatment?*

When describing the legal protection that functionally equivalent IP assets must have to qualify under the Modified Nexus Approach, BEPS Action 5 states that 'legal protection includes exclusive rights to use the IP asset [...]' (emphasis added).[548] *An exclusive licence would fulfil this requirement since the licensee has the right to exclude others (including the licensor) from using the licensed asset within a specific geographic area. The same should also be true when it comes to patents. Accordingly, also an exclusive licensee should be allowed to receive preferential treatment. This corresponds to a substance-over-form approach for which the legal arrangements do not have an impact on the granting of tax benefits (i.e., in the aforementioned example, the legal ownership of the patent could also be split between Companies A and B so that Company A becomes the patent holder in its respective jurisdiction and Company B becomes the patent holder in its respective jurisdiction).*[549],[550] *The inclusion of exclusive licences as qualifying assets can also be observed in the patent box regimes that some countries have already implemented.*[551] *Of course, an exclusive licence alone is not sufficient to effectively receive benefits under the Modified Nexus Approach since the licensor still has*

546. A CCA is 'a contractual arrangement among business enterprises to share the contributions and risks involved in the joint development, production or the obtaining of intangibles, tangible assets or services with the understanding that such intangibles, tangible assets or services are expected to create benefits for the individual businesses of each of the participants', *see* OECD TPG 2017 Mn 8.3.
547. For the possibilities on how ownership rights and rights of use can be arranged under a CCA, *see Storck/Stradinger* in *Bernegger/Rosar/Rosenberger* 497f.
548. BEPS Action 5, 41 FN 5; *see also* FN 510.
549. *See also Storck/Stradinger* in *Bernegger/Rosar/Rosenberger* 497f.
550. *See also Koch/Küttel/Trüssel*, TPI 2018, 156; this solution may also be indicated in the example provided in BEPS Action 5, 41 FN 3 and the statement in Mn 31: '[T]he nexus approach was not designed to disadvantage arrangements where different entities are engaged in activities contributing to the development of IP assets.'
551. For example, Switzerland, *see Koch/Küttel/Trüssel*, TPI 2018, 156; likewise, the UK, *see Robertson*, Time to Revisit the U.K. Patent Box?, TNI 2019, 843 (843); the UK also has the following peculiarity: 'A company that is party to a cost-sharing arrangement might be treated as holding another party's rights if specific criteria are met, even if the company does not legally hold the right or an exclusive license for the right itself', *see Robertson*, TNI 2019, 844; the OECD reviewed the UK's revised patent box regime with the above-mentioned feature and did classify it as not harmful, *see OECD*, Harmful Tax Practices – Peer Review Results on Preferential Regimes (2018) 3 (available at http://www.oecd.org/tax/beps/update-harmful-tax-practices-2017-progress-report-on-preferential-regimes.pdf).

to fulfil the stipulated substance requirements (which will be discussed in the following sections).[552]

3.2.6 Nexus Ratio and Substance

3.2.6.1 Introduction

The Modified Nexus Approach looks at the level of an entity (entity-perspective) which expenditures it incurred in the development of a qualifying IP asset and distinguishes these expenditures in qualifying expenditures and overall expenditures (or does not consider them at all).[553] On the one hand, qualifying expenditures are such where it is assumed that the underlying activity of the taxpayer that caused the respective expenditures created value. On the other hand, overall expenditures also include additional expenditure items where it is assumed that the underlying value-creating activity was not directly performed by the taxpayer (although the taxpayer has ultimately borne the expenditures of the respective activities).

The ratio of qualifying expenditures to overall expenditures, the so-called nexus ratio, is used to determine the value creation and hence the substance of a taxpayer in the development of a qualifying IP asset. Accordingly, '[e]xpenditures [...] act as a proxy for substantial activities'.[554] However, '[i]t is not the *amount* of expenditures that acts as a direct proxy for the amount of activities' but 'the *proportion* of expenditures directly related to development activities that demonstrates real value added by the taxpayer and acts as a proxy for how much substantial activity the taxpayer undertook'.[555]

The nexus ratio follows an additive approach.[556] That is, it includes all qualifying expenditures and overall expenditures incurred by a taxpayer over the life of the IP asset. Therefore, the relevant numbers 'increase every time a taxpayer incurs expenditure that would qualify for either category. The proportion of the cumulative numbers will then determine the percentage to be applied to overall income earned each year'.[557]

3.2.6.2 Qualifying Expenditures

Due to a lack of an internationally harmonized tax law, the OECD can only provide guiding principles that states have to follow when defining qualifying expenditures.[558] Their concrete formulation, however, is left to countries.[559]

552. *See also Matteotti/Roth*, ASA 2014/2015, 773.
553. *See also* BEPS Action 5, Mn 31.
554. BEPS Action 5, Mn 29.
555. BEPS Action 5, Mn 29.
556. BEPS Action 5, Mn 45; *see also* BEPS Action 5, Mn 60 and the example in Annex A, 71f.
557. BEPS Action 5, Mn 45.
558. *Becker*, IStR 2014, 707.
559. *See* BEPS Action 5, Mn 39: 'Jurisdictions will provide their own definitions of qualifying expenditures [...].'

Accordingly, BEPS Action 5 sets the following requirements for qualifying expenditures:

- they must be incurred by a qualifying taxpayer;
- they must be directly connected to the IP asset;
- they only include expenditures that are incurred for the purpose of actual R&D activities; and
- they must be included in the nexus ratio at the time they are incurred.[560]

The focus on qualifying expenditures incurred by the qualifying taxpayer follows the purpose of the Modified Nexus Approach 'to grant benefits only to income that arises from IP where the *actual R&D activity was undertaken by the taxpayer itself*' (emphasis added).[561]

Concerning the relevant connection between qualifying expenditures and IP assets, BEPS Action 5 makes a reference to input incentives. It states that qualifying expenditures 'would include the types of expenditures that currently qualify for R&D credits under the tax laws of multiple jurisdictions'.[562] Therefore, they could include 'salary and wages, direct costs, overhead costs directly associated with R&D facilities, and cost of supplies [...]'.[563] However, expenditures that are explicitly excluded are 'interest payments, building costs, acquisition costs, or any costs that could not be directly linked to a specific IP asset'.[564]

Expenditures have to arise out of actual R&D activities which means 'activities undertaken to advance the understanding of scientific relations or technologies, address known scientific or technological obstacles, or otherwise increase knowledge or develop new applications'.[565] It is striking that the OECD has not referred to its Frascati Manual when defining the relevant R&D activities as the manual provides 'internationally accepted definitions of R&D and classifications of its component activities'.[566] This is all the more surprising when considering that many countries seem to already orientate themselves by the Frascati Manual (or the Oslo Manual)[567] when implementing R&D tax incentives into their domestic laws.[568] However, while BEPS Action 5 does not directly refer to the Frascati Manual, their understanding of R&D activities appears to be congruent.[569]

560. BEPS Action 5, Mn 39.
561. BEPS Action 5, Mn 29.
562. BEPS Action 5, Mn 39.
563. BEPS Action 5, 41f FN 10; on a differentiation between direct costs and indirect costs, *see also* OECD TPG 2017 Mn 2.53.
564. BEPS Action 5, Mn 39.
565. BEPS Action 5, 41f FN 10.
566. *OECD*, Frascati Manual 2015 – Guidelines for Collecting and Reporting Data on Research and Experimental Development (2015) 3.
567. *OECD/Eurostat*, Oslo Manual 2018 – Guidelines for Collecting, Reporting and Using Data on Innovation (2018).
568. *Danon* in *IFA* 29.
569. *See Danon* in *IFA* 31; *see* the definition of R&D in *OECD*, Frascati Manual 2015 – Guidelines for Collecting and Reporting Data on Research and Experimental Development (2015) Mn 2.5:

With its focus on actual R&D activities, the Modified Nexus Approach emphasizes the relevance of activities on the operational level (day-to-day activities) in contrast to management activities (strategical and tactical level).[570] Qualifying expenditures may therefore include, for example, expenditures for the R&D personnel, expenditures for the necessary R&D equipment, or expenditures for materials needed to conduct the R&D.

Additionally, a peculiarity exists regarding the expenditures for general and speculative R&D.[571] By their very nature, such expenditures may have links to more than one IP asset. Thus, when such expenditures 'cannot be included in the qualifying expenditures of a specific IP asset to which they have a direct link, they could be divided pro rata across IP assets or products'.[572] That is, whereas a direct link between expenditures and IP assets is generally affirmed in the case of general and speculative R&D, such a direct link is negated in the case of, for example, building costs. This conclusion is not comprehensible in its generality when one thinks of a case where a qualifying taxpayer builds or rents a new building to conduct a specific R&D project in it and its results eventually lead to a patent.[573]

Qualifying expenditures have to be included in the nexus ratio at the time they are incurred; their treatment for accounting or other tax purposes is irrelevant under the Modified Nexus Approach.[574] That is, it does not matter whether expenditures are

---

'Research and experimental development [...] comprise creative and systematic work undertaken in order to increase the stock of knowledge – including knowledge of humankind, culture and society – and to devise new applications of available knowledge.'

570. *See also Theophilou*, Patent Boxes: The Rise, the Change or the Fall?, BIT 2019, 286 (291) who states that the substance requirements of BEPS Action 5 are 'are effectively in line with the location of the scientists who are basically developing the IP [...]'.
571. BEPS Action 5 does not provide a definition for general and speculative R&D; it is questionable whether the term 'basic research' ('experimental or theoretical work undertaken primarily to acquire new knowledge of the underlying foundations of phenomena and observable facts, without any particular application or use in view') and the corresponding explanations to it provided in *OECD*, Frascati Manual 2015 – Guidelines for Collecting and Reporting Data on Research and Experimental Development (2015) Mn 2.9 and 2.25ff, can provide further insights here.
572. BEPS Action 5, Mn 39; furthermore, when 'R&D expenditures were incurred by the taxpayer or outsourced to unrelated parties in connection with a larger R&D project that produced an income-generating IP asset, then an IP regime may also include all such R&D expenditures in qualifying expenditures and not just those R&D expenditures that, with the benefit of hindsight, directly contributed to IP income. These expenditures could be treated the same as general or speculative R&D and either divided pro rata across IP assets or included in qualifying expenditures if a direct link between the IP asset and the expenditures could be established'; however, apart from that, '[e]xpenditures for unsuccessful R&D will typically not be included in the nexus ratio, which is consistent with the purposes of IP regimes that grant benefits to income, since unsuccessful R&D by definition does not generate any income', *see* BEPS Action 5, Mn 44.
573. *See also Hinny*, IFF 2016, 214 FN 111, according to whom expenditures such as interest payments and building costs should be considered as relevant expenditures under the Modified Nexus Approach provided that they are sufficiently specific for the development of an IP asset like the construction of a new laboratory for the development of a certain new substance that is eventually patented.
574. BEPS Action 5, Mn 39.

classified as current expenditures (e.g., salary) or capital expenditures (e.g., expenditures for equipment) since, in both cases, they have to be fully included in the nexus ratio in the year in which they were incurred (and not spread over their depreciation period).

The Modified Nexus Approach requires a qualifying taxpayer to undertake actual R&D activity itself in order to be eligible for preferential treatment. The qualifying expenditures serve as a proxy for the R&D activity carried out by a qualifying taxpayer and, accordingly, the value created by the taxpayer (when set into proportion with the overall expenditures). As a result, 'mere capital contribution or expenditures for *substantial R&D activity by parties other than the taxpayer*' do not, in principle, count as qualifying expenditures (emphasis added).[575] Of course, this raises the question of when the R&D activity of a party other than the taxpayer is classified as substantial and, hence, the corresponding expenditures must not be included under qualifying expenditures. In this regard, the Modified Nexus Approach contains special provisions for outsourcing and acquired IP as will be shown in the following sections.

3.2.6.3 Outsourcing

BEPS Action 5 distinguishes between outsourcing to:

- unrelated parties; or
- related parties.[576]

Depending on which of those two forms of outsourcing is at hand, the relevant expenditures incurred are treated differently.

On the one hand, expenditures incurred for R&D activities outsourced to unrelated parties are treated as qualifying expenditures. This applies irrespective of whether the unrelated party conducts the R&D within or outside the jurisdiction offering the preferential regime.[577] The rationale for this treatment is that 'it is unlikely that a company will outsource the fundamental value-creating activities to an unrelated party, regardless of where that unrelated party is located'.[578] Furthermore, '[a]s a matter of business practice, unlimited outsourcing to unrelated parties should not provide many opportunities for taxpayers to receive benefits without themselves engaging in substantial activities'.[579] In this regard, BEPS Action 5 acknowledges that the 'vast majority of the value of an IP asset rests in *both the R&D undertaken to create it and the information necessary to undertake such R&D*' (emphasis added),[580] i.e., day-to-day activities (operational level) and management activities (strategical and

575. BEPS Action 5, Mn 29.
576. *See* BEPS Action 5, Mn 49ff; it is not defined when a party is considered to be a related party, *see also Schwarz Martínez,* IP Box Regime im Europäischen Steuerrecht (2017) 191; against this background, it cannot be said whether the criteria stipulated in Art. 9 OECD MC (participation in the management, control, or capital of an enterprise) are relevant.
577. BEPS Action 5, Mn 49.
578. BEPS Action 5, Mn 50.
579. BEPS Action 5, Mn 50.
580. BEPS Action 5, Mn 50.

tactical level). Accordingly, the treatment of expenditures incurred for outsourced R&D to unrelated parties as qualifying expenditures 'achieves the goal of the nexus approach to only grant tax benefits to income arising from the substantive R&D activities in which the taxpayer itself engaged that contributed to the income'.[581]

Conversely, expenditures for R&D activities outsourced to related parties are not included in the qualifying expenditures.[582] This applies, again, irrespective of whether the related parties are within or outside the country offering the preferential regime.[583] This difference in treatment compared to expenditures for unrelated party outsourcing is justified by stating that 'a company may outsource the full spectrum of R&D activities to a related party, [while] the same is typically not true of an unrelated party'.[584]

Ultimately, under the Modified Nexus Approach, it is decisive to whom R&D is outsourced (unrelated or related party). By contrast, it is generally irrelevant where the outsourced R&D activity takes place (within or outside the jurisdiction offering a patent box regime). However, there is a peculiarity for non-EU member countries. Such countries may allow that expenditures incurred for the outsourcing to related parties being treated as qualifying expenditures if the related parties are resident[585] in their territory.[586] Therefore, the Modified Nexus Approach is designed as a 'territorial approach' for non-EU members (i.e., substance is tested on a territorial level) and as a 'personal approach' for EU members (i.e., substance is tested on an individual

581. BEPS Action 5, Mn 50.
582. BEPS Action 5, Mn 49; this should also apply when R&D is 'outsourced' to foreign PEs (but the IP asset is allocated to the head office), *see* the convincing arguments in *Arginelli*, Innovation through R&D Tax Incentives: Ideas for a Fair and Transparent Tax Policy, WTJ 2015, 3 (56f); however, within the EU, the different treatment of expenditures for R&D conducted in foreign PEs or in domestic establishments of the head office would possibly be an infringement of the freedom of establishment, *see Bañuelos*, The Nexus Approach and Its Compatibility With EU Law, Journal of International Taxation 2016, 28 (36).
583. For this reason, it is criticized that the Modified Nexus Approach disadvantages smaller countries compared to larger countries, *see Hinny*, IFF 2016, 210; *see* already FN 482; this is because certain activities of an R&D project are, by their very nature, only executable in larger countries (e.g., if a big population for clinical trials is needed), *see Müller*, Inputförderung: Forschung und Entwicklung im Ausland, Expert Focus 2016, 800 (800), concerning input incentives, but the same considerations also apply in the case of the Modified Nexus Approach; furthermore, the bigger a country is, the easier it is to source R&D from the domestic market simply because of a larger labour force, *see also Hinny*, IFF 2016, 216 FN 120.
584. BEPS Action 5, Mn 50.
585. Although the term 'resident' – if understood according to the OECD MC 2017 – may indicate that only taxpayers that are subject to unlimited tax liability fall under this category (*see* already the considerations in sec. 3.2.3 concerning resident companies as qualifying taxpayers), it appears to make sense for understanding the term more broadly in this context so that it is consistent with the definition of qualifying taxpayers; that is, it should also encompass domestic PEs of foreign companies and foreign PEs of resident companies when the credit method is applicable; otherwise, it would be possible that a domestic PE of a foreign company outsources R&D to a resident company, and the respective expenditures would be treated as qualifying expenditures whereas, in the reverse case, the expenditures would not qualify; *see also Danon* in *IFA* 50.
586. BEPS Action 5, 48 FN 16.

level).[587] The territorial approach is even more in line with the desired policy objective to promote R&D within a country since it provides an incentive to outsource R&D only to resident-related parties instead of non-resident-related parties. However, within the EU, the territorial approach would have been incompatible with the fundamental freedoms, which is why this distinction was made.[588]

3.2.6.4 Acquisition of IP

Concerning the acquisition of IP, the basic principle is that 'only the expenditures incurred for improving the IP asset after it was acquired should be treated as qualifying expenditures', whereas the acquisition costs themselves do not qualify.[589] This is comprehensible since expenditures for acquired IP are not based on any R&D activity of the acquiring taxpayer.[590] This rationale applies notwithstanding from whom IP is acquired. Consequently, unlike in the case of outsourcing, expenditures for the acquisition of IP are treated the same irrespective of whether the IP asset is acquired from a related or an unrelated party.

This treatment of acquisition costs has an impact on cases when the acquired IP is directly exploited (no preferential treatment) or cases when the acquired IP is used as a platform for further development (preferential treatment depends on the extent of the qualifying taxpayer's activity after the acquisition of the IP). However, when IP is acquired that is helpful or even necessary for the subsequent development of another IP asset but that itself is not further developed, this case is not encompassed. For example, at a certain stage in the R&D development process of a drug, a taxpayer active in the pharmaceutical sector might buy the right to use software that enables the monitoring of test results.[591] Of course, the R&D expenditures incurred prior to the acquisition of the software would still be included under qualifying expenditures in such a case, and the acquisition costs for the software should also qualify.[592] In this regard, BEPS Action 5 states that acquisition costs 'would include, among other

587. *See also Danon* in *IFA* 27ff; under the reasoning of the personal approach 'expenses pertaining to outsourcing of R&D functions to a foreign related party are not denied because these functions are carried out abroad but rather because they are not performed by the taxpayer itself', *see Danon* in *IFA* 49.
588. For more details, *see Danon* in *IFA* 27ff; critical *Kaul*, Der Nexus-Ansatz: Auswirkungen auf IP-Boxen und Alternativansätze (2018) 16, according to whom the personal approach should also apply to non-EU members in order to ensure international consistency and to avoid fuelling new fire in international tax competition; according to *Danon* in *IFA* 36f, the personal approach could also be extended to input incentives within the EU to avoid double deductions for R&D expenditures in different countries (i.e., only the taxpayer that conducts actual R&D activities should be favoured and not the principal of R&D).
589. BEPS Action 5, Mn 52.
590. *See also Pross/Radmanesh*, IStR 2015, 583.
591. For similar considerations, *see Kaul*, Der Nexus-Ansatz: Auswirkungen auf IP-Boxen und Alternativansätze (2018) 18.
592. In a similar direction, BEPS Action 5, 42 FN 17 distinguishes between outsourcing and the buying-in of components from a party that owns the IP to those components; the acquisition of the software as presented above would be considered as a buying-in of components.

expenditures, those that were incurred to obtain rights to research'.[593] Therefore, the right to use an IP is not sufficient for characterizing the respective expenditures as acquisition costs, but the right to further develop (and exploit) an IP has to be transferred.[594]

On the other hand, it does not make a difference whether IP is acquired outright or licensed. In both scenarios, the respective expenditures are equally considered as acquisition costs. Furthermore, care should be taken that 'taxpayers are not able to circumvent this treatment of acquisition costs by acquiring entities that own IP assets'.[595]

The potential IP assets within the scope of the acquisition costs coincide with the abstract definition of qualifying IP assets under the Modified Nexus Approach. For example, a company may acquire a patent and conduct further developments that lead to a new patent. In this case, the acquisition costs for the patent would obviously be treated as acquisition costs and hence not be included under qualifying expenditures. Likewise, a company that does not meet the SME threshold[596] may acquire know-how and, based on it, develop a patent. While the know-how itself would not be a qualifying asset for the company in this case since it does not meet the SME threshold, the patent certainly is. It would be inconsistent with the purpose of the Modified Nexus Approach ('to grant benefits only to income that arises from IP where the actual R&D activity was undertaken by the taxpayer itself')[597] if the costs for acquiring the know-how would not be treated as acquisition costs. Furthermore, expenditures for the acquisition of the know-how were also incurred in order to obtain rights to research (and rights to exploit). Therefore, acquisition costs for IP should comprise all of the IP assets that are abstractly qualifying IP assets under the Modified Nexus Approach (irrespective of whether the acquired IP is a qualifying IP asset for a company in a concrete case).

3.2.6.5 Uplift

As already stated above, the initial proposal of the Nexus Approach did not find acceptance among all countries.[598] In particular, concerns were expressed about the calculation of qualifying expenditures.[599] The Nexus Approach was perceived by some as being too strict with regard to the treatment of outsourcing to related parties and

593. BEPS Action 5, Mn 52.
594. Admittedly, BEPS Action 5, Mn 52 also states that '[a]cquisitions include any transfer of rights [...]'; however, this phrase is more concerned with the point in time when IP is considered as acquired and not necessarily with what can be regarded as an acquisition of IP; *see also* sec. 3.2.6.6.
595. BEPS Action 5, 42 FN 18; in this context, *see also P. Schoueri*, Conflicts of International Legal Frameworks in the Area of Harmful Tax Competition: The Modified Nexus Approach (2019) 108 and 116, who highlights that BEPS Action 5 does not provide any information on how to proceed in merger situations.
596. *See* sec. 3.2.4.
597. BEPS Action 5, Mn 29; *see* sec. 3.2.6.2.
598. *See* sec. 3.2.1.
599. *OECD*, Action 5: Agreement on Modified Nexus Approach for IP Regimes (2015) 3.

acquisition costs (both entirely excluded from qualifying expenditures).[600] Eventually, the initial proposal was slightly modified to account for these concerns (hence the title Modified Nexus Approach).[601]

Accordingly, jurisdictions may allow taxpayers to lift up their qualifying expenditures by up to 30%.[602] That is, expenditures for related party outsourcing and acquisition costs are not directly included under qualifying expenditures - the same considerations as presented above still apply -[603] but they are indirectly taken into account via this uplift (i.e., the qualifying expenditures are multiplied by 1.3). However, '[t]his up-lift may increase qualifying expenditures but only to the extent that the taxpayer has non-qualifying expenditures. In other words, the increased amount of qualifying expenditures may not exceed the taxpayer's overall expenditures'.[604]

The OECD justifies the uplift by stating that MNEs might face restructuring costs due to the new requirements in case they want to continue profiting from a patent box regime. Additionally, it is stated that disregarding 'any IP acquisition costs at all might have an impact on commercial decisions'.[605] Consequently, the stated purpose of the uplift is 'to ensure that the nexus approach does not penalise taxpayers excessively for acquiring IP or outsourcing R&D activities to related parties'.[606] Nevertheless, the uplift would continue to ensure that taxpayers only receive benefits if they have carried out R&D activities themselves, but 'it acknowledges that taxpayers that acquired IP or outsourced a portion of the R&D to a related party may themselves still be responsible for much of the value creation that contributed to IP income'.[607]

This is, in principle, the same rationale that also applies in the case of outsourcing to unrelated parties.[608] However, while expenditures for outsourcing to unrelated parties are directly considered as qualifying expenditures, the expenditures for related party outsourcing are only accounted for via an uplift of the qualifying expenditures. Therefore, in the case of related party outsourcing, a qualifying taxpayer still needs to perform an activity that leads to qualifying expenditures. To provide a simplified example: A taxpayer that outsources all of the actual R&D to an unrelated party would still have a nexus ratio of 1 because the expenditures for the outsourcing to the unrelated party are considered as qualifying expenditures (based on the assumption that the taxpayer provided the information necessary to undertake the R&D). However, a taxpayer that outsources all of the actual R&D to a related party would have a nexus ratio of 0 since - according to the Modified Nexus Approach - it did not engage in any substantial R&D activity and, hence, did not incur any qualifying expenditures (0 plus

600. *See OECD*, Countering Harmful Tax Practices More Effectively, Taking into Account Transparency and Substance - Action 5: 2014 Deliverable (2014) 51 FN 7 where it is stated that Spain and the UK maintained a reservation with regard to the section dealing with outsourcing.
601. *See* already sec. 3.2.1.
602. *OECD*, Action 5: Agreement on Modified Nexus Approach for IP Regimes (2015) 3; *see also* BEPS Action 5, Mn 40.
603. *See* secs 3.2.6.3 and 3.2.6.4.
604. BEPS Action 5, Mn 40.
605. *OECD*, Action 5: Agreement on Modified Nexus Approach for IP Regimes (2015) 3.
606. BEPS Action 5, Mn 41.
607. BEPS Action 5, Mn 41.
608. *See* sec. 3.2.6.3.

the uplift of 30% is still 0). Therefore, in this case, it still depends on a taxpayer's own actual R&D activity (in relation to the R&D activity of the related party) how high the nexus ratio is.[609]

3.2.6.6 *Overall Expenditures*

Overall expenditures are defined as 'the sum of all expenditures that would count as qualifying expenditures if they were undertaken by the taxpayer itself'.[610] It follows from this that 'any expenditures that would not be included in qualifying expenditures even if incurred by the taxpayer itself (e.g. interest payments, building costs, and other costs that do not represent actual R&D activities) cannot be included in overall expenditures'.[611]

However, there is one exception to this rule, namely, the acquisition costs of IP.[612] While they are not treated as qualifying expenditures,[613] they are considered in the overall expenditures. This treatment is justified by stating that acquisition costs are 'a proxy for expenditures incurred by a non-qualifying taxpayer'.[614]

In this context, it is also stated that 'no expenditures incurred by any party prior to acquisition will be included in either qualifying expenditures or overall expenditures'.[615] However, again, there is a peculiarity for non-EU members who 'could modify this limitation so that the acquisition of a taxpayer that incurred qualifying expenditures in the jurisdiction providing the IP regime allowed those expenditures to be included in the qualifying expenditures of the acquirer'.[616] That is, the qualifying expenditures of a taxpayer who acquires the IP would include the qualifying expenditures incurred by the seller to develop the IP asset. At the same time, the overall expenditures of the acquirer can contain the acquisition costs or all of the overall expenditures that the seller incurred to develop the IP asset (if the seller has 'engaged in complete tracking and tracing to ensure that all overall expenditures are included').[617] In the end, this means that, in the case of non-EU members, the acquisition of IP assets may not have a negative influence on the nexus ratio of the acquirer (when the seller did not outsource R&D to related parties abroad or did not acquire IP assets from parties abroad). As a result, it may not make a difference in the case of non-EU members whether R&D is outsourced to a domestic party or acquired from a domestic party, which is again based on a territorial approach[618] that is applicable for non-EU members.

---

609. Therefore, it can be argued that the uplift is in line with the rationale of the Modified Nexus Approach (*see* sec. 3.2.6.2); opposing view *Matteotti/Roth*, ASA 2014/2015, 768.
610. BEPS Action 5, Mn 42.
611. BEPS Action 5, Mn 42.
612. Otherwise, it would be possible to acquire IP, develop it just a little further, and then enjoy preferential treatment for the corresponding income.
613. *See* sec. 3.2.6.4.
614. BEPS Action 5, Mn 42.
615. BEPS Action 5, Mn 52.
616. BEPS Action 5, 42 FN 19.
617. BEPS Action 5, 42 FN 19.
618. *See* already sec. 3.2.6.3.

Like in the case of qualifying expenditures,[619] overall expenditures have to be included in the nexus ratio at the time they are incurred.[620] However, concerning acquisition costs of IP, it is stated that '[a]cquisitions include any transfer of rights *regardless of whether a payment was actually made*' (emphasis added).[621] Therefore, acquisition costs have to be included in the nexus ratio at the time the rights in an intangible are transferred. The reason for this different treatment seems to be to counteract arrangements between related parties when no payment is made.[622]

In short, overall expenditures include all qualifying expenditures (i.e., expenditures for the taxpayer's own actual R&D activities and for the outsourcing to unrelated parties) plus expenditures for outsourcing to related parties and acquisition costs of IP.[623] Therefore, the Modified Nexus Approach 'does not include all expenditures ever incurred in the development of an IP asset in overall expenditures. Instead, it only adds two things to qualifying expenditures [...]'.[624]

BEPS Action 5 provides the following illustration for the nexus ratio:[625]

$$\frac{a + b}{a + b + c + d}$$

Accordingly, 'a represents R&D expenditures incurred by the taxpayer itself, b represents expenditures for unrelated-party outsourcing, c represents acquisition costs, and d represents expenditures for related-party outsourcing'.[626]

In the end, the relevant expenditures that are considered in the nexus ratio (i.e., qualifying expenditures and overall expenditures) are limited in two ways: First, in objective terms since expenditures are excluded when it is not possible to establish a direct link between them and a specific IP asset.[627] However, it is not explicitly stated that such expenditures might not be relevant in the development of an IP asset but just that they cannot be reconciled to a specific IP asset.[628] That is, they are not generally overlooked because they are not important when developing an IP asset but rather because a link between them and an IP asset cannot be established.[629] Still, this entails that such expenditures are not considered as creating value under the Modified Nexus Approach.

619. *See* already sec. 3.2.6.2.
620. *See* BEPS Action 5, Mn 44.
621. *See* BEPS Action 5, Mn 52.
622. *See also Kaul*, Der Nexus-Ansatz: Auswirkungen auf IP-Boxen und Alternativansätze (2018) 18; furthermore, the author points out that it is not specified when a transfer of rights occurred.
623. BEPS Action 5, Mn 42.
624. BEPS Action 5, Mn 43.
625. BEPS Action 5, Mn 43.
626. BEPS Action 5, Mn 44.
627. *See* sec. 3.2.6.2.
628. *See* BEPS Action 5, 42 FN 11: 'Building costs or other non-separable capital costs would not be included because it would be impossible to establish a direct link between the cost of an entire building and different IP assets created in that building.'
629. On criticism of this assumption (i.e., impossibility of establishing a link between certain expenditures and a certain IP asset) in its generality, *see* already sec. 3.2.6.2, especially FN 573.

Second, relevant expenditures are also limited in subjective terms since the nexus ratio 'only includes qualifying and overall expenditures *incurred by the entity*. It therefore does not consider all expenditures ever incurred in the development of the IP asset' (emphasis added).[630] BEPS Action 5 provides an example as an illustration where three companies, Company A, Company B, and Company C, work together to develop an IP asset.[631] That is, R&D is not outsourced from one of the companies to the others, but all companies jointly develop an IP asset.[632] Company A is in a jurisdiction that offers an IP regime. Concerning the development of the IP asset, 'Company A contributes 30% of the R&D and 3 000 of the R&D funding, Company B contributes 30% of the R&D and 3 000 of the R&D funding, and Company C contributes 40% of the R&D and 4 000 of the R&D funding.'[633] The development is successful, and the IP asset generates 100.000 in income of which 30.000 is allocated to Company A.[634] In this regard, BEPS Action 5 states that '[i]f Company A did not pay to outsource to a related company or to acquire any IP assets, then the nexus ratio that would apply to that 30 000 before the up-lift is 3 000/3 000 (or 100%). The entire 30 000 would therefore qualify for the IP regime in Company A's jurisdiction.'[635]

That is, although the total expenditures to develop the IP amount to 100.000 and Company A only incurred 30.000 of it, it still has a nexus ratio of 1. This is because only the expenditures at the level of an entity are examined (and distinguished in qualifying expenditures, overall expenditures, or not considered at all).[636] In the case of the joint development of an IP asset, expenditures incurred for R&D are distributed among the various companies participating in it. Therefore, to come back to the above example, although the activity of Company B and Company C certainly contributed to the value creation of the IP asset, their respective expenditures were not borne by Company A which is why they are not considered in Company A's nexus ratio. This is, however, consistent with the purpose of the Modified Nexus Approach to 'grant benefits only to income that arises from IP where the actual R&D activity was undertaken by the taxpayer itself'.[637] Concerning the 30.000 of Company A, 100% of them can be treated preferentially as this income is – according to the Modified Nexus Approach – completely based on an activity of Company A because Company A did not outsource R&D to related parties or acquire any IP asset.[638] Ultimately, as long as a taxpayer's

630. BEPS Action 5, Mn 31.
631. *See* BEPS Action 5, 41 FN 3.
632. Within the OECD TPG, this endeavour would be classified as a development CCA since 'all parties make contributions and share in the consequences of risks materialising in relation to the development of the intangible and decide that each of them, through those contributions, acquires a right in the intangible'; *see* OECD TPG 2017 Mn 8.12; however, the provided example does not say whether the mentioned companies are associated.
633. BEPS Action 5, 41 FN 3.
634. That is, according to the DEMPE Approach, Company A's contribution to the value creation of the intangible amounts to 30% (under the assumption that the mentioned companies are associated).
635. *See* BEPS Action 5, 41 FN 3.
636. *See* already sec. 3.2.6.1.
637. BEPS Action 5, Mn 29; *see* already sec. 3.2.6.2.
638. *See also* BEPS Action 5, Mn 44: '[T]he only way that the [nexus] ratio can be decreased from 100% is if the taxpayer outsourced the R&D to related parties or acquired the R&D.'

expenditures for the outsourcing to related parties and the acquisition of IP do not exceed the 30% uplift of its qualifying expenditures, the nexus ratio will be 1.

3.2.6.7 Synopsis

For the overall income from a qualifying IP asset to be taxed preferentially, a qualifying taxpayer must:

- incur expenditures for its own R&D activity;[639] and/or
- incur expenditures for the outsourcing to unrelated parties;[640] and the
- expenditures incurred for the outsourcing to related parties, and the acquisition of IP must not exceed these above-mentioned expenditures by more than 30%.[641]

The Modified Nexus Approach requires a link (nexus) between expenditures (proxy for activities) and IP income.[642] Accordingly, a taxpayer's activity - as expressed by the nexus ratio - is relevant for the amount of income eligible for preferential treatment.[643] Therefore, the Modified Nexus Approach is an activity-based concept.[644] By contrast, the Modified Nexus Approach intends to 'prevent mere capital contribution [...] from qualifying the subsequent income for benefits under an IP regime'.[645]

Value creation under the Modified Nexus Approach is primarily concerned with actual R&D activities (day-to-day activities), i.e., activities on the operational level.[646] However, it is also acknowledged that the 'vast majority of the value of an IP asset rests in both the R&D undertaken to create it and the information necessary to undertake such R&D'.[647] For this reason, expenditures for the outsourcing to unrelated parties are qualifying expenditures because it is assumed that the qualifying taxpayer provided the necessary information to undertake the R&D.[648] Therefore, in this case, management activities (activities on the strategical and tactical level) are considered as value-creating activities (like under the DEMPE Approach).[649] By contrast, expenditures for outsourcing to related parties are not qualifying expenditures (only overall expendi

639. *See* sec. 3.2.6.2.
640. *See* sec. 3.2.6.3.
641. *See* secs 3.2.6.3, 3.2.6.4 and 3.2.6.5.
642. *See also* BEPS Action 5, Mn 55.
643. *See also* BEPS Action 5, Mn 28: 'This focus on expenditures aligns with the underlying purpose of IP regimes by ensuring that the regimes that are intended to encourage R&D activity only provide benefits to taxpayers that in fact engage in such activity.'
644. *See also Chand/Malek*, BTR 2019, 415f.
645. BEPS Action 5, Mn 29.
646. *See* sec. 3.2.6.2.
647. BEPS Action 5, Mn 50; *see* already sec. 3.2.6.3.
648. There is the possibility that jurisdictions 'only permit unrelated outsourcing up to a certain percentage or proportion', *see* BEPS Action 5, Mn 51; however, this possible limitation is inconsistent with the assumption that the R&D activity conducted by unrelated parties is generally insubstantial - accordingly, there would not be a reason for this limitation, *see also Kaul*, Der Nexus-Ansatz: Auswirkungen auf IP-Boxen und Alternativansätze (2018) 15.
649. *See* sec. 2.5.5.

tures)[650] because it is assumed that value is created by the related parties' R&D activities (activities on the operational level). A bridge between these two understandings of value creation – activities on the operational level vs activities on the strategical and tactical level – is built by the uplift as 'it acknowledges that taxpayers that [...] outsourced a portion of the R&D to a related party may themselves still be responsible for much of the value creation that contributed to IP income'.[651] Yet, a qualifying taxpayer still has to have expenditures for its own actual R&D activity to make use of the uplift.[652]

The Modified Nexus Approach is a quantitative approach to determine substance as the fulfilment of the relevant criteria (i.e., distinguishing expenditures incurred in qualifying expenditures and overall expenditures) can be objectively assessed.[653] The Modified Nexus Approach operates under the assumption that the significance of an activity for the creation of value is reflected in the expenditures incurred in the performance of said activity. While it is true that conclusions about a taxpayer's involvement in value creation cannot be directly drawn from the amount of its qualifying expenditures – they still have to be set in proportion to the overall expenditures to determine the nexus ratio – the amount of its qualifying expenditures does certainly affect the nexus ratio. Stated differently, if an activity increases the qualifying expenditures by 2 and a different activity increases the overall expenditures by 1, it is assumed that the first-mentioned activity created more value. To formulate it bluntly, what costs more is considered worth more.[654] It therefore does not depend on the relevant facts and circumstances which activity has actually created more value.

Under the Modified Nexus Approach, a typical structure with an IP Principal[655] that has contract R&D arrangements with related parties in different jurisdictions will not be able to claim preferential tax treatment. This is precisely the intention behind the different treatment of expenditures for related party outsourcing and expenditures for unrelated party outsourcing. MNEs shall not have the possibility to outsource R&D to related parties in high-tax jurisdictions and, at the same time, have the corresponding income preferentially taxed in a jurisdiction with a patent box regime.[656] Effectively, this means that outsourcing to related parties is under a general suspicion of abuse under the Modified Nexus Approach.[657] At the same time, however, this may create an incentive to outsource certain routine R&D activities to unrelated parties instead of related parties. Furthermore, there is an incentive to shift people that perform

650. *See* sec. 3.2.6.6.
651. BEPS Action 5, Mn 41.
652. Or expenditures for outsourcing to unrelated parties, respectively, *see* already sec. 3.2.6.5.
653. *See* already sec. 1.1.
654. Therefore, at least in theory, countries with high wage levels that offer a nexus-compliant IP regime may be at an advantage compared to countries where wage levels are lower. If the same activity costs 10 in one country and 5 in another country, the Modified Nexus Approach assumes that more value was created in the first-mentioned country because the expenditures incurred were higher.
655. *See* sec. 1.5 (especially FN 80).
656. *See Becker/Hoeck* in *Kofler/Schnitger* 322; *Gupta*, TNI 2015, 1129.
657. *See also Pross/Radmanesh*, IStR 2015, 583.

operational R&D activities to the jurisdiction of the IP Principal to sustain the tax planning structure.[658]

3.2.7 Overall Income

Like in the case of qualifying expenditures,[659] BEPS Action 5 does not provide a concrete definition of overall income but only provides certain principles. According to them:

- the OECD TPG have to be followed;
- overall income is only a net amount; and
- overall income only includes income derived from an IP asset.

BEPS Action 5 states that '[j]urisdictions will define "overall income" consistent with their domestic laws on income definition *after the application of transfer pricing rules*' (emphasis added).[660] Although it is not specified which transfer pricing rules are exactly referred to - domestic transfer pricing rules may deviate from the OECD standards - one can likely assume that the TPG of the OECD (as changed in the BEPS Project) are meant.[661] In the case that an IP asset is used in controlled transactions, this entails that the DEMPE Approach sets the limit of how much income may benefit from a preferential IP regime (i.e., a consideration that goes beyond the arm's-length principle cannot be taxed preferentially).

Additionally, countries have to ensure that overall income is only a net amount; that is, it should be 'calculated by subtracting IP expenditures allocable to IP income and incurred in the year from gross IP income earned in the year' (so-called net approach).[662,663] The wording 'IP expenditures allocable to IP income' suggests that the expenditures to be deducted must not necessarily be qualifying expenditures. As such, qualifying expenditures are costs that 'arise out of activities undertaken to advance the understanding of scientific relations or technologies, address known scientific or technological obstacles, or otherwise increase knowledge or develop new applications'.[664] This stems from the fact that the Modified Nexus Approach is only concerned with the development or enhancement (and possibly maintenance) of an IP asset.[665] By contrast, expenditures for the protection or the exploitation of an IP asset are irrelevant for determining the nexus ratio (i.e., these activities are not considered as relevant

658. *See also Danon* in *IFA* 49: '[A]s a result of the application of the modified nexus approach, certain IP structures will have to be reorganized and an increased centralization of R&D functions is likely to take place.'
659. *See* already 3.2.6.2.
660. *See* BEPS Action 5, Mn 46.
661. This is indicated in BEPS Action 5, 42 FN 15, where a reference to the 'transfer pricing principles as updated through the report on Actions 8-10 of the BEPS Action Plan' is made.
662. *See Luts*, EC Tax Review 2014, 259f; *Mang*, ET 2015, 78; by contrast, a gross-approach would allow deducting the respective expenditures from income that is taxed at the regular corporate tax rate.
663. BEPS Action 5, Mn 47.
664. BEPS Action 5, 41f FN 10; *see* already sec. 3.2.6.2.
665. *See also* Hinny, IFF 2016, 214 FN 111.

substance under the Modified Nexus Approach).[666] Yet, expenditures for these activities are obviously IP expenditures allocable to IP income, and they must hence be deducted when determining overall income.

Furthermore, IP expenditures have to be calculated by applying the ordinary domestic tax provisions.[667] This is to avoid a double benefit that may arise, for example, when a country offers an input incentive in addition to a patent box regime (i.e., enhanced allowances are only granted under the input incentive).[668] Likewise, any remaining losses in this calculation must not be offset against income that is taxed at the regular rate.[669]

These specifications, however, only concern current expenditures (i.e., expenditures incurred in the same year as the year in which IP income is earned), whereas it is left unanswered how historic expenditures for the development of a qualifying IP asset should be treated.[670] Such expenditures were usually previously deducted from income that is taxed at the normal tax rate. However, when an IP asset is successfully developed and a qualifying taxpayer applies for a preferential IP regime, the respective income will be taxed at a preferential rate. On the one hand, a country could simply accept this asymmetrical treatment of R&D expenditures and IP income.[671] On the other hand, if a country wants to align the tax treatment of R&D expenditures and IP income *ex post*, there are generally two prevalent options:[672] First, a country may foresee that the previous expenditures are capitalized at the moment that a qualifying taxpayer opts into the IP regime; i.e., they would be added back to the taxable profit in the year of the entry into the IP regime and taxed at the normal rate (capitalization approach).[673] Under the second approach, the historic R&D expenditures are recaptured by taxing IP

---

666. *See also* OECD, Frascati Manual 2015 – Guidelines for Collecting and Reporting Data on Research and Experimental Development (2015) Mn 2.47: 'Care must be taken to exclude activities that, although part of the innovation process, do not satisfy the criteria required to be classified as R&D. For example, patent application and licensing activity [...] are not in their own right R&D activities and cannot be assumed to be part of an R&D project.'
667. BEPS Action 5, 42 FN 14.
668. *See Kaul*, Der Nexus-Ansatz: Auswirkungen auf IP-Boxen und Alternativansätze (2018) 19; apart from this requirement, BEPS Action 5 does not specify anything on the interaction between input incentives and output incentives, *see also Danon* in *IFA* 46.
669. BEPS Action 5, 42 FN 14.
670. *See also Danon* in *IFA* 46.
671. *See also Evers/Miller/Spengel*, Intellectual property box regimes: effective tax rates and tax policy considerations, International Tax and Public Finance 2015, 502 (509); *Luts*, EC Tax Review 2014, 260.
672. *See also Mang*, ET 2015, 79; *Evers/Miller/Spengel*, International Tax and Public Finance 2015, 509f; on the alignment of R&D expenditures and IP income *ex ante*, *see Evers/Miller/Spengel*, ZEW Discussion Paper No. 13-070, 15f (available at http://ftp.zew.de/pub/zew-docs/dp/dp13070.pdf).
673. Countries could provide a time limit on expenditures to be taken into account (e.g., expenditures of the last three years) or a limit on the amount (e.g., capped with the market value of the IP asset); if the capitalized expenditures are depreciated, a depreciation is only possible against income that is taxed preferentially since these are 'IP expenditures allocable to IP income', *see also Hinny*, IFF 2016, 218f; furthermore, countries could provide that the resulting tax liability is not due immediately on the entry into the IP regime but within a certain number of years, *see also Hausmann/Widler/Spillmann*, Gesamtüberblick über die Patentbox, Expert Focus 2016, 821 (824); *Hausmann/Roth/Meyer-Nandi*, Expert Focus 2016, 194.

income at the normal rate until the IP income exceeds the historic R&D expenditures (recapture approach). That is, only when IP income exceeds the historic R&D expenditures is it taxed at a preferential rate.

Another principle to be observed is that overall income only includes 'income that is derived from the IP asset. This may include royalties, capital gains and other income from the sale of an IP asset, and embedded IP income from the sale of products and the use of processes directly related to the IP asset'.[674]

A concrete definition of royalties and capital gains is not provided. Against the background that BEPS Action 5 states that '[j]urisdictions will define "overall income" consistent with their domestic laws on income definition [...]',[675] it is questionable whether the definition[676] or understanding[677] of those terms in the OECD MC and its Commentary are applicable here. Nonetheless, they can provide a useful orientation aid. This would mean, for example, that not only payments made under a licence but also compensation for the infringement of rights in a qualifying IP asset would be characterized as royalties and hence eligible income.[678]

Besides royalties and capital gains, the sale of products that are protected by an IP asset is also encompassed ('embedded IP income from the sale of products [...] directly related to the IP asset').[679] This concerns cases when either the whole product or only a part of it is protected by an IP asset. Furthermore, the income from process patents is also eligible for preferential treatment ('embedded IP income from [...] the use of processes directly related to the IP asset').[680] In such a case, not a product itself or a part of it is protected by an IP asset, but a patent is used in the manufacturing process of a product. To provide a borrowed example:[681] In order to grind coffee according to the specific standards of certain customers, a lot of know-how and special processes may be needed. While the coffee itself may not be protected by an IP asset, the proprietary processes to grind it may be with a process patent. As a result, (part of) the income from the sale of the coffee can also be taxed preferentially.[682]

Likewise, the same should also be true when a qualifying IP asset is used in the performance of a service, for example, if a company uses a proprietary software when

674. BEPS Action 5, Mn 48.
675. BEPS Action 5, Mn 46.
676. For the definition of royalties in the OECD MC, *see* Art. 12(2) OECD MC 2017; *see also* FN 815.
677. The term 'capital gains' is not defined in the OECD MC 2017, *see* Art. 13 Mn 5 OECD Commentary 2017; however, in the same Mn, it is stated that '[t]he words "alienation of property" are used to cover in particular capital gains resulting from the sale or exchange of property and also from a partial alienation, the expropriation, the transfer to a company in exchange for stock, the sale of a right, the gift and even the passing of property on death'; according to *Reimer* in *Reimer/Rust*, Klaus Vogel on Double Taxation Conventions[4] (2015) Art. 13 Mn 20, the term 'gain' has to be interpreted autonomously and is 'any advantage in money or in kind that constitutes a consideration (a quid pro quo) for the alienation of the underlying asset'.
678. *See* Art. 12 Mn 8 OECD Commentary 2017; affirmative, *Koch*, Expert Focus 2016, 833.
679. On embedded intangibles, *see* already sec. 2.2.
680. *See also Koch/Küttel/Trüssel*, TPI 2018, 155; *Koch*, Expert Focus 2016, 830.
681. Taken from *Koch/Küttel/Trüssel*, TPI 2018, 155.
682. Interesting in this context, the considerations in *Koch*, Expert Focus 2016, 830, who is cautious about whether copyrighted software is a qualifying process patent for a product in all cases.

it provides certain services to a customer.[683] Otherwise, a company would be forced to license or sell the rights in the software in order to benefit from an IP regime.[684]

When a country decides to grant benefits to embedded IP income, it 'must implement a consistent and coherent method for separating income unrelated to IP (e.g. marketing and manufacturing returns) from the income arising from IP'.[685] It has to be mentioned that BEPS Action 5 generally does not provide a specific method on how to achieve this separation.[686] It is only stated that '[o]ne method that would achieve this outcome could, for example, be based on transfer pricing principles'.[687]

3.2.8 Illustrative Example

The following simplified example illustrates the application of the Modified Nexus Approach:[688]

> An IP Company acquires IP for 10. Afterwards, it incurs expenditures of 100 for its own R&D activities to improve the acquired IP asset. Furthermore, for the outsourcing of some R&D activities to a related party, the IP Company incurs expenditures of 40. The R&D project is successful and a patent is granted.

In total, the overall expenditures incurred for developing the patent amount to 150 (10 acquisition costs, 100 for own R&D activities, and 40 for related party outsourcing). However, not all of these expenditures are qualifying expenditures; namely, the acquisition costs and the expenditures for related party outsourcing do not fall under this category. Therefore, the qualifying expenditures are 100 (expenditures for the IP Company's own R&D activity). By applying the uplift, the qualifying expenditures can be increased by 30% (30) to 130.[689] The division of the qualifying expenditures (increased by the uplift) by the overall expenditures results in a nexus ratio of 86.7% (130/150). That is, 86.7% of the overall (net)[690] income generated with

683. *See also Arginelli*, WTJ 2015, 61; the eligibility of service income is implicitly addressed in BEPS Action 5, 42 FN 20 where a reference is made to 'certain industries that produce services or other outputs other than products [...]', and it is stated that 'product families could include functional equivalents [...]'.
684. In this context, *see* the comments of *Robertson*, TNI 2019, 844 concerning the UK's patent box regime: 'When a company derives income from exploiting a qualifying IP right that is not covered by the above categories (which may include service income), a percentage of that income is treated as relevant IP income (the notional royalty regime). Generally, the percentage is the arm's length royalty that would be paid to an unrelated party for use of the right.'
685. BEPS Action 5, Mn 48.
686. *See also Hinny*, IFF 2016, 216 FN 122.
687. BEPS Action 5, Mn 48; for an example on how overall IP income is calculated under the Swiss IP regime, *see Koch*, Expert Focus 2016, 833ff.
688. Based on the example in BEPS Action 5, Mn 40.
689. The taxpayer can increase qualifying expenditures only up to the amount of the overall expenditures at the maximum; that is, if, in the example above, acquisition costs were only 5 and expenditures for related party outsourcing only 20, the uplift would increase the qualifying expenditures by only 25 – which leads to a nexus ratio of 100% – and not by 30; *see also* Example B in BEPS Action 5, Mn 40.
690. Expenditures incurred in the same fiscal year that are allocable to the IP income have to be deducted, *see* already sec. 3.2.7.

the patent can be taxed at a preferential rate, whereas the other 13.3% has to be taxed at the regular rate.

It has to be kept in mind that the nexus ratio is not set in stone indefinitely, but it has to be calculated for each fiscal year (additive approach).[691] This means that the relevant expenditures incurred in the fiscal year concerned are added to the relevant expenditures of previous fiscal years. Assuming that the IP Company incurs 30 for their own R&D activities and 10 for outsourcing to related parties in the following year, the overall expenditures would amount to 190 (150 from the previous fiscal year, 30 for their own R&D activities, and 10 for related party outsourcing, both incurred in the current fiscal year). The qualifying expenditures, on the other hand, would amount to 130 (100 from the previous year and 30 from the current year for the IP Company's own R&D activities). Again, applying an uplift of 30% (39) on the qualifying expenditures would result in 169. Therefore, the nexus ratio would be 88.9% (169/190) in the following year which would be applied to the overall (net) income generated with the patent in that year.

3.2.9 Tracking

The Modified Nexus Approach is a quantitative approach for determining the substance of a taxpayer (i.e., the nexus ratio) since the fulfilment of the relevant criteria can, in principle, be objectively assessed.[692] While a general advantage of a quantitative approach to determine substance is the easier applicability in practice,[693] this is not the case under the Modified Nexus Approach.

Since the Modified Nexus Approach requires a link between expenditures, IP assets, and income,[694] 'taxpayers that want to benefit from an IP regime must track expenditures, IP assets, and income [...]' and 'provide evidence of this [link] to their tax administrations'.[695] Otherwise, they will not be able to avail themselves of an IP regime.[696] This entails that the tracking of the relevant components has to be reviewed on a case-by-case basis which is a burdensome exercise not only for taxpayers but also for tax administrations.[697]

The tracking itself might be fairly easy when a company owns only one IP asset that the company has fully self-developed (i.e., without any outsourcing or acquisition).[698] However, in the practice of an MNE that has an abundance of patents and when many entities contribute to the IP development process, it is often very difficult to track the relevant qualifying and overall expenditures incurred for and the income

691. *See* already sec. 3.2.6.1; *see also* the example provided in BEPS Action 5, 71f, Annex A.
692. *See* already sec. 3.2.6.7.
693. On the strengths and weaknesses of a quantitative approach to define substance, *see* sec. 1.1.
694. BEPS Action 5, Mn 55, *see* already sec. 3.2.6.7.
695. BEPS Action 5, Mn 53.
696. However, taxpayers are still able to earn IP income, of course, which is determined according to the DEMPE Approach; *see also* BEPS Action 5, Mn 53.
697. *See Becker/Hoeck* in *Kofler/Schnitger* 324.
698. BEPS Action 5, Mn 30 and 53.

generated by an IP asset.[699] Furthermore, it is criticized that it is extremely difficult or even impossible to link expenditures and income to a particular IP asset.[700]

In general, the Modified Nexus Approach requires the tracking of expenditures and income to individual IP assets (*IP asset-based approach*).[701]

However, R&D activities in a company are often not structured on an IP-asset-by-IP-asset basis.[702] In order to take this into account, BEPS Action 5 leaves it at the discretion of countries to allow the tracking of expenditures and income at the level of a product (*product-based approach*).[703] The application of the product-based approach is possible when multiple IP assets are incorporated into one product since, in this case, tracking at the level of an IP asset 'would be unrealistic and require arbitrary judgements'.[704] It entails that a link is established 'between expenditures, products arising from IP assets, and income'.[705] Consequently, taxpayers have to 'include all qualifying expenditures linked to the development of all IP assets that contributed to the product in "qualifying expenditures" and to include all overall expenditures linked to the development of all IP assets that contributed to the product in "overall expenditures"'. Afterwards, this ratio would be 'applied to overall income from the product that was directly linked to all the underlying IP assets'.[706] While, under the IP asset-based approach, benefits may be granted for as long as patent protection exists,[707] BEPS Action 5 is rather vague concerning the expiration of benefits under the product-based approach. It is simply stated that jurisdictions must ensure 'that benefits expire at a fair and reasonable time (e.g. the average life of all IP assets)'.[708] However, it is unclear how the lifetime of the individual IP assets should be determined and

699. BEPS Action 5 acknowledges this difficulty (Mn 30 and 53) but, at the same time, states that 'taxpayers are willing to comply with certain often complex requirements when an optional tax benefit is made conditional on such requirements'; furthermore, it is stated that the Modified Nexus Approach will lead to a standardization of eligibility criteria that 'may in the long term reduce the overall complexity that taxpayers that are benefiting from multiple IP regimes currently face' (Mn 54); on the use of a three- or five-year rolling average to calculate the nexus ratio as a transitional measure to ensure that taxpayers have sufficient time to adapt to the tracking requirement, *see* BEPS Action 5, Mn 60 and the example in Annex A.

700. *See Fensby*, The Dangers Posed by the OECD's Approach to Preferential Tax Regimes, TNI 2018, 953 (955): 'The tracking and tracing required under the nexus rule is destined to produce arbitrary results. [...] How do you link income and expenses to a particular asset or distinguish between intangible-related returns and normal returns? What about when ongoing research and development relates to many projects that affect multiple streams of income? What about blue sky research — that is, research that does not have a specific, immediate commercial goal? The nexus approach's complexity makes defining appropriate returns for various functions, assets, and risks under the OECD's transfer pricing guidelines look simple in comparison.'

701. BEPS Action 5, Mn 55; *see also Hausmann/Widler/Spillmann*, Expert Focus 2016, 822; *Hausmann/Roth/Meyer-Nandi*, Expert Focus 2016, 192.

702. *See also* BEPS Action 5, Mn 56: 'This is because R&D programmes and projects are generally focused on answering research questions or solving technical problems and it is only in a subsequent stage that there is any discussion of how to provide legal protection to the results of these projects. Often, the results of these projects will contribute to multiple IP assets.'

703. BEPS Action 5, Mn 55ff.

704. BEPS Action 5, Mn 55f.

705. BEPS Action 5, Mn 55.

706. BEPS Action 5, Mn 55.

707. *See* sec. 3.2.5.

708. BEPS Action 5, Mn 55.

whether adjustments have to be made when the projected lifetime does not correspond to the actual lifetime.[709]

The concrete definition of 'product' is left to the countries.[710] BEPS Action 5 only provides a few indications in this respect: From two examples provided by the OECD, it can be concluded that the R&D and related IP assets underlying the different value-driving components have to sufficiently overlap[711] and that tracking should not require a level of detail that did not relate to the actual innovation.[712] Furthermore, it seems to be important how R&D activities are organized within a company[713] and whether common scientific, technological, or engineering challenges are underlying the R&D expenditures and income.[714] Consequently, it is stated that taxpayers may track to products when 'these groupings include all the IP assets that arose from overlapping expenditures and contributed to overlapping streams of income'.[715]

Finally, tracking may also be done at the level of product families if there are only minor variations between the individual products (e.g., different colours or sizes), and the individual products contain the same IP (*product family-based approach*).[716] Therefore, the definition of products can include 'product families such as components for printer or computer producers, active compounds for the chemical industry, and therapeutic areas or narrower disease categories for the pharmaceutical industry'.[717]

In the end, the OECD's remarks on the product definition are vague and, hence, possibly susceptible to manipulation by taxpayers as well as countries.[718] Admittedly,

709. *Kaul*, Der Nexus-Ansatz: Auswirkungen auf IP-Boxen und Alternativansätze (2018) 21.
710. BEPS Action 5, Mn 57.
711. In this regard, the OECD provides an example of a company that produces multiple components for a truck which it (i.e., the truck) then sells. In this case, a product definition that permitted tracking to the whole truck would be too broad since 'the R&D and related IP assets underlying the different value driving components would not sufficiently overlap'. Rather, the tracking should take place at the level of the relevant components, *see* BEPS Action 5, Mn 57.
712. In this regard, the OECD provides an example of a company that 'produces hinges that are used in hundreds of industries'. In this case, 'a product definition that required the taxpayer to track and trace to the specific type of hinge built for a specific type of truck would be too narrow as it would require the taxpayer to track and trace to a level of detail that did not relate to the actual innovation'. Rather, the tracking should take place at the level of the group of hinges that share the same IP assets, *see* BEPS Action 5, Mn 57.
713. *See* Example A in BEPS Action 5, Mn 59, where the 'R&D responsible for [...] two patents was undertaken by different project teams' and, hence, tracking should be done on an IP-asset basis; *see also* Example B in BEPS Action 5, Mn 59, where 'employees track their research time according to which product family they are working on' and, hence, tracking should take place at the level of product families.
714. *See* Example C in BEPS Action 5, Mn 59, where tracking should be done at the level of diseases that a company's products are designed to treat (i.e., there is a common scientific challenge [curing the disease] underlying the R&D expenditures and income).
715. *See* BEPS Action 5, Mn 57.
716. BEPS Action 5, Mn 57; *see also* Example B in BEPS Action 5, Mn 59, where tracking is done to product families.
717. BEPS Action 5, Mn 57; functional equivalent groupings shall apply for industries that produce services or other outputs other than products, *see* BEPS Action 5, 42 FN 20.
718. Critical also *Kaul*, Der Nexus-Ansatz: Auswirkungen auf IP-Boxen und Alternativansätze (2018) 22; BEPS Action 5 requires a jurisdiction to request certain documentation from taxpayers that benefit from its IP regime in order to prevent manipulation; for more details, *see* BEPS Action 5, Mn 58 and 61.

differences between different sectors and industries may not allow for a uniform product definition.[719] However, considering that the income eligible for benefits under the product-based approach may deviate substantially from the income eligible for benefits under the IP asset-based approach, further information would be desirable.[720]

To sum up, the Modified Nexus Approach requires a link between expenditures, income, and either an IP asset, a product, or a product family. This means that, depending on the circumstances, the substance of a taxpayer (i.e., the expenditures incurred) is tested with regard to only one IP asset (IP asset-based approach) or with regard to multiple IP assets that are relevant for a product (product-based approach) or a product family (product family-based approach), respectively.

3.2.10 Rebuttable Presumption

BEPS Action 5 allows countries to treat the nexus ratio as a rebuttal presumption.[721] Income receiving tax benefits should, at first, always be calculated by using the nexus ratio. However, it would be possible to prove that more income should qualify for preferential treatment provided that:

- a taxpayer has undertaken substantial qualifying R&D activity in developing a qualifying IP asset or product; and
- the taxpayer can demonstrate that, because of exceptional circumstances, the application of the nexus ratio leads to an outcome where the level of income eligible for tax benefits is not commensurate with the level of the taxpayer's R&D activity.[722]

The requirement of a substantial qualifying R&D activity undertaken by the taxpayer in developing a qualifying IP asset or product is met when the calculated nexus ratio (excluding the uplift) of a taxpayer equals or exceeds 25 %.[723]

Furthermore, a taxpayer would need to establish that 'because of exceptional circumstances the application of the nexus ratio would result in an outcome that was inconsistent with the principle of the nexus approach'.[724] BEPS Action 5 is rather vague about when such exceptional circumstances are at hand.[725] It only states that they could include 'for instance, a complete or partial write down of acquired IP in the taxpayer's financial statements or other instances of an exceptional nature where a *taxpayer can demonstrate that it engaged in greater value creating activity than is reflected in the nexus calculation*' (emphasis added).[726]

719. Similar *Kaul*, Der Nexus-Ansatz: Auswirkungen auf IP-Boxen und Alternativansätze (2018) 22.
720. For a contrasting example of the two approaches and the possible different results, *see Kaul*, Der Nexus-Ansatz: Auswirkungen auf IP-Boxen und Alternativansätze (2018) 88.
721. BEPS Action 5, Mn 56.
722. BEPS Action 5, Mn 67.
723. BEPS Action 5, Mn 68.
724. BEPS Action 5, Mn 68.
725. *See also Kaul*, Der Nexus-Ansatz: Auswirkungen auf IP-Boxen und Alternativansätze (2018) 24.
726. BEPS Action 5, Mn 67.

Thus, this concerns cases where the value creation of a taxpayer is not adequately reflected in the nexus ratio; i.e., the nexus ratio shows less substance than the taxpayer actually has. Leaving aside the question of what 'instances of an exceptional nature'[727] could be (besides the example of a write down of acquired IP), it is also interesting to consider how a taxpayer 'can demonstrate that it engaged in greater value creating activity than is reflected in the nexus calculation'. An obvious solution would be to consider the value created by a taxpayer according to the DEMPE Approach. However, since the OECD also contemplated a Transfer Pricing Approach to determine the Substantial Activity Requirement but, in the end, decided against it - as it would not have imposed any additional substance requirements compared to those that are already stipulated by the arm's-length principle -[728] it is difficult to imagine that the DEMPE Approach could eventually be enforced by using the detour of the rebuttable presumption.

Still, it would be conceivable to shift the focus of the analysis from expenditures that are regarded as a proxy for value creation under the Modified Nexus Approach to the value that is actually created by an activity as under transfer pricing principles.[729] Compared to replacing the Modified Nexus Approach by the DEMPE Approach,[730] this would not change the yardstick for assessing what creates value but would only weigh the underlying attributes differently. Effectively, this would be a switch from a quantitative approach to determine substance to a qualitative approach.[731] However, then again, it is said that 'any adjustments to the nexus ratio must result in outcomes that are commensurate with the level of the taxpayer's R&D activity, consistent with the fundamental principle of the nexus approach'[732] and that '[t]he fundamental principle underlying the nexus approach is that income should only benefit from an IP regime to the extent that the *taxpayer itself incurred the R&D expenditures* that contributed to that IP' (emphasis added).[733] Therefore, it might be argued that, even in the case of a rebuttal, the focus is still on the R&D expenditures incurred by a taxpayer.

Then it would only be possible to increase a taxpayer's substance by either increasing a taxpayer's qualifying expenditures (with the argument that the expenditures do not do justice to the value created by the taxpayer or that certain expenditures are not included in qualifying expenditures that should be included since they created value) or decreasing (respectively, excluding) certain expenditures included in the overall expenditures (because the expenditures for the activity were higher than the value created by it or it did not create any value at all).[734] How such adjustments should

727. Tax administrations have to annually review whether exceptional circumstances are still present; for more details *see* BEPS Action 5, Mn 67.
728. *See* already sec. 3.2.1, especially FN 479.
729. *See* already sec. 3.2.6.7.
730. For a comparison between the DEMPE Approach and the Modified Nexus Approach, *see* sec. 5.1.1.
731. On the different approaches to determine substance, *see* already sec. 1.1.
732. BEPS Action 5, Mn 67.
733. BEPS Action 5, Mn 55.
734. In this context, *see Shi*, ET 2016, 380 who states that the rebuttal 'may be important for enterprises that conduct further development on the basis of existing IP assets, where issues may arise as to whether certain ex post development expenditures could be included in

be made without ultimately resorting to the OECD TPG, however, is also not readily apparent.

Should a taxpayer decide to rebut the nexus ratio, the possibility of the uplift is dropped.[735] Therefore, a taxpayer has to choose between the uplift that allows for a lump sum increase of a taxpayer's value creation activity or 'rebutting the nexus ratio on the basis of IP asset, product, or product family, and taxpayers may not choose based on a narrower grouping than that used for tracking and tracing'.[736] Again, it is unclear whether this means that a taxpayer's qualifying expenditures can generally not be subject to any uplift or whether they only cannot be uplifted by the lump sum 30% in the case of a rebuttal.[737] If the taxpayer's qualifying expenditures can be increased by a higher uplift, then the rebuttal would be more a rebuttal of the 30% uplift than of the nexus ratio per se (i.e., the taxpayer would argue that an uplift of only 30% does not adequately account for his respective value creation and, hence, the uplift should be higher, e.g., 40%). If a taxpayer's qualifying expenditures can generally not be subject to any uplift, then a taxpayer would need to demonstrate, as stated above, that certain qualifying expenditures incurred should be increased to account for the value created by them or that certain expenditures that are compensated by the 30% uplift but are generally not included in qualifying expenditures should be included in qualifying expenditures (e.g., expenditures for the outsourcing to related parties).[738]

In the end, the requirements for successfully rebutting the Modified Nexus Approach are everything but clear and largely left to the discretion of the individual countries.[739] As a result, BEPS Action 5 requires jurisdictions to submit certain information to the FHTP should they decide to implement the possibility of a rebuttal in their patent box regime.[740] This information is intended to enable the FHTP to 'monitor whether jurisdictions were only permitting taxpayers to rebut the nexus ratio in exceptional circumstances'.[741] However, since the requirements of BEPS Action 5 concerning the rebuttable presumption are so vague, it is questionable how the FHTP will assess whether jurisdictions are still within the boundaries of unharmful tax competition.[742]

---

qualifying expenditures and how much IP income is attributable to such further development in the event IP is acquired from a third party'.

735. *See* BEPS Action 5, 42f FN 21.
736. BEPS Action 5, 42f FN 21.
737. *See* the wording in BEPS Action 5, 42f FN 21: '[T]axpayers could not both rebut the nexus ratio and benefit from the *30%* up-lift' (emphasis added).
738. With the uplift, the OECD 'acknowledges that taxpayers that acquired IP or outsourced a portion of the R&D to a related party may themselves still be responsible for much of the value creation that contributed to IP income', *see* already sec. 3.2.6.5.
739. *See also Kaul*, Der Nexus-Ansatz: Auswirkungen auf IP-Boxen und Alternativansätze (2018) 24.
740. E.g. 'a list of the exceptional circumstances [...] that permitted taxpayers to rebut the nexus ratio', for more details, *see* BEPS Action 5, Mn 69.
741. BEPS Action 5, Mn 69.
742. *See also Kaul*, Der Nexus-Ansatz: Auswirkungen auf IP-Boxen und Alternativansätze (2018) 24f.

3.3 THE SUBSTANTIAL ACTIVITY REQUIREMENT WITH REGARD TO NO OR ONLY NOMINAL TAX JURISDICTIONS: CORE INCOME GENERATING ACTIVITIES

3.3.1 Core Income Generating Activities for Preferential Non-IP Regimes as a Starting Point

The Modified Nexus Approach was specifically designed to determine the Substantial Activity Requirement in the context of preferential IP regimes.[743] However, 'Action 5 requires substantial activity not only for IP regimes but for all preferential regimes.'[744] Thus, BEPS Action 5 foresees that the same principle ('to link income and activities')[745] as that under the Modified Nexus Approach shall also apply in the context of non-IP regimes.[746] Nevertheless, in this case, the OECD uses the concept of Core Income Generating Activities to determine the Substantial Activity Requirement. Accordingly, 'such regimes would only be found to meet the substantial activity requirement if they also granted benefits only to qualifying taxpayers *to the extent those taxpayers undertook the core income generating activities required to produce the type of business income covered by the preferential regime*' (emphasis added).[747]

The nature of the Core Income Generating Activities always depends on the respective type of preferential regime (i.e., which income is treated preferentially).[748] For example, in the case of leasing regimes - regimes that grant preferential tax treatment to income from leasing activities -[749] the Core Income Generating Activities could include 'agreeing funding terms; identifying and acquiring assets to be leased [...]; setting the terms and duration of any [...] leasing; monitoring and revising any agreements; and managing any risks'.[750]

Besides an exemplary enumeration of activities that could constitute Core Income Activities under different non-IP regimes,[751] there is no further guidance on this concept in BEPS Action 5. However, in 2017, the OECD published its Progress Report on the implementation of BEPS Action 5[752] in which some additional remarks were made on the concept. There, it is stated that Core Income Generating Activities 'presuppose having an *adequate number of full-time employees with necessary qualifications* and *incurring an adequate amount of operating expenditures to undertake such*

743. BEPS Action 5, 9.
744. BEPS Action 5, Mn 70.
745. BEPS Action 5, Mn 72; *see also* sec. 3.2.6.7.
746. BEPS Action 5, Mn 71; for the specific regimes that are addressed, *see* BEPS Action 5, 43 FN 23 and Mn 74ff.
747. BEPS Action 5, Mn 71; *see also* OECD, Harmful Tax Practices - 2017 Progress Report on Preferential Regimes (2017) 40 Mn 7.
748. BEPS Action 5, Mn 73.
749. BEPS Action 5, Mn 78.
750. BEPS Action 5, Mn 79.
751. *See* BEPS Action 5, Mn 74ff.
752. *OECD*, Harmful Tax Practices - 2017 Progress Report on Preferential Regimes (2017).

activities' (emphasis added).[753] Furthermore, two examples concerning the application of the Substantial Activity Requirement to non-IP regimes were provided.[754] Regarding the case of a compliant leasing regime, the following is stated:[755]

> A regime requires benefitting taxpayers to undertake the leasing activities and operations in the jurisdiction, including identifying and acquiring the assets to be leased, negotiating the leasing terms, and managing the leases. *The regime further requires that benefitting taxpayers incur at least EUR 5 million in annual business spending and employ an adequate number of qualified full-time employees to undertake the core activities (and at least three such employees) in the jurisdiction.* The jurisdiction requires the taxpayer to report information annually on the income benefitting from the regime, as well as the type and level of activity performed to generate the income. Taxpayers which do not meet the requirements are denied the regime's benefits. This regime demonstrates that the core income generating activities occur in the jurisdiction and has a robust follow-up mechanism to ensure compliance. It therefore satisfies the requirement for having substantial activities in the jurisdiction (emphasis added).

That is, contrary to the Modified Nexus Approach, a reference to the number of employees (and their qualification) is made to determine a substantial activity under the Core Income Generating Activities.

Furthermore, while under the Modified Nexus Approach, not the total amount of expenditures is decisive, but the ratio between qualifying expenditures and overall expenditures determines a taxpayer's substance,[756] this is different under the Core Income Generating Activities where apparently exceeding a certain expenditure threshold (i.e., the total amount of expenditures) is relevant. However, under the Core Income Generating Activities, a 'disproportionately large net income relative to benefitting core activities may indicate that other non-benefitting activities/value drivers may be responsible for the reported net income' and, eventually, benefits could be denied.[757]

Effectively, the OECD combines a qualitative approach with a quantitative approach to define substance in the case of the Core Income Generating Activities.[758]

---

753. *OECD*, Harmful Tax Practices – 2017 Progress Report on Preferential Regimes (2017) 40 Mn 8; *see also OECD*, Harmful Tax Practices – 2017 Progress Report on Preferential Regimes (2017) 42 Mn 10.
754. These examples concern financing and leasing regimes and headquarters regimes, *see OECD*, Harmful Tax Practices – 2017 Progress Report on Preferential Regimes (2017) 42 Mn 13; *see also OECD*, Harmful Tax Practices – 2017 Progress Report on Preferential Regimes (2017) 44 FN 4, where it is stated that '[t]hese examples are for illustrative purposes only and are not intended to set minimum standards.'
755. *OECD*, Harmful Tax Practices – 2017 Progress Report on Preferential Regimes (2017) 42 Mn 13.
756. *See* already sec. 3.2.6.1.
757. *OECD*, Harmful Tax Practices – 2017 Progress Report on Preferential Regimes (2017) 42 Mn 10.
758. *See also OECD*, Harmful Tax Practices – 2017 Progress Report on Preferential Regimes (2017) 43 Mn 14 where it is stated that jurisdictions have to report to the FHTP the 'type of core activities undertaken by taxpayers benefitting from the regime' and 'the quantity of core activities undertaken by taxpayers benefitting from the regime (as measured by the number of full-time employees and the amount of operating expenditures associated with these activities)'; on a side note, in Mn 15, it is stated that 'monitoring would be required only with respect to taxpayers that are members of multinational enterprise groups with annual revenues in the

On the one hand, it is debatable which activities are the core activities that generate income as the OECD only provides examples what they could be (qualitative approach).[759] On the other hand, taxpayers have to undertake the Core Income Generating Activities with a specified number of employees and incur a specified amount of expenditures (quantitative approach).[760] This is, of course, different under the Modified Nexus Approach where only a quantitative approach is applied.[761]

What is more, the Modified Nexus Approach establishes a link between expenditures (as a proxy for a substantial activity) and income whereas, under the Core Income Generating Activities, a link is established between the activities themselves - the core activities - and the income. This also entails different legal consequences under the two concepts. While, under the Modified Nexus Approach, the income benefitting from preferential treatment is proportionate (i.e., according to a taxpayer's nexus ratio), it appears as if, under the Core Income Generating Activities, it is only possible that either the total amount of the income is treated preferentially or there is no preferential treatment at all.

Still, even after these further remarks in the Progress Report 2017, the guidance on the concept of the Core Income Generating Activities remains scarce, especially when compared to the very detailed guidance under the Modified Nexus Approach. In this regard, the Progress Report 2017 states:[762]

> The 2015 Report on Action 5 *[...]* contained detailed guidance on the application of the substantial activities criterion to IP regimes as well as more general guidance for the application of the substantial activities criterion to non-IP regimes. In part *this recognised that applying the substantial activities criterion to non-IP regimes is a relatively more straightforward and simpler exercise as the value creation is primarily driven by the services provided rather than a separate IP asset that can be shifted* (emphasis added).

In the end, it appears as if the concept of Core Income Generating Activities 'comes down to no more than a traditional transfer-pricing-type functional analysis'[763] supplemented by a quantitative element.

---

preceding year of EUR 750 million or more - that is, taxpayers which are constituent entities of MNE groups required to file CbC reports'; that is, for MNEs below this threshold, the compliance with the Core Income Generating Activities will not be monitored.

759. *See also OECD*, Harmful Tax Practices - 2017 Progress Report on Preferential Regimes (2017) 43 Mn 14 where it is stated that jurisdictions have to 'notify the FHTP of how they define core income generating activities' which already indicates that different views may exist about what constitutes Core Income Generating Activities; furthermore, in the above-mentioned example of a compliant leasing regime, the use of the word 'including' when describing the relevant activities may indicate that the following enumeration is not exhaustive.
760. *See* the above-mentioned example of a compliant leasing regime where it is required that benefitting taxpayers employ at least three employees in the respective jurisdiction and that they incur at least EUR 5 million in annual business spending.
761. *See* already sec. 3.2.6.7.
762. *OECD*, Harmful Tax Practices - 2017 Progress Report on Preferential Regimes (2017) 39.
763. *Larking*, TNI 2018, 330.

3.3.2 Core Income Generating Activities for No or Only Nominal Tax Jurisdictions

With the elevation of the Substantial Activity Requirement for preferential tax regimes, a potential incoherence within the framework to identify harmful tax practices became apparent.[764] On the one hand, MNEs would have to fulfil the Substantial Activity Requirement (Modified Nexus Approach or Core Income Generating Activities) to avail themselves of a preferential regime. On the other hand, if a jurisdiction generally does not levy any taxes or only nominal taxes (no or only nominal tax jurisdictions)[765] – i.e., not only within the framework of a preferential tax regime – the Substantial Activity Requirement would not be applicable.[766] Therefore, MNEs could simply relocate to no or only nominal tax jurisdictions, or countries could reduce their general tax rate instead of introducing a preferential regime to circumvent the Substantial Activity Requirement.[767]

To remedy this inconsistency, the OECD issued guidance on the resumption of the Substantial Activity Requirement to no or only nominal tax jurisdictions in 2018.[768] As stated, this guidance applies to 'jurisdictions which do not impose a corporate income tax' and 'jurisdictions which impose only nominal corporate income tax to avoid the requirements'.[769] However, a specific minimum tax rate is not provided.[770] As of now, it appears that the OECD has only reviewed no tax jurisdictions (e.g., Bermuda, Cayman Islands, etc.) under this criterion.[771]

Furthermore, activities within the scope of the guidance are 'geographically mobile activities, such as financial and other service activities, including the provision of intangibles'.[772] Similar to BEPS Action 5,[773] the guidance generally distinguishes

764. *See also OECD*, Resumption of Application of Substantial Activities Factor to No or only Nominal Tax Jurisdictions (2018) Mn 16.
765. In the 1998 Report on Harmful Tax Competition, such jurisdictions were addressed as tax havens, *see also OECD*, Resumption of Application of Substantial Activities Factor to No or only Nominal Tax Jurisdictions (2018) Mn 1.
766. This is because the aim of BEPS Action 5 only was to establish a Substantial Activity Requirement for preferential regimes, *see OECD*, Action Plan on Base Erosion and Profit Shifting (2013) 18; *Becker/Hoeck* in *Kofler/Schnitger* 318.
767. *See also OECD*, Resumption of Application of Substantial Activities Factor to No or only Nominal Tax Jurisdictions (2018) Mn 17.
768. *OECD*, Resumption of Application of Substantial Activities Factor or No or only Nominal Tax Jurisdictions (2018) [in the following: OECD Resumption]; *see also Finley*, OECD Forum to Scrutinize Tax Havens' Substance Requirements, TNI 2018, 821 (821ff).
769. OECD Resumption, Mn 21; *see also* OECD Resumption, 20 FN 7: 'The purpose of considering nominal tax jurisdictions along with zero tax jurisdictions is to ensure that there is not an incentive for zero rate jurisdictions to shift to a rate near zero.'
770. *See also* OECD Resumption, 20 FN 7.
771. *See OECD*, Harmful Tax Practices – Peer Review Results (2020) 21f (available at https://www.oecd.org/tax/beps/harmful-tax-practices-peer-review-results-on-preferential-regimes.pdf); *see also Johnston*, Tax Havens Make the Grade On OECD Substance Requirements, TNI 2019, 445 (445f).
772. OECD Resumption, Mn 22; *see* already *OECD*, Harmful Tax Competition: An Emerging Global Issue (1998) Mn 6; furthermore, it is stated that these types of mobile activities typically fall into the categories of 'headquarters, distribution centres, service centres, financing, leasing, fund

between IP income and non-IP income.[774] However, whereas under BEPS Action 5 different concepts are provided for the respective category (i.e., Modified Nexus Approach or Core Income Generating Activities), the guidance applies the concept of Core Income Generating Activities to both categories.[775]

The reason for this is that, in the case of no or only nominal tax jurisdictions, the Modified Nexus Approach comes to its limits as it is designed for a tax system that provides for both a regular tax rate and a preferential tax rate.[776] Since no or only nominal tax jurisdictions do not levy any taxes at all (or only at a considerable low rate), the formula of the Modified Nexus Approach would be ineffective. That is, even if income is not eligible to be taxed preferentially according to the nexus formula (i.e., when the nexus ratio is below 1), it would nonetheless remain untaxed because there is no other tax rate that could be applied.[777] Therefore, the OECD decided to use the concept of Core Income Generating Activities – a concept used under BEPS Action 5 to determine the Substantial Activity Requirement for non-IP regimes – to determine the required substance with regard to IP income in cases of no or only nominal tax jurisdictions.[778]

If the Substantial Activity Requirement is not met, no or only nominal tax jurisdictions should impose appropriate sanctions that are 'rigorous, effective and dissuasive' like striking an entity off the company register (since the possibility of applying a higher tax rate, as in the case of preferential regimes, does not exist).[779]

3.3.3 Core Income Generating Activities with Regard to IP Income

The guidance applies when an entity is earning income from exploiting an IP asset.[780] In this regard, the term 'IP assets' includes the same assets as those under the Modified Nexus Approach.[781]

management, banking, insurance, shipping, holding companies and the provision of intangibles', *see* OECD Resumption, Mn 22.

773. *See* BEPS Action 5, Mn 26ff (IP regimes) and 70ff (non-IP regimes).
774. OECD Resumption, Mn 23ff.
775. *See* OECD Resumption, Mn 24 (non-IP income) and 28 (IP income); *see* already sec. 1.3.3.
776. OECD Resumption, Mn 27.
777. OECD Resumption, Mn 26.
778. OECD Resumption, Mn 28.
779. OECD Resumption, Mn 42; furthermore, no or only nominal tax jurisdictions have to introduce mechanisms to ensure compliance with the Substantial Activity Requirement, *see also McLoughlin*, Tax Havens May Need Resources To Satisfy OECD Substance Standard, TNI 2019, 1206 (1206ff); what is more, the guidance also foresees an enhanced exchange of information; *see*, for more details, OECD Resumption, Mn 43ff; *see also OECD*, Substantial Activities in No or Only Nominal Tax Jurisdictions: Guidance for the Spontaneous Exchange of Information (2019); *Finley*, OECD Issues Information Exchange Rules For No-Tax Jurisdictions, TNI 2019, 454 (454ff).
780. *See* OECD Resumption, Mn 30; as an example, *see* the situation in the Cayman Islands, *Tax Information Authority*, Economic Substance for Geographically Mobile Activities – Guidance (2020) 6ff (available at http://www.tia.gov.ky/pdf/Economic_Substance_-_Guidance_-_v2.0.pdf).
781. OECD Resumption, Mn 30; on IP assets in the context of the Modified Nexus Approach, *see* already sec. 3.2.4.

The guidance states that '[t]he core income generating activities in this context would be conducting research and development (rather than simply acquiring or outsourcing it), which reflects the same concept as the nexus approach'.[782] Furthermore, 'the entity should demonstrate that it has conducted the core income generating activities with the *adequate number of qualified full-time employees* and *adequate amount of operating expenditures*' (emphasis added).[783] That is, different from the Core Income Generating Activities for non-IP regimes, a reference to a concrete number of employees or a concrete amount of operating expenditures is not made.[784] This is, however, similar to the Modified Nexus Approach. Nonetheless, while the Modified Nexus Approach is a quantitative approach to define substance, the Core Income Generating Activities with regard to IP income applies a qualitative approach.

Under the Core Income Generating Activities, it is tested whether the taxpayer performed the Core Income Generating Activities required to produce the IP income. That is, unlike in the Modified Nexus Approach, expenditures might not necessarily be decisive for assessing whether the taxpayer undertook Core Income Generating Activities.[785] For example, if a taxpayer in a no or only nominal tax jurisdiction incurs expenditures of 100 for its own R&D activity and expenditures of 100 for the outsourcing of R&D to related parties, it cannot automatically be concluded that it performed the Core Income Generating Activities. Instead, it has to be assessed on the basis of the facts and circumstances which activities were the Core Income Generating Activities required to produce the IP income in this specific case.[786] Furthermore – as will be seen – it is possible that an entity could, in fact, be conducting substantial

782. OECD Resumption, Mn 30; *see also* the statement in OECD Resumption, Mn 29: 'At the outset, in all cases, the substantial activities requirements for IP income would always be insufficient if the entity only passively held IP assets which had been created and exploited on the basis of decisions made and activities performed outside of the jurisdiction. Similarly, the test would never be met if the only activities contributing to the income were the periodic decisions of non-resident board members in the jurisdiction.'
783. OECD Resumption, Mn 30.
784. *See* already sec. 3.3.1; *see also*, as an example, the situation in the Cayman Islands, *Tax Information Authority*, Economic Substance for Geographically Mobile Activities – Guidance (2020) 30 (available at http://www.tia.gov.ky/pdf/Economic_Substance_-_Guidance_-_v2.0.pdf): 'This Guidance does not prescribe a minimum number of full time employees or other personnel for a particular level of relevant income either generally or for any particular type of relevant activity because that would be arbitrary and would prove uneconomical in many cases.'
785. Still, expenditures might provide a useful indication; in this direction *OECD*, Substantial Activities in No or Only Nominal Tax Jurisdictions: Guidance for the Spontaneous Exchange of Information (2019) 60 (template for cases of non-compliance) and 65 (template for high-risk scenarios) where it is distinguished between operating expenditures directly incurred and outsourcing expenditure.
786. Again, *see* the situation in the Cayman Islands, *Tax Information Authority*, Economic Substance for Geographically Mobile Activities – Guidance (2020) 14 (available at http://www.tia.gov.ky/pdf/Economic_Substance_-_Guidance_-_v2.0.pdf): 'The elements listed in the definition of Cayman Islands [Core Income Generating Activities] in relation to each relevant activity are neither exhaustive nor mandatory. It is a question of fact in each case which elements are actually undertaken to generate relevant income.'

activities even if it did not perform actual R&D.[787] This also shows that Core Income Generating Activities always depend on the facts and circumstances.[788]

On top of that, the substantive scope under the Core Income Generating Activities for no or only nominal tax jurisdictions is broader than under the Modified Nexus Approach because it also encompasses marketing intangibles.[789] Again, this is because no or only nominal tax jurisdictions do not have another tax rate to which they could subject income from marketing intangibles.[790] The application of the same principle as that under the Modified Nexus Approach would mean that 'entities in a no or only nominal tax jurisdiction would not be allowed to hold and receive returns on marketing intangibles at all', which is considered disproportionate.[791] Therefore, with regard to marketing intangibles, entities in no or only nominal tax jurisdictions also have to fulfil certain substance requirements (i.e., Core Income Generating Activities) from the perspective of harmful tax practices.[792] The respective Core Income Generating Activities in this case are 'branding, marketing, and distribution'.[793]

Like the guidance on the Core Income Generating Activities for non-IP regimes,[794] the guidance on the Core Income Generating Activities for no or only nominal tax jurisdictions is scarce, especially when compared to the very detailed guidance under the Modified Nexus Approach. However, whereas in the case of non-IP regimes, this was justified by stating that 'applying the substantial activities criterion to non-IP regimes is a relatively more straightforward and simpler exercise as the value creation is primarily driven by the services provided rather than a separate IP asset that can be shifted',[795] this is not the case concerning IP income earned in no or only nominal tax jurisdictions. Therefore, it is not comprehensible why the OECD did not provide more detailed guidance.

787. *See* sec. 3.3.4.
788. Different under the Modified Nexus Approach where a more expensive activity is always perceived to have created more value than a less expensive activity, *see* already sec. 3.2.6.7.
789. OECD Resumption, Mn 31.
790. *See* already sec. 3.3.2.
791. OECD Resumption, 20 FN 9.
792. Since marketing intangibles are never qualifying IP assets under a nexus-compliant preferential IP regime, the same substance requirements do not exist for IP income concerning no or only nominal tax jurisdictions and preferential IP regimes (from the perspective of harmful tax practices); interestingly, the requirement of substantial activities for no or only nominal tax jurisdictions and not for preferential regimes (at least not as a key factor, *see* already FN 462) under the 1998 Report on Harmful Tax Competition was ultimately the reason why the Substantial Activity Requirement was not applied (no or nominal tax jurisdictions argued that they do not want to be worse off than OECD members with preferential regimes); however, here it is the other way around as no or only nominal tax jurisdictions are in a 'better' position compared to preferential regimes since income from marketing intangibles is within the scope.
793. OECD Resumption, Mn 31.
794. *See* already sec. 3.3.1.
795. *OECD*, Harmful Tax Practices - 2017 Progress Report on Preferential Regimes (2017) 39.

3.3.4 Exceptional Cases and Rebuttable Presumption

According to the guidance, it may exceptionally[796] be 'possible that an entity exploiting IP assets in a no or only nominal tax jurisdiction could in fact be conducting substantial activities, even if this did not involve research and development (for patents and similar assets) or branding, marketing and distribution (for marketing IP assets)'.[797] In this regard, 'such activities could include conducting the strategic decision-making, managing and bearing the principal risks relating to the development and subsequent exploitation of the IP asset, or carrying on the underlying trading activities through which the asset is exploited'.[798] Effectively, this means that entities may conduct other types of activities than the generally stipulated as Core Income Generating Activities (i.e., conducting R&D or branding, marketing, and distribution, respectively) and still meet the Substantial Activity Requirement in the case of no or only nominal tax jurisdictions.

However, for so-called higher-risk scenarios, there is a presumption that an entity has not conducted a substantial activity when it has not performed the generally stipulated Core Income Generating Activities.[799] Higher-risk scenarios are cases in which:[800]

> (i) the entity has acquired the IP asset from related parties or through the entity funding research and development activities which took place outside the no or only nominal tax jurisdiction; and
> (ii) the IP asset is licensed or sold to related parties, or the exploitation is conducted by related parties outside the jurisdiction [...].

That is, higher-risk scenarios comprise cases in which foreign related parties are involved in the development and the exploitation of an IP asset. More precisely, the guidance seems to have IP Companies in mind as they are often not responsible for the operative performance of R&D and the subsequent direct exploitation of developed IP assets.[801] The use of the word 'and' as well as the provided example ('foreign related parties are paid to develop and sell a product in which the intangible asset is embedded')[802] suggests that both requirements have to be fulfilled cumulatively for a higher-risk scenario to exist.

Nevertheless, an entity can still demonstrate that it has conducted substantial activities in higher-risk scenarios (i.e., the presumption is rebuttable)[803] 'by providing evidence that the income generated is directly linked to activities undertaken in the local jurisdiction rather than in a foreign jurisdiction'.[804] Accordingly, entities 'would

796. Further information is not provided when such an exception may be at hand.
797. OECD Resumption, Mn 32.
798. OECD Resumption, Mn 32.
799. OECD Resumption, Mn 33.
800. OECD Resumption, Mn 34.
801. *See* already sec. 1.5.
802. OECD Resumption, Mn 34.
803. OECD Resumption, Mn 35.
804. OECD Resumption, Mn 36.

need to provide evidence that there was, and historically has been, a high degree of *control over the development, exploitation, maintenance, enhancement and protection* of the intangible asset, exercised by an adequate number of full-time employees with the necessary qualifications that permanently reside and perform their activities within the jurisdiction' (emphasis added).[805] Even though the relevant components are listed in a different order, this is obviously a reference to the DEMPE Approach.[806] Therefore, it appears as if an entity can use the DEMPE Approach (i.e., substance in the area of Transfer Pricing)[807] to fulfil the Substantial Activity Requirement in cases of no or only nominal tax jurisdictions.[808]

Furthermore, for a successful rebuttal, entities have to provide additional information about their employees (e.g., level of experience), evidence that decision-making takes place in the no or only nominal tax jurisdiction, and demonstrate the commercial rationale for holding the IP assets in the respective jurisdiction.[809] Again, the provision of information about the qualification of employees resembles more the procedure of a transfer pricing analysis because, under the Modified Nexus Approach, the qualification of employees is never specifically tested (it is simply assumed that the R&D activities for which expenditures were incurred were performed by qualified people). Likewise, decision-making is crucial under the DEMPE Approach,[810] but not under the Modified Nexus Approach. In the same manner, explaining the commercial rationale for holding an IP asset is not necessary under the Modified Nexus Approach, whereas under the DEMPE Approach, a commercial rationality test is known.[811]

Last but not least, the focus on the exploitation as one of the two requirements for a higher-risk scenario as well as the possibility for the rebuttal of the presumption is not comprehensible (at least for patents and similar assets) because, under the Modified Nexus Approach, the role in the exploitation is not relevant for determining the necessary substance of a taxpayer.[812] Maybe these inconsistencies are the reason that the rebuttable presumption will be subject to review by the FHTP no later than 2020.[813]

805. OECD Resumption, Mn 37.
806. *See also* OECD Resumption, 15 Figure 1.
807. Interestingly, concerning the Core Income Generating Activities for non-IP regimes, the *OECD*, Harmful Tax Practices - 2017 Progress Report on Preferential Regimes (2017) 43 Mn 14 states that '[t]he purpose of such monitoring [i.e. the monitoring procedures that jurisdictions have to establish to ensure that taxpayers are compliant with the Substantial Activity Requirement] is *not to conduct a transfer pricing analysis* but instead to confirm that the regime continues to operate consistently with the type and level of activities upon which the previous findings of the FHTP were based' (emphasis added).
808. However, it is not clear how high the degree of involvement in the DEMPE of an intangible has to be; in OECD Resumption, Mn 35, it is stated that, in higher-risk scenarios, it is presumed that the Substantial Activity Requirement has not been met when the generally stipulated Core Income Generating Activities are not performed by an entity, 'notwithstanding that a transfer pricing analysis would allocate *some* profits to the entity' (emphasis added).
809. OECD Resumption, Mn 37.
810. *See* already sec. 2.5.3.2.
811. *See* already sec. 2.6.
812. *See also Shi*, ET 2016, 337; *see* already sec. 3.2.7.
813. OECD Resumption, Mn 38.

3.4 PRELIMINARY CONCLUSIONS

- The Substantial Activity Requirement is concerned with the preferential taxation and the no or only nominal taxation of income from an IP asset.
- To this end, two concepts are used to determine the Substantial Activity Requirement: The Modified Nexus Approach for preferential IP regimes and the Core Income Generating Activities for no or only nominal tax jurisdictions.
- The Modified Nexus Approach is a quantitative approach for defining substance.
- It applies a formula to determine how much of the income that a qualifying taxpayer receives from a qualifying IP asset may be taxed preferentially; according to this formula, expenditures are a proxy for substantial activities; the ratio of qualifying expenditures to overall expenditures (nexus ratio) is used to determine the value creation and hence the substance of a taxpayer in the development of a qualifying IP asset.
- Qualifying expenditures are such when it is assumed that the underlying activity of the taxpayer that caused the respective expenditures created value; overall expenditures also include additional expenditure items for which it is assumed that the underlying value-creating activity was not directly performed by the taxpayer itself.
- The legal owner of a qualifying IP asset is expected to incur expenditures only for its own actual R&D activity and for outsourcing R&D to unrelated parties; by contrast, outsourcing to related parties and the acquisition of IP is generally harmful; however, unless a taxpayer's expenditures for outsourcing to related parties and the acquisition of IP do not exceed his expenditures for his own actual R&D activity and for outsourcing R&D to unrelated parties by more than 30% (uplift), the overall IP income may be taxed preferentially.
- According to the Modified Nexus Approach, value is primarily created by the performance of activities on the operational level (day-to-day activities); however, it is also acknowledged that activities on the strategical and tactical level (management activities) play an important role in creating value for an IP asset; in this regard, the uplift functions as a bridge between these two understandings of value creation.
- By contrast, mere capital contribution is not regarded as creating value; therefore, the Modified Nexus Approach is an activity-based concept (link between expenditures that serve as a proxy for activity and income).
- When establishing an IP Company, MNEs have to make sure that they locate people that perform operational R&D activities in the jurisdiction of the IP Company; an IP Company that is only responsible for the management of the R&D process while the operational R&D activities are performed by related parties in different jurisdictions will not be able to claim preferential tax treatment.

- The Modified Nexus Approach requires tracking expenditures and income and linking them to individual IP assets, a product or a product family; in practice, this is often a very difficult task.
- In exceptional circumstances, it is possible to rebut the nexus ratio; however, the requirements for a successful rebuttal are anything but clear.
- The Core Income Generating Activities with regard to IP income is a qualitative approach for defining substance.
- It expects an entity in a no or only nominal tax jurisdiction that earns IP income to perform the Core Income Generating Activities required to produce the IP income.
- In this context, the Core Income Generating Activities would be conducting R&D (rather than simply acquiring or outsourcing it); therefore, the Core Income Generating Activities is also an activity-based concept (link between activity and income).
- Furthermore, while the Modified Nexus Approach has a rather narrow definition of a qualifying IP asset, the Core Income Generating Activities apply a broader definition that also encompasses marketing intangibles.
- With regard to marketing intangibles, the Core Income Generating Activities would be branding, marketing, and distribution.
- However, in exceptional circumstances, an entity may demonstrate that it performed the Core Income Generating Activities even if it did not conduct R&D or branding, marketing, and distribution, respectively; in this regard, the substance requirements under the DEMPE Approach may be used to provide evidence of Core Income Generating Activities.

CHAPTER 4
Substance in the Area of Tax Treaties: Beneficial Ownership[814]

4.1 INTRODUCTION

Article 12 OECD MC deals with the taxation of cross-border royalties.[815] Accordingly, the residence state generally has the exclusive right to tax. However, if the beneficial owner of the royalties is not a resident of the residence state, the source state may levy withholding taxes.[816]

In light of the high relevance of cross-border payments of royalties as well as dividends and interest,[817] it is surprising that there is still so much confusion surrounding the Beneficial Ownership Test.[818] The reason for this becomes apparent when looking at the historical evolution of the concept:

The Beneficial Ownership Test was already introduced into the OECD MC in 1977. However, over 40 years later, the OECD MC and Commentary still do not contain a clear definition of the term 'beneficial owner'.[819]

---

814. The author already dealt with the topic of beneficial ownership in *Navisotschnigg*, The Beneficial Ownership Test, in *Lang/Pistone/Rust/Schuch/Staringer* (Eds), Tax Treaty Entitlement (2019) 91 (91ff); this chapter is partly based on this contribution.
815. According to Art. 12(2) OECD MC 2017, royalties are 'payments of any kind received as a consideration for the use of, or the right to use, any copyright of literary, artistic or scientific work including cinematograph films, any patent, trade mark, design or model, plan, secret formula or process, or for information concerning industrial, commercial or scientific experience'; for more details, *see Valta* in *Reimer/Rust*, Klaus Vogel on Double Taxation Conventions[4] (2015) Art. 12 Mn 8ff.
816. *See* already sec. 1.4.
817. The beneficial ownership requirement can be found in the Arts 10, 11, and 12 of the OECD MC 2017; as this thesis examines substance requirements concerning intangibles, its focus will be on Art. 12 OECD MC and beneficial ownership of royalties; however, considerations concerning beneficial ownership in Art. 12 OECD MC are also applicable in the context of Art. 10 and Art. 11 OECD MC, *see* already sec. 1.4.
818. *See also du Toit*, BIT 2010, 500.
819. *See also Poiret*, Beneficial Ownership: Concept, History and Perspective, ET 2016, 274 (274): 'The term "beneficial owner" in the OECD Model (2014) has no precise or clear definition.

Nevertheless, over the course of time, the OECD has broadly expanded its Commentary on the issue of beneficial ownership. At the same time, though, it left the relevant articles in the MC more or less unchanged. Undoubtedly, it is problematic when issues regarding the meaning of a term are addressed only by amending the OECD Commentary and not the OECD MC itself.[820] This is all the more true when the amendments are not just clarifications, but they introduce new concepts.[821]

Additionally, the OECD dealt with beneficial ownership not only in its Commentary but also in other reports. As will be seen, however, the notion of the concept is not aligned across these publications which further exacerbates a common understanding.

Against this background, it comes as no surprise that the notion of beneficial ownership considerably varies in scholarly discussion and in case law. At the same time, however, the reasons outlined above make it clear that knowledge of the historical evolution of the Beneficial Ownership Test is essential for its understanding. In other words, an analysis of the OECD documents dealing with beneficial ownership in tax treaty law is not an end in itself. Rather, it is indispensable in order to comprehend the different views often expressed on the Beneficial Ownership Test.

However, the primary purpose of this chapter is not to revisit court decisions[822] or to elaborate exhaustively on different opinions that have been expressed in literature on the Beneficial Ownership Test.[823] Instead, the focus is put on the relevant OECD documents in order to examine the different directions in which they tend to go. This will help to understand not only how the Beneficial Ownership Test itself has evolved over time but also whether the notion of substance in international tax law has changed with the BEPS Project. Nonetheless, case law and scholarly opinions are, of course, consulted where appropriate.

4.2 HISTORICAL EVOLUTION

4.2.1 1977: Introduction into the OECD MC

4.2.1.1 Background

Initially, the wording of Article 12(1) was as follows in the OECD MC 1963:

> Royalties arising in a Contracting State and paid to a resident of the other Contracting State shall be taxable only in that other State.

While this may not have been an issue in 1977, the increasing use of the concept over the last decade has highlighted the lack of a clear and universal definition.'

820. *See also du Toit*, BIT 2010, 509.
821. On the relevance of changes in the OECD Commentary for the interpretation of DTCs, *see* fundamentally *Lang*, Introduction to the Law of Double Taxation Conventions (2013) Mn 93ff; *see also* FN 403.
822. For a comprehensive analysis of the relevant case law, *see Meindl-Ringler*, Beneficial Ownership in International Tax Law (2016) 95ff.
823. For an overview of the scholarly discussion, *see Meindl-Ringler*, Beneficial Ownership in International Tax Law (2016) 77ff.

Evidently, the United Kingdom, which played the leading role in the introduction of the Beneficial Ownership Test into the OECD MC 1977,[824] had issues with this wording.[825] In fact, the first time the Beneficial Ownership Test was implemented in a tax treaty in relation to income[826] was in the 1966 protocol[827] to the United Kingdom-United States Income Tax Treaty 1945.[828,829] Subsequently, the United Kingdom started to renegotiate many of its tax treaties (e.g., with New Zealand) and thereby regularly proposed to insert the beneficial ownership requirement in the articles on passive income.[830] Eventually, the United Kingdom also suggested the insertion of a beneficial ownership clause into the OECD MC (or alternatively a subject-to-tax clause).[831]

The reason for this seems to have been a peculiarity in the United Kingdom's domestic law.[832] Accordingly, a person could be taxed on merely receiving income without being entitled to it (i.e., a nominee that simply received income would have been liable to tax on that income despite not being entitled to it).[833] However, a

824. *See Avery Jones*, The United Kingdom's Influence on the OECD Model Tax Convention, BTR 2011, 653 (682): 'The UK can claim to have introduced beneficial ownership into the Model although it might have been better if it had not, given all the problems that it has caused.'
825. *See OECD*, Preliminary Report on suggested amendments to Articles 11 and 12 of the Draft Convention, relating to interest and royalties, respectively, FC/WP27(68)1 (1968) 14: 'The United Kingdom Delegation considers that the drafting of the Articles on dividends, interest, and royalties "is defective [...]". In its view the relief provided for under these Articles ought to apply only if the beneficial owner of the income in question is resident in the other contracting State.'
826. The term has already been used in DTCs prior to this but not in relation to income, *see Vann*, Beneficial Ownership: What Does History (and Maybe Policy) Tell Us, in *Lang/Pistone/Schuch /Staringer/Storck* (Eds), Beneficial Ownership: Recent Trends (2013) 267 (271ff).
827. Supplementary Protocol between the Government of the United Kingdom of Great Britain and Northern Ireland and the Government of the United States of America Amending the Convention between the United States of America and the United Kingdom of Great Britain and Northern Ireland for the Avoidance of Double Taxation and the Prevention of Fiscal Evasion with Respect to Taxes on Income (1966).
828. Convention between the United States of America and the United Kingdom of Great Britain and Northern Ireland for the Avoidance of Double Taxation and the Prevention of Fiscal Evasion with respect to Taxes on Income (1945).
829. *See Avery Jones/De Broe/Ellis/van Raad/Le Gall/Goldberg/Killius/Maisto/Miyatake/Torrione/ Vann/Ward/Wiman*, The Origins of Concepts and Expressions Used in the OECD Model and Their Adoption by States, BIT 2006, 220 (249).
830. *Vann* in *Lang/Pistone/Schuch/Staringer/Storck* 276.
831. *See OECD*, Observations of Member Countries on Difficulties Raised by the OECD Draft Convention on Income and Capital, TFD/FC/216 (1967) 14; *OECD*, Consolidated List of Outstanding Points Concerning the OECD Draft Convention on Income and Capital, TFD/FC/218 (1967) 31; *see also Ng*, The Concept of Beneficial Ownership, in *Ecker/Ressler* (Eds), History of Tax Treaties: The Relevance of the OECD Documents for the Interpretation of Tax Treaties (2011) 509 (522); a subject-to-tax clause was rejected as being 'contrary to the spirit and general arrangement of the Draft Convention' as relief from withholding taxes in the source country would be dependent on the effective taxation in the residence state, *see OECD*, Report on suggested amendments to Articles 11 and 12 of the Draft Convention, relating to interest and royalties, respectively, FC/WP27(70)1 (1970) 13.
832. *Vann* in *Lang/Pistone/Schuch/Staringer/Storck* 285f.
833. For more details, *see Avery Jones*, The Beneficial Ownership Concept Was Never Necessary in the Model, in *Lang/Pistone/Schuch/Staringer/Storck* (Eds), Beneficial Ownership: Recent Trends (2013) 333 (335ff), who suspects that 'this provision is unusual, perhaps unique, in tax systems'.

nominee for a non-UK resident was only liable to tax on domestic income but not on foreign income he received. As tax treaties drafted according to the OECD MC 1963 were also applicable in the case of limited tax liability in one contracting state – the second sentence of Article 4(1) of the OECD MC[834] was only introduced with the 1977 OECD MC – such a nominee was considered a treaty resident and, hence, could claim treaty benefits. Thus, '[t]he United Kingdom [...] may have been concerned about reducing its withholding tax in its capacity as source state if the treaty partner state had similar taxing rules and the income was beneficially owned by a person who was not a resident of that state'.[835] In other words, the United Kingdom was worried that third-country residents could interpose a nominee in one of its treaty partner countries (that had comparable domestic law provisions) and thereby obtain treaty benefits that would otherwise not be available to them.[836] To remedy this situation, the United Kingdom included a subject-to-tax clause and later a beneficial ownership requirement in all of its tax treaties. Presumably to save arguments when negotiating DTCs, the United Kingdom wanted the Beneficial Ownership Test to be inserted into the OECD MC.[837]

4.2.1.2 Content

With the OECD MC 1977, Article 12(1) was amended as follows:

> Royalties arising in a Contracting State and paid to a resident of the other Contracting State shall be taxable only in that other State *if such resident is the beneficial owner of the royalties* (emphasis added).

Furthermore, the following paragraph was inserted into the OECD Commentary:[838]

> Under paragraph 1, *the exemption from tax in the State of source is not available when an intermediary, such as an agent or a nominee, is interposed between the beneficiary and the payer, unless the beneficial owner is a resident of the other Contracting State*. States which wish to make this more explicit are free to do so during bilateral negotiations. The term 'paid' has a very wide meaning, since the concept of payment means the fulfilment of the obligation to put funds at the disposal of the creditor in the manner required by contract or custom (emphasis added).

834. *See* the second sentence of Art. 4(1) OECD MC 1977: 'This term, however, does not include any person who is liable to tax in that State in respect only of income from sources in that State or capital situated therein.'
835. *Vann* in *Lang/Pistone/Schuch/Staringer/Storck* 285.
836. *See OECD*, Observations of Member Countries on Difficulties Raised by the OECD Draft Convention on Income and Capital, TFD/FC/216 (1967) 14.
837. *Avery Jones* in *Lang/Pistone/Schuch/Staringer/Storck* 338.
838. *See* Art. 12 Mn 4 OECD Commentary 1977; *see also* the corresponding statements in Art. 10 Mn 12 and Art. 11 Mn 8 OECD Commentary 1977.

4.2.1.3 *Analysis: Normative Meaning of the Concept?*

In general, tax treaties 'do not provide any autonomous rules with respect to the attribution of income but rather follow the classification of the contracting states'.[839] However, the allocation rules of tax treaties use different terms to 'denote the connection between income and a person' (e.g., 'paid to' as in Article 12(1) OECD MC 1977).[840] That is, the application of the allocation rules presupposes that income is attributed to a person according to the domestic law (i.e., the wording 'paid to' encompasses the attribution of income under domestic law).[841]

The introduction of the Beneficial Ownership Test into the OECD MC 1977, therefore, seems to suggest that there is an additional requirement - beyond the attribution of income - that taxpayers have to fulfil to obtain treaty benefits with regard to passive income.[842] However, when looking at the history of origins of the term, a different picture emerges.

At the outset, it should be noted that a 'great deal is now known about the early history of the introduction of the beneficial ownership limitation into the OECD Model'.[843] However, this was not always the case as access to informative documents was often restricted.[844] Only in later years did these documents became available to the public.[845] Nevertheless, even such documents may be considered in the interpretation process.[846]

As already stated above, the first time the beneficial ownership requirement was used in relation to income in a tax treaty was in the 1966 protocol to the United

839. *Lang*, Introduction to the Law of Double Taxation Conventions (2013) Mn 416; *see also* FN 188; different opinion *Baumgartner*, Das Konzept des beneficial owner im internationalen Steuerrecht der Schweiz: Unter besonderer Berücksichtigung der Weiterleitung von abkommensbegünstigten Dividenden- und Zinseinkünften in Reich/Simonek (Eds), Schriften zum Steuerrecht (2010) 162ff with further references.
840. *Wheeler*, The Attribution of Income to a Person for Tax Treaty Purposes, BIT 2005, 477 (477f); *see also Danon*, Switzerland's direct and international taxation of private express trusts: With particular references to US, Canadian and New Zealand trust taxation, in Oberson (Ed.), Droit fiscal Suisse et international (2004) 296f.
841. *Canete/Pamperl*, Einkünftezurechnung und Beneficial Ownership, in *Lang/Schuch/Staringer* (Eds), Einkünftezurechnung im Internationalen Steuerrecht (2012) 73 (79).
842. *See also Wheeler*, BIT 2005, 478; *Ng* in *Ecker/Ressler* 511.
843. *Baker* in Maisto 88.
844. *See du Toit*, Beneficial Ownership of Royalties in Bilateral Tax Treaties (1999) 179: '[T]he documentation is regarded as confidential and the OECD is not willing to disclose it. [...] There is some documentation available from that period, but it would not be right to refer to such documentation. In the absence of access to all the documentation from the period, the limited available information may be misleading as to the true intentions of the drafters of the OECD Model.'
845. In this regard, *see also OECD*, Resolution of the Council on the Historical Archives of the Organisation, C(91)132/FINAL (1991); *OECD*, Council Resolution on the Classification and Declassification of Information, C(97)64/FINAL (1997).
846. For further considerations on this issue, *see Lang*, Kommunalsteuer und DBA, SWI 2005, 16 (16ff).

Kingdom-United States Income Tax Treaty (1945).[847] In this regard, the United States noted the following:[848]

> *While the protocol is the first entered into by the United States which specifically states that the dividend must be beneficially owned by a resident of the country to qualify for the reduced rate of tax on dividends, this limitation on treaty benefits has been considered implicit in all of this country's prior conventions. Therefore, the addition of this language to the article is not intended to reduce the scope of this article as compared to corresponding articles of prior conventions (emphasis added).*

Furthermore, records of the treaty negotiations between the United Kingdom and New Zealand are also instructive:[849]

> New Zealand *doubted whether these words [note: beneficially owned] were necessary* as, under New Zealand law, a nominee could not be said to derive a dividend, he was simply acting as an agent for his principal who was the person who derived the income (emphasis added).

Therefore, the United States and New Zealand seem to have been of the opinion that the addition of the Beneficial Ownership Test to the treaty is superfluous as it is already implicitly included.[850]

Likewise, historical documents of the discussion at the OECD show that '[t]he Delegate for Germany found *no trouble with the existing text* and would prefer to make it clear in the commentaries that the recipient must be the beneficial owner' (emphasis added).[851] Consequently, the German position seems to correspond to the position of the United States and New Zealand which view beneficial ownership as implied throughout the treaty.[852]

Similarly, the United Kingdom's suggestion that beneficial ownership should be inserted 'not necessarily in Articles 10, 11 and 12, but possibly as a general provision

847. *See* sec. 4.2.1.1.
848. *See* United States, Technical Memorandum of Treasury Department Concerning Proposed Protocol Amending the Income Tax Convention between the United States and the United Kingdom (1966), Document 93-30729B, as cited in *Vann* in *Lang/Pistone/Schuch/Staringer /Storck* 275; besides, it is worth noting that the United Kingdom-United States Income Tax Treaty was also the first tax treaty to use a provision comparable to Art. 3(2) of the OECD MC (*lex fori* rule), *see Lang*, Die Bedeutung des Musterabkommens und des Kommentars des OECD-Steuerausschusses für die Auslegung von Doppelbesteuerungsabkommen, in *Gassner/Lang/Lechner* (Eds), Aktuelle Entwicklungen im internationalen Steuerrecht: Das neue Musterabkommen der OECD (1994) 11 (35); this provision is widely considered to have no normative meaning, for a discussion of the different views regarding Art. 3(2) OECD MC, *see Lang* in *IFA* 207ff.
849. *See* The National Archives (UK) Public Record Office, File IR 40/17246, 14 Feb. 1966, as cited in *Vann* in *Lang/Pistone/Schuch/Staringer/Storck* 276.
850. *Vann* in *Lang/Pistone/Schuch/Staringer/Storck* 277.
851. *OECD*, Note on the Discussion of the first report of Working Party No. 27 of the Fiscal Committee on interest and royalties during the 31st session of the Fiscal Committee held from 10th to 13th June, DAF/FC/69.10 (1969) 6.
852. *See also Vann* in *Lang/Pistone/Schuch/Staringer/Storck* 284.

in a separate Article'[853] indicates that it had an issue with the OECD MC as such and not only its Articles 10-12.[854]

In the end, 'history shows that all countries except the United Kingdom seemed to consider obvious that a person who is not the legal owner of income (because he acts as an agent or nominee) may not have access to treaty benefits'.[855] Stated differently, as income is regularly not attributed to agents and nominees under domestic law,[856] they cannot claim treaty benefits and, hence, the Beneficial Ownership Test just clarified what was the case anyway.[857]

Consequently, opinions are voiced in literature that 'the concept of beneficial ownership is a basic principle of income taxation: the beneficial owner of income is the person who should be taxed on the income. Accordingly, this basic principle of taxation on the basis of beneficial ownership is implicit in all of the distributive articles of the tax treaty and, to that extent, the explicit reference to "beneficial owner" in Arts. 10, 11, and 12 of the OECD Model *does not add anything*' (emphasis added).[858]

Similarly, *Lang* takes the view that the term has no normative meaning but is merely an 'indication that one has to apply an economic – and not a formal – approach in interpreting tax treaties'.[859] The reason why beneficial ownership is only expressly

853. *OECD,* Note on the Discussion of the first report of Working Party No. 27 of the Fiscal Committee on interest and royalties during the 31st session of the Fiscal Committee held from 10th to 13th June, DAF/FC/69.10 (1969) 6; *see also Vann* in *Lang/Pistone/Schuch/Staringer /Storck* 284: '[T]his was never adopted although people have wondered why it is restricted to dividends, interest and royalties. The outcome is understandable, if not fully thought through, as these articles are the only ones (apart from those on pensions and government service, which are not normally paid to agents or trustees) that depend on payment rather than income being derived, they are the only articles in the Model with a reduction to a fixed rate limit for source taxation and also dividends, interest and royalties are commonly paid to intermediaries.'

854. As stated already above (*see* sec. 4.2.1.1), a nominee for a non-UK resident was liable to tax on domestic income but not on any foreign income he received; as a consequence, *Avery Jones* in *Lang/Pistone/Schuch/Staringer/Storck* 335 FN 10 states: 'This treatment of foreign income may be why the United Kingdom proposed that beneficial ownership be applied to all tax treaty articles.'

855. *Gutmann,* The 2011 Discussion Draft on Beneficial Ownership: What Next for the OECD?, in *Lang/Pistone/Schuch/Staringer/Storck* (Eds), Beneficial Ownership: Recent Trends (2013) 341 (341).

856. *Lang,* VwGH zur Verweigerung der Abkommensberechtigung, SWI 2000, 423 (427); *see also Wheeler,* General Report, in *IFA* (Ed.), Cahiers de droit fiscal international, Vol. 92b Conflicts in the attribution of income to a person (2007) 17 (36f).

857. *See also Vann* in *Lang/Pistone/Schuch/Staringer/Storck* 287: 'The history in WP27 of the insertion of beneficial ownership into the OECD Model suggests that there was not a great deal of enthusiasm for it, that it confirmed to most countries what was the case anyway, but that it did no harm.'

858. *Arnold,* Tax Treaty News, BIT 2010, 306 (308); *see also Arnold,* Tax Treaties and Tax Avoidance: The 2003 Revisions to the Commentary to the OECD Model, BIT 2004, 244 (248); *Arnold,* Tax Treaty News, BIT 2008, 263 (263); *Arnold,* Tax Treaty News, BIT 2011, 555 (556).

859. *Lang,* Interpretation of the Term 'Beneficial Ownership' The Prévost Case – Tax Court of Canada, in *The Chamber of Tax Consultants* (Eds), International Taxation – A Compendium: Volume 1 (2008) 592 (601); *see also* the considerations in *Lang,* Die Stiftung im internationalen Ertragsteuerrecht, in *Csoklich/Müller* (Eds), Die Stiftung als Unternehmer (1990) 185 (201f); *Lang,* 'Treaty Shopping' – Der Mißbrauch von Doppelbesteuerungsabkommen, SWI 1991, 55 (60).

mentioned in Articles 10-12 OECD MC is that these articles deal with the types of income that are the most susceptible to abuse.[860] However, 'the usage of the term "beneficial ownership" makes it clear for all other tax treaty provisions as well that tax treaty terms have to be interpreted applying an economic approach'.[861]

A similar approach was taken in the Aiken Industries case – although concerning a conduit company and not an agent or nominee, respectively – where a US Court had to interpret the terms 'received by'[862] *included in the relevant distributive article (the DTC in question did not contain a beneficial ownership requirement).*[863] *The court did not follow the plain wording of the terms but rather determined that 'received by' means 'interest received by a corporation of either of the contracting States as its own and not with the obligation to transmit it to another. The words "received by" refer not merely to the obtaining of physical possession on a temporary basis of funds representing interest payments from a corporation of a contracting State, but contemplate complete dominion and control over the funds'. That is, although the relevant DTC did not contain a beneficial ownership requirement, the court still denied treaty benefits based on an economic approach in interpreting the wording 'received by'.*[864]

To sum up, it appears that the Beneficial Ownership Test was a mere clarification of a self-evident principle when it was first introduced into the OECD MC in 1977. Therefore, except maybe for the United Kingdom with the above-mentioned peculiarity in its legal system – although one could argue that, by way of an economic approach in the interpretation of DTCs, the same result could have been achieved – the concept did not have any normative meaning.[865]

Curiously enough, even from the United Kingdom's point of view, the beneficial ownership requirement was no longer necessary when it was included in the OECD MC 1977.[866] Since that version made clear that a tax treaty is only applicable when a person

860. *Lang* in *The Chamber of Tax Consultants* 601; *see also Wheeler*, BIT 2005, 479.
861. *Lang* in *The Chamber of Tax Consultants* 601; for a similar opinion, *see* Mooji's comment in *Walser*, The Concept of Beneficial Ownership in Tax Treaties, in *IFA* (Ed.), The OECD Model Convention – 1998 and Beyond: The Concept of Beneficial Ownership in Tax Treaties (2000) 15 (32).
862. Contrarily, the OECD MC 1963 contained the wording 'paid to' in its Art. 11; for this reason, *Wardzynski*, The 2014 Update to the OECD Commentary: A Targeted Hybrid Approach to Beneficial Ownership, Intertax 2015, 179 (183) argues that it is disputable whether the reasoning of the case can be extrapolated to other cases.
863. United States Tax Court, 5. 8. 1971, 56 TC 925, Aiken Industries, Inc. v. Commissioner of Internal Revenue; for more details, *see Brauner*, Beneficial Ownership in and outside US Tax Treaties, in *Lang/Pistone/Schuch/Staringer/Storck* (Eds), Beneficial Ownership: Recent Trends (2013) 143 (146ff).
864. Interesting in this regard, *Vogel*, Klaus Vogel on Double Taxation Conventions^3 (1997) Preface to Arts 10-12 Mn 14: 'In DTCs that do not use the term "beneficial owner" the general principles concerning "treaty shopping" [...] normally produce the same results [...]. In other words, all that the concept of "beneficial ownership" brings about is to clarify the situation as it already existed under the earlier DTCs and can be expected to continue to exist in future.'
865. *See also Ng* in *Ecker/Ressler* 539, who distinguishes between the meaning of the term in common law countries and in civil law countries and states: 'For bilateral tax treaties signed after 1977 and before 1986 involving civil law countries, the expression ought to be interpreted as being irrelevant for tax treaty purposes as the intention of inserting the expression was only to assist UK and other common law countries to attribute income to the rightful owner.'
866. *See Avery Jones* in *Lang/Pistone/Schuch/Staringer/Storck* 333 and 339.

is fully liable to tax in at least one contracting state,[867] a nominee for a non-UK resident - who was only subject to limited tax liability because he was only liable on UK source income - was no longer a treaty resident. Therefore, the problem the United Kingdom was initially worried about was not existent anymore.

4.2.2 1986: OECD Conduit Companies Report

4.2.2.1 Background

In 1986, the OECD published a report dubbed 'Double Taxation Conventions and the Use of Conduit Companies' (Conduit Companies Report) in which it dealt with issues raised by conduit companies. Such companies are situated in a treaty country and act 'as a conduit for channeling income economically accruing to a person in another State who is thereby able to take advantage "improperly" of the benefits provided by a tax treaty'.[868] In this report, the OECD examined, *inter alia*, whether the Beneficial Ownership Test is a suitable tool for tackling conduit company structures.[869]

4.2.2.2 Content

Under the heading anti-avoidance provisions, the report made the following comments:[870]

> Articles 10 to 12 of the OECD Model deny the limitation of tax in the State of source on dividends, interest and royalties if the conduit company is not its 'beneficial owner'. Thus the limitation is not available when, *economically, it would benefit a person not entitled to it* who interposed the conduit company as an intermediary between himself and the payer of the income (paragraphs 12, 8 and 4 of the Commentary to Articles 10, 11 and 12 respectively). The Commentaries mention the case of a nominee or agent. The provisions would, however, *apply also to other cases where a person enters into contracts or takes over obligations under which he has a similar function to those of a nominee or an agent. Thus a conduit company can normally not be regarded as the beneficial owner if, though the formal owner of certain assets, it has very narrow powers which render it a mere fiduciary or an administrator acting on account of the interested parties* (most likely the shareholders of the conduit company). In practice, however, it will usually be difficult for the country of source to show that the conduit company is not the beneficial owner. *The fact that its main function is to hold assets or rights is not itself sufficient to categorise it as a mere intermediary*, although this may indicate that

867. *See* the second sentence of Art. 4(1) OECD MC 1977; *see* already FN 834.
868. *OECD*, Double Taxation Conventions and the Use of Conduit Companies (1986) Mn 2; furthermore, the Conduit Companies Report distinguishes between direct conduits (income received by the conduit company is tax-exempt in its residence state, e.g., because of a participation exemption) and 'stepping stone' conduits (income received by the conduit company is not tax-exempt in its residence state but because of high deductible expenses to a related company, the conduit company is only subject to insubstantial taxation, if any), *see OECD*, Double Taxation Conventions and the Use of Conduit Companies (1986) Mn 4f.
869. *See OECD*, Double Taxation Conventions and the Use of Conduit Companies (1986) Mn 14.
870. *OECD*, Double Taxation Conventions and the Use of Conduit Companies (1986) Mn 14.

further examination is necessary. This examination will in any case be highly burdensome for the country of source and not even the country of residence of the conduit company may have the necessary information regarding the shareholders of the conduit company, the company's relationships to the shareholders or other interested parties or the decision-making process of the conduit company. So even an exchange of information between the country of source and the country of the conduit company may not solve the problem. *It is apparently in view of these difficulties that the Commentaries on the 1977 OECD Model mentioned the possibility of defining more specifically during bilateral negotiations the treatment that should be applicable to such companies* (cf. paragraph 22 of the Commentary on Article 10) (emphasis added).

4.2.2.3 Analysis: New Direction for the Beneficial Ownership Test

In light of the history of origin of beneficial ownership as presented above, it is interesting that the Conduit Companies Report refers to the Beneficial Ownership Test as an anti-avoidance provision.[871] On the contrary, history suggests that – as a basic principle – 'beneficial ownership is confined to agent/nominee situations'.[872] Consequently, the OECD Commentary 1977 explicitly excluded agents and nominees as beneficial owners.[873] The Conduit Companies Report, on the other hand, extends the beneficial ownership concept to conduit companies.[874]

However, whereas income is regularly not attributed to agents and nominees under domestic law,[875] this is generally not true for conduit companies (i.e., income is attributed to them).[876] This entails that agents and nominees can usually not claim treaty benefits – even if a treaty does not contain the Beneficial Ownership Test –[877] while this is different in the case of conduit companies.[878] As a result, the Conduit

871. *See also Meindl-Ringler*, Beneficial Ownership in International Tax Law (2016) 31: 'Although the U.K. delegate initially talked about abuse by using intermediaries, tax avoidance was not an issue'; additionally, the report also denotes the second sentence of Art. 4 (1) OECD MC 1977 as an anti-avoidance provision to tackle conduit company structures, *see OECD*, Double Taxation Conventions and the Use of Conduit Companies (1986) Mn 14.
872. *See Vann* in *Lang/Pistone/Schuch/Staringer/Storck* 288 and 296.
873. *See* sec. 4.2.1.2; however, according to *De Broe*, International Tax Planning and Prevention of Abuse (2008) 664 and 681ff; *Wardzynski*, Intertax 2015, 181f; *Polivanova-Rosenauer*, Das Konzept des Nutzungsberechtigten aus abkommensrechtlicher Sicht, SWI 2001, 257 (262) and *du Toit*, Beneficial Ownership of Royalties in Bilateral Tax Treaties (1999) 215ff, the OECD Commentary does not intend to restrict the application of the Beneficial Ownership Test to agents and nominees only since, otherwise, a more explicit wording then 'such as' would have been used.
874. *See also Vann* in *Lang/Pistone/Schuch/Staringer/Storck* 298; *Ng* in *Ecker/Ressler* 536.
875. *See* already FN 856.
876. *See also De Broe*, International Tax Planning and Prevention of Abuse (2008) 684: '[U]nlike an agent or nominee, a conduit has a personal entitlement to the income which it collects in its own name and for its own account.'
877. *See also Yoshimura*, Clarifying the Meaning of 'Beneficial Owner' in Tax Treaties, Tax Analysts 2013, 761 (762).
878. *See also OECD*, Double Taxation Conventions and the Use of Conduit Companies (1986) Mn 13: 'Normally under the OECD Model the conduit company is regarded as a person [...] resident in the State of conduit [...]. It is therefore entitled to claim the benefits of the treaty in its own name.'

Companies Report turns the Beneficial Ownership Test into a new direction,[879] as it ascribes a normative meaning to it.

This is, to a certain extent, even implicitly acknowledged in the Conduit Companies Report when it is stated that '[t]he new provisions of the 1977 OECD Model [note: amongst others the Beneficial Ownership Test] thus deal with the conduit situation in a rudimentary way, *expressing only a general concern that improper use of treaties should be avoided*' (emphasis added).[880] Against this background, the legal relevance of the report for the interpretation of DTCs (more precisely, the Beneficial Ownership Test) can be questioned,[881] even more than what is usually the case for OECD reports.[882] However, what the report certainly did was making 'the term now more uncertain in operation'.[883]

4.2.3 1995/1997: Update of the OECD MC

4.2.3.1 Background

The wording of Articles 10-12 OECD MC 1977 distinguished between the recipient of a payment, on the one hand, and its beneficial owner on the other hand.[884] Apparently, this distinction was perceived as problematic when the recipient and the beneficial owner of a payment are two different persons. There was the fear that, in such cases, neither of the two could claim a reduction of withholding taxes.[885] To account for this issue, the wording of Articles 10(2) and 11(2) was amended in 1995,[886] and the wording of Article 12(1) OECD MC was amended in 1997.[887]

4.2.3.2 Content

The wording of Article 12(1) was amended as follows:

> Royalties arising in a Contracting State and *beneficially owned* by a resident of the other Contracting State shall be taxable only in that other State (emphasis added).

879. *Vann* in *Lang/Pistone/Schuch/Staringer/Storck* 297f; *Ng* in *Ecker/Ressler* 536.
880. *OECD*, Double Taxation Conventions and the Use of Conduit Companies (1986) Mn 15.
881. In this regard, *see also Eynatten/De Haen/Hostyn*, The Concept of 'Beneficial Owner' under Belgian Tax Law: Legal Interpretation is Maintained, Intertax 2003, 523 (537 and 546) and *Pijl*, The Definition of 'Beneficial Owner' under Dutch Law, BIT 2000, 256 (260), according to whom the Conduit Companies Report cannot be considered for the interpretation of DTCs (admittedly, however, they argue that beneficial ownership should be interpreted according to domestic law); different *De Broe*, International Tax Planning and Prevention of Abuse (2008) 683, who would consider the Conduit Companies Report for interpretation purposes.
882. *See Lang*, Introduction to the Law of Double Taxation Conventions (2013) Mn 108: '[T]he assumption that the negotiators of the DTC followed the opinion represented in an OECD report is not as obvious as it is when it comes to the Commentary.'
883. *Vann* in *Lang/Pistone/Schuch/Staringer/Storck* 298.
884. For the wording of Art. 12(1) OECD MC 1977, *see* sec. 4.2.1.2.
885. *See Lang*, Die Bedeutung der 1995 erfolgten Änderungen des OECD-Musterabkommens und des Kommentars des OECD-Steuerausschusses für die Doppelbesteuerungsabkommen, in *Lang/Loukota /Lüthi* (Eds), Die Weiterentwicklung des OECD-Musterabkommens (1996) 39 (40f).
886. *OECD*, The 1995 Update to the Model Tax Convention, DAFFE/CFA/WP1(94)9 (1994) 6f.
887. *OECD*, Next Update to the Model Convention, DAFFE/CFA/WP1(97)6 (1997) 4.

This is still the wording in the current OECD MC 2017.[888]

Furthermore, a note concerning this amendment was added in brackets to Article 12 Mn 4 OECD Commentary 1997:

> [T]he text of the Model was amended in 1995 [sic][889] to clarify this point, which has been the consistent position of all Member countries.

4.2.3.3 Analysis: Beneficial Ownership Tested on a Territorial Level

The update is supposed to make clear that the withholding tax reduction is still available when the recipient of a cross-border payment is not its beneficial owner, but the beneficial owner is resident in the same country as the recipient.[890]

As stated above, DTCs link to the attribution of income under domestic law.[891] On the treaty level, income always has to be assigned to one of the allocation rules.[892] In the case that income cannot be assigned to a specific allocation rule, Article 21(1) OECD MC contains a blanket clause for 'other income'. Accordingly, '[i]tems of income of a resident of a Contracting State, wherever arising, not dealt with in the foregoing Articles of this Convention shall be taxable only in that State' (i.e., exclusive taxing right of the residence state).

With respect to the Beneficial Ownership Test, this means that it has to be analysed whether income is attributed to a person under domestic law in the first place,[893] and, in a second step, whether this person is the beneficial owner of that income.[894] Accordingly, if royalties (Article 12(2) OECD MC) are attributed to a taxpayer under domestic law but the respective taxpayer is not the beneficial owner of

888. Contrarily, the wording of Art. 10(2) and Art. 11(2) was marginally amended in 2014 to further clarify this issue, *see OECD*, 2014 Update to the OECD Model Tax Convention (2014) Mn 5f, 34 and 41; *see also* Art. 10 Mn 12.7 and Art. 11 Mn 11 OECD Commentary 2017.
889. Initially, Art. 12 should have been updated together with Arts 10 and 11 in 1995 (*see OECD*, The 1995 Update to the Model Tax Convention, DAFFE/CFA/WP1(94)9 (1994) 8); however, discussions concerning the amended wording of Art. 12 postponed its update to 1997; nevertheless, the exact same sentence pointing out the changes that were made was adopted for all three articles in the Commentary; for more details, *see Meindl-Ringler*, Beneficial Ownership in International Tax Law (2016) 33; with the update of the Commentary in 2014, the date was rectified (i.e., 1997), *see OECD*, 2014 Update to the OECD Model Tax Convention (2014) Mn 48; *see also* Art. 12 Mn 4.6 OECD Commentary 2017.
890. *Meindl-Ringler*, Beneficial Ownership in International Tax Law (2016) 33; *see also OECD*, OECD Model Tax Convention: Revised proposals concerning the meaning of 'beneficial owner' in Articles 10, 11 and 12 (2012) Mn 30: '[T]he 1995 change [...] addressed the issue where the direct recipient and the beneficial owner of the dividends are both residents of the same State.'
891. *See* sec. 4.2.1.3.
892. *Lang*, Introduction to the Law of Double Taxation Conventions (2013) Mn 174.
893. In the opinion of *Danon* in *Oberson* 309ff, the attribution of income according to the domestic law of the residence state is decisive for the source state (i.e., the source state must follow the attribution of income of the residence state when applying a tax treaty); however, *Canete/Pamperl* in *Lang/Schuch/Staringer* 81 argue convincingly that either the attribution of income according to the domestic law of the residence state or the source state is relevant depending on where treaty benefits are claimed; on this issue, *see also* sec. 4.2.5.3.
894. *Canete/Pamperl* in *Lang/Schuch/Staringer* 83.

these royalties, Article 12 OECD MC - and not Article 21(1) OECD MC -[895] is still applicable.[896] However, in such a case, the elimination of withholding taxes is only granted when the beneficial owner is also a resident of the other contracting state.[897]

Therefore, similar as under the Modified Nexus Approach for non-EU members,[898] a territorial approach is applied; i.e., it is tested whether the beneficial owner is a resident of the same country as the person to whom the royalties are attributed. Stated differently, the person to whom income is attributed and the beneficial owner can diverge, and treaty benefits may nonetheless be granted as long as they both reside in the other contracting state.

However, when the person to whom income is attributed and the beneficial owner reside in different countries, it is not possible for either of them to claim treaty benefits.[899] On the one hand, the person to whom income is attributed is not eligible for a reduction of withholding taxes because he is not the beneficial owner (or the beneficial owner does not reside in the other contracting state, respectively). On the other hand, the beneficial owner is not eligible as income is not attributed to him and, therefore, a potential DTC between his residence state and the source state cannot have any limiting effects in this case.[900] Furthermore, it can also not be said that a recharacterization takes place in the sense that the Beneficial Ownership Test changes the attribution of income under domestic law so that income is attributed to the beneficial owner who may hence claim treaty benefits in the above-mentioned case.[901] This is because tax treaties can generally only restrict taxing rights existing under domestic law, but they cannot generate any tax liability on their own.[902] However, '[i]f tax treaties [note: in this case the Beneficial Ownership Test] were to attribute income

895. Apparently, this was the fear expressed by France, *see OECD*, Working Party Proposals for Preparing for the 1995+ Update, DAFFE/CFA/WP1(95)5/REV3 (1995) Mn 10; for further considerations on this issue, *see also Vogel*, Klaus Vogel on Double Taxation Conventions[3] (1997) Preface to Arts 10-12 Mn 11.
896. *Canete/Pamperl* in *Lang/Schuch/Staringer* 82f.
897. If this is not the case, the taxpayer may still enjoy treaty benefits with regard to other forms of income, for example, business income (Art. 7 OECD MC) or income from capital gains (Art. 13 OECD MC), *see also Blum*, Treaty shopping and prevention in a post-BEPS world, International Tax Report 11/2017, 1 (11).
898. *See* sec. 3.2.6.3.
899. Different *Danon/Salomé*, The BEPS Multilateral Instrument: General overview and focus on treaty abuse, IFF 2017, 197 (218); *Pijl*, Beneficial Ownership and Second Tier Beneficial Owners in Tax Treaties of the Netherlands, Intertax 2003, 353 (360); *Yoshimura*, Tax Analysts 2013, 780 FN 84; all of the above authors base their opinion on later versions of the OECD Commentary (*see* sec. 4.2.8.2 [Mn 4.6]); however, since the respective OECD Commentary versions refer to intermediaries such as agents or nominees that are interposed in a third state and, at the same time, state that income is not attributed to agents and nominees, this conclusion is not convincing.
900. The distributive articles of a DTC - in this case, Art. 12 OECD MC - are only applicable to persons to whom income is domestically attributed, *see Canete/Pamperl* in *Lang/Schuch /Staringer* 78; in this context, *see also* the position of the Netherlands Secretary of State for Finance as cited in *Pijl*, Intertax 2003, 359: 'Tax credit or repayment can only be claimed by the recipient of the dividend because he or she is the person subjected to dividend withholding tax in the first instance. Therefore, the actual economic beneficiary cannot claim tax credit or repayment.'
901. In this direction, *Danon/Salomé*, IFF 2017, 218.
902. *See* already FN 405.

to a different person than the domestic laws of the contracting states, they would actually create new taxing rights at the level of that person, which would be contrary to the basic functioning of tax treaties'.[903]

Overall, it has to be stressed that all of the above-mentioned considerations come only into play when a normative meaning is assigned to the Beneficial Ownership Test. At this stage, however, this cannot be claimed.

4.2.4 1998: OECD Report on Harmful Tax Competition

4.2.4.1 Background

In its Report on Harmful Tax Competition, the OECD not only discussed factors that it would use for identifying tax havens and harmful preferential tax regimes,[904] but it also provided recommendations on how countries can use their tax treaties to counter harmful tax practices.[905] The report recommends that 'countries consider including in their tax conventions provisions aimed at restricting the entitlement to treaty benefits for entities and income covered by measures constituting harmful tax practices and *consider how the existing provisions of their tax conventions can be applied for the same purpose* [...]' (emphasis added).[906] In this context, the report also mentions the Beneficial Ownership Test.

4.2.4.2 Content

The report starts by stating that a 'wide treaty network may [...] have the unintended consequence of opening up the benefits of harmful preferential tax regimes offered by treaty partners'.[907] Then, it highlights that '[v]arious approaches have been used by countries to reduce that risk' with one of them being the Beneficial Ownership Test.[908]

In this regard, the report states the following:[909]

> Another example [note: for countries' approaches] involves denying companies with *no real economic function* treaty benefits because these companies are not considered as beneficial owner of certain income formally attributed to them (emphasis added).

4.2.4.3 Analysis: Beneficial Ownership as a General Anti-avoidance Rule?

As *Vann* rightly points out, it is 'apparent from the history [of the Beneficial Ownership Test] that there was nothing to suggest that it was dealing with tax regimes deliberately

903. *Schaffer*, Domestic Attribution of Income and Taxation of International Entertainers and Sportspersons: Theory and Practice of Art. 17 OECD Model Convention (2017) 27.
904. *See* already sec. 3.1.
905. *OECD*, Harmful Tax Competition: An Emerging Global Issue (1998) Mn 113ff.
906. *OECD*, Harmful Tax Competition: An Emerging Global Issue (1998) Mn 117.
907. *OECD*, Harmful Tax Competition: An Emerging Global Issue (1998) Mn 118.
908. *OECD*, Harmful Tax Competition: An Emerging Global Issue (1998) Mn 119.
909. *OECD*, Harmful Tax Competition: An Emerging Global Issue (1998) Mn 119.

created by one country to impinge unfairly on the tax system of other countries'.[910] Furthermore, the understanding of beneficial ownership in this report goes beyond the previous understanding of the term in the OECD MC and Commentary 1977.[911] Therefore, it would not be appropriate to consider its statements for the interpretation of DTCs.[912] What is more, the OECD did not further pursue this position when it updated its Commentary in 2003.[913]

Nonetheless, it is interesting to examine the understanding of beneficial ownership that the report carries. As it seems, the report understands the concept of beneficial ownership as a test to determine whether a company has any real economic function besides the alleged achievement of a tax saving.[914] This would make the Beneficial Ownership Test similar to a general anti-avoidance rule.

Occasionally, this opinion is also expressed in literature. For example, *Jain* argues that 'courts can decide conduit company cases more convincingly if they apply the beneficial ownership test as if it were a general anti-avoidance rule'.[915] Accordingly, 'courts can refuse treaty benefits if they find no practical reason for the existence of the interposed company in a corporate structure, other than to obtain source state withholding tax reduction'.[916]

Similar positions can also be found in case law. For example, in the *Spanish Real Madrid* cases,[917] the court understood beneficial ownership as a business purpose test

910. *Vann* in *Lang/Pistone/Schuch/Staringer/Storck* 299.
911. *See* sec. 4.2.1.3.
912. *See also Vann* in *Lang/Pistone/Schuch/Staringer/Storck* 299: 'The approach seems to be to retrofit the new policy change to existing tax treaties by interpretation which would seem to go beyond the legitimate sphere of interpretation.'
913. *See* sec. 4.2.6.2; the wording 'no real economic function' was not used in the updated 2003 Commentary, although the Report on Harmful Tax Competition and its comments concerning beneficial ownership were mentioned in the update document, *see OECD*, Restricting the Entitlement to Treaty Benefits (2002) Mn 1ff.
914. It would also be conceivable that the report understands the beneficial ownership test as an instrument to target companies that do not perform any functions, *see Jain*, Effectiveness of the Beneficial Ownership Test in Conduit Company Cases (2013) 79; however, in this context, the report already mentions the application of transfer pricing rules to counteract harmful tax competition: 'Measures that constitute harmful tax competition often result in significant income being attributed to a foreign entity which performs few, if any, real activities. The application of transfer pricing rules, which typically start from an analysis of the true functions performed by each part of a group of associated enterprises, does, in that respect, constitute a useful counteracting measure'; *see OECD*, Harmful Tax Competition: An Emerging Global Issue (1998) Mn 166.
915. *Jain*, Effectiveness of the Beneficial Ownership Test in Conduit Company Cases (2013) 214.
916. *Jain*, Effectiveness of the Beneficial Ownership Test in Conduit Company Cases (2013) 204.
917. Audiencia Nacional (National Court, AN), 18 July 2006, JUR\2006\204307, JUR\2007\8915 and JUR\2007\16549; AN, 20 July 2006, JUR\2007\16526; AN, 10 Nov. 2006, JUR\2006\284679; AN, 13 Nov. 2006, JUR\2006\284618; AN, 26 Mar. 2007, JUR\2007\10187710 as cited in *Jiménez*, Beneficial Ownership as a Broad Anti-Avoidance Provision: Decisions by Spanish Courts and the OECD's Discussion Draft, in *Lang/Pistone/Schuch/Staringer/Storck* (Eds), Beneficial Ownership: Recent Trends (2013) 127 (128 FN 6).

and asked whether 'there is a business reason to place an entity between the payer and the final recipient of the income beyond reduction of withholding taxes in Spain'.[918]

Likewise, in the *Bank of Scotland* case,[919] the French Supreme Administrative Court concluded that 'the sole purpose [of a usufruct agreement to shares was] to obtain abusively the benefit of favourable provisions of the France-UK tax treaty'.[920] As a result, the court denied the beneficial ownership status of the recipient of the dividends (Bank of Scotland), although the Bank of Scotland was 'not acting as an agent or a nominee and therefore did not fall within the scope of the traditional understanding of the beneficial ownership concept in the sense of the OECD Model and Commentary'.[921]

However, 'there are no significant indications in the historical and current OECD material that beneficial ownership should be construed as a broad anti-avoidance rule'[922] (besides maybe the Report on Harmful Tax Competition for which legal relevance – as stated above – can seriously be questioned).[923] Consequently, many scholars[924] negate such a broad anti-abuse meaning of the Beneficial Ownership Test.

On a related note, in analysing the *Bank of Scotland* case, *Gutmann* concludes that it shows the 'need to include an intentional element in the definition of beneficial ownership'.[925] Otherwise, 'the risk of over-extending the meaning of beneficial ownership is to deny treaty benefits to persons who have not tried to circumvent any tax rule'.[926] However, then again, neither the wording of Articles 10-12 OECD MC nor the OECD Commentary on the respective articles – even in its current version – suggests

918. *See Jiménez* in *Lang/Pistone/Schuch/Staringer/Storck* 130f; however, the court relied on the updated 2003 OECD Commentary as well as the Conduit Companies Report in its judgment, *see Jiménez* in *Lang/Pistone/Schuch/Staringer/Storck* 130f.
919. French Supreme Administrative Court (Conseil d'État), 29. 12. 2006, No. 283314, Bank of Scotland v. Ministre de l'Economie, des Finances et de l'Industrie; for more details, *see Gibert/Ouamrane*, Beneficial Ownership – A French Perspective, ET 2008, 2 (6ff).
920. *Gibert/Ouamrane*, ET 2008, 6.
921. *Gutmann*, Beneficial Ownership as Anti-Abuse Provision: The Bank of Scotland Case, in *Lang/Pistone/Schuch/Staringer/Storck* (Eds), Beneficial Ownership: Recent Trends (2013) 167 (171); furthermore, the author explains that 'the Bank of Scotland had the full right to use and enjoy the dividends that it received. It had no obligation to pass the dividends to anyone else. It was therefore the beneficial owner in the sense of the 2011 "clarification" suggested by the Committee of Fiscal Affairs of the OECD'; however, *Castro*, The Concept of Beneficial Owner in Tax Treaties: Separating the Wheat from the Chaff Through Case Law Method Internationally, International Tax Journal 2013, 21 (28f) points out that the case 'was more related to [a] treaty shopping case than to a beneficial owner case [...]' and therefore 'it cannot be considered as a proper beneficial owner precedent [...]'.
922. *Meindl-Ringler*, Beneficial Ownership in International Tax Law (2016) 322.
923. *See also Navisotschnigg* in *Lang/Pistone/Rust/Schuch/Staringer* 98.
924. *See inter alia Meindl-Ringler*, Beneficial Ownership in International Tax Law (2016) 322f; *Baker* in *United Nations Economic and Social Council*, Note by the Coordinator of the Subcommittee on Improper Use of treaties: Proposed amendments – Addendum: Progress Report of Subcommittee on Improper Use of Tax Treaties: Beneficial Ownership (2008) Mn 14; *Avery Jones/Vann/Wheeler*, Response to the 2011 OECD Discussion Draft 'Clarification of the Meaning of "Beneficial Owner" in the OECD Model Tax Convention' (2011) 5f (available at http://www.oecd.org/tax/treaties/48420432.pdf); *Jiménez*, Beneficial Ownership: Current Trends, WTJ 2010, 35 (52ff); *Wardzynski*, Intertax 2015, 186.
925. *Gutmann* in *Lang/Pistone/Schuch/Staringer/Storck* 172.
926. *Gutmann* in *Lang/Pistone/Schuch/Staringer/Storck* 171.

that subjective intentions play any role in the Beneficial Ownership Test.[927] Consequently, the consideration of such is predominantly rejected.[928]

4.2.5 1999: OECD Partnership Report

4.2.5.1 Background

The OECD Partnership Report dealt with issues in the application of the OECD MC to partnerships.[929] In this context, the Beneficial Ownership Test is used as a means to solve conflicts of income allocation between partners and partnerships (i.e., when the source state attributes income to the partners but the resident state attributes income to the partnership or vice versa).

4.2.5.2 Content

To remedy such conflicts of income allocation, *the report proposes, inter alia, the following:*[930]

> [One] approach would involve consideration of the terms of the distributive rules in the relevant Articles of the Convention. Under that analysis, in the case of dividends, interest and royalties, the inquiry would be *whether or not the recipient of the item of income was the beneficial owner of the income under the laws of the State of residence of the taxpayer claiming treaty benefits and thus the taxpayer in relation to the income.* In the case of a partnership treated as transparent under the laws of the source State but as a taxable entity under the laws of the residence State, the entity itself and not the partners would be treated as the beneficial owner. *Because of the treatment of the income in the State of residence, the partners would not be the beneficial owners of the income for purposes of the treaty.* Thus the partners would not be entitled to treaty benefits in those circumstances and whether the entity was so entitled would depend on whether it independently qualified as a resident. [...] (emphasis added).

4.2.5.3 Analysis: Beneficial Ownership as an Attribution-of-Income Rule?

The Partnership Report understands the Beneficial Ownership Test as an attribution-of-income rule.[931] That is, it 'equates being liable to tax in the residence state on a specific item of income with being the beneficial owner of that income'.[932] This view is

927. *See also Danon*, BIT 2018, 34 and 36; *Blum*, International Tax Report 11/2017, 10.
928. *Jiménez*, WTJ 2010, 54; *Lang*, Schweizer Grundsatzurteil zum Beneficial Owner nach DBA-Recht, SWI 2012, 226 (228); *De Broe*, International Tax Planning and Prevention of Abuse (2008) 689f and 713; *Danon*, BIT 2018, 34 and 36.
929. *See OECD*, The Application of the OECD Model Tax Convention to Partnerships (1999) Mn 1.
930. *OECD*, The Application of the OECD Model Tax Convention to Partnerships (1999) Mn 54; *see also* the statements in *OECD*, The Application of the OECD Model Tax Convention to Partnerships (1999) Mn 61, 71 and 73.
931. *Meindl-Ringler*, Beneficial Ownership in International Tax Law (2016) 55.
932. *See Wheeler*, The Missing Keystone of Income Tax Treaties, WTJ 2011, 274.

also widely held in literature.[933] The main argument brought forward in this regard is that double taxation can only occur when the recipient of a payment arising in the source state is also liable to tax on that payment in the residence state.[934]

There is also case law in which this approach was applied. For example, in a Spanish case,[935] it was ruled that a foreign society for the management of copyrights and authors' rights could not be regarded as the beneficial owner of royalties received from Spanish sources since it 'could only manage the rights of other parties (the authors), and the real owners of the rights had not attributed further powers to the societies apart from those related to receiving the income in their name'.[936] To come to this conclusion, the Spanish Court examined the powers of such societies from the point of view of the Spanish legislation on author's rights. In this respect, *Jiménez* states that the Beneficial Ownership Test was applied 'as a sort of rule on attribution of income: the income was obtained by the authors and not the societies and, therefore, the residence of the owner of the income should be proved in order to have access to reduced withholding tax rates under tax treaties'.[937]

Similarly, in the Canadian *Prévost* case,[938] the court assessed the power of a Netherlands holding company over a received dividend according to Netherlands commercial and tax law. The court concluded that the Netherlands holding company was the beneficial owner since it was the owner of the dividend according to Netherlands legislation and thereby 'left the meaning of beneficial ownership confined to something of an attribution of income rule'.[939]

Even in treaty practice, it can be observed that some DTCs define beneficial ownership by referring to the attribution of income under the domestic law of one of the contracting states.[940] For example, in the DTC between Germany and Sweden,[941]

933. *Meindl-Ringler*, Beneficial Ownership in International Tax Law (2016) 385; *Jiménez*, WTJ 2010, 55; Ault's position in *Walser* in *IFA* 21f; other authors suggest a two-step approach where the attribution of income in the residence state has to be tested in the first step, *see Avery Jones/Vann/Wheeler*, Response to the 2011 OECD Discussion Draft 'Clarification of the Meaning of "Beneficial Owner" in the OECD Model Tax Convention' (2011) 5 (available at http://www.oecd.org/tax/treaties/48420432.pdf); *De Broe*, International Tax Planning and Prevention of Abuse (2008) 722; Libin's position in *Oliver/Libin/van Weeghel/du Toit*, Beneficial Ownership, BIT 2000, 310 (322f).
934. *De Broe*, International Tax Planning and Prevention of Abuse (2008) 691; *Jiménez*, WTJ 2010, 55; Libin's comment in *Oliver/Libin/van Weeghel/du Toit*, BIT 2000, 322; Ault's comment in *Walser* in *IFA* 22.
935. Spanish Central Economic-Administrative Court (Tribunal Económico Administrativo Central), 22. 9. 2000, RG 6294/1996.
936. *Jiménez*, Beneficial Ownership as an Attribution-of-Income Rule in Spain: Source and Residence Country Perspectives, in *Lang/Pistone/Schuch/Staringer/Storck* (Eds), Beneficial Ownership: Recent Trends (2013) 199 (201).
937. *Jiménez* in *Lang/Pistone/Schuch/Staringer/Storck* 201; it should be noted that the Spanish Court took into account the law of the source state to determine the beneficial owner; however, according to *Jiménez*, WTJ 2010, 37 the court 'probably did not mean that when searching for the beneficial owner, the legislation of the source state is relevant' but rather 'simply sought a way to facilitate [its] decision'.
938. Tax Court of Canada, 22. 4. 2008, 2008 TCC 231, Prévost Car Inc. v. Her Majesty the Queen, Mn 100ff.
939. *Jiménez*, WTJ 2010, 48.
940. *See also* the examples in *Wheeler*, BIT 2005, 481.

the term 'beneficial owner' is (primarily) defined as the person to whom income is attributed according to the domestic law of the residence state.[942] Conversely, according to the Germany-United States DTC,[943] the beneficial owner is the person to whom income is attributed according to the domestic law of the source state.

However, such an attribution-of-income approach would require the source state to have knowledge about the domestic law of potentially every other state with which it has concluded a DTC - obviously a very burdensome task.[944]

Furthermore, the premise itself that the tax treatment in the residence state is decisive for the entitlement to treaty benefits in the source state can be challenged:[945]

> According to a well accepted principle of treaty application, tax treaties restrict the imposition of taxes provided for by domestic tax law. Therefore, it is the domestic taxpayer who is entitled to the treaty benefits: *If the taxes are imposed on the taxpayer, the tax treaty can only function properly if the same taxpayer is entitled to the treaty benefits*. Therefore, it makes sense to assume that it is not up to the residence State to decide who shall be entitled to the treaty benefits in the source State. It is the source State that decides on the taxpayer status. Therefore, this decision should be considered relevant for treaty application purposes (emphasis added).

Additionally, in the rare case that a residence state attributes income to an agent or a nominee - as this apparently was the situation for the United Kingdom -[946] this would lead to an outcome that is at odds with the OECD Commentary which explicitly excludes agents and nominees as beneficial owners.[947]

941. Art. 43(3) DTC Germany-Sweden states: 'A resident of a Contracting State shall be deemed the beneficial owner of dividends, interest and royalties within the meaning of Articles 10 to 12 if they are attributable for tax purposes to that resident under the laws of that State. Such resident, however, shall not be deemed the beneficial owner if according to the law of the other State such income is attributed to other persons who own the usufruct thereof and are not residents of the first-mentioned State.'
942. In this context, *see also Wheeler* in *IFA* 23: 'In some countries, application of the beneficial ownership concept generally gives the same result as the attribution of income under domestic law (Austria, Belgium, Brazil, Malaysia, Norway, Spain).'
943. Art. 10 of the Protocol to the DTC Germany-US states: 'A Contracting State shall deem the recipient of dividends, interest, or royalties who is a resident of the other Contracting State to be the beneficial owner for the purposes of Articles 10, 11, and 12 if the recipient is the person to which the income is attributable for tax purposes under the laws of the first-mentioned State.'
944. *See also Lang*, Personengesellschaften im DBA-Recht, SWI 2000, 60 (63); according to *Meindl-Ringler*, Beneficial Ownership in International Tax Law (2016) 336 and 371 and *Jiménez* in *Lang/Pistone/Schuch/Staringer/Storck* 205 this task could nonetheless be manageable as the relevant legal situation could be communicated via an exchange of information; in this context, it should be mentioned that Art. 1(2) that was introduced into the OECD MC 2017 requires the source state to consider the domestic law of the residence state; for more details, *see Lang*, Einkünftezurechnung im Lichte des Entwurfs zu Art 1 Abs 2 OECD-MA, SWI 2015, 153 (161f); on the relationship between Art. 1(2) OECD MC 2017 and the Beneficial Ownership Test, *see* FN 949.
945. *Lang*, The Application of the OECD Model Tax Convention to Partnerships: a critical analysis of the report prepared by the OECD Committee on Fiscal Affairs (2000) 38.
946. *See* sec. 4.2.1.1.
947. For similar considerations, even though in a slightly different context (arguing against an interpretation of beneficial ownership according to domestic law), *see Canete/Staringer*,

Therefore, the considerations of the Partnership Report should be disregarded for the interpretation of the Beneficial Ownership Test.[948] This also seems to be the position of the OECD itself since, in subsequent amendments to the Commentary on the Beneficial Ownership Test, a reference to the Partnership Report was never made[949] whereas, for example, the Conduit Companies Report is referenced.[950] Consistently, the practice in individual states does not follow this approach.[951]

4.2.6 2003: Update of the Commentary

4.2.6.1 Background

Already in the Conduit Companies Report, it was stated that the 'provisions mentioned in paragraph 14 above [note: inter alia the Beneficial Ownership Test] and/or the Commentaries should be revised in order to solve any existing difficulties and doubts'.[952] However, it was only in 2003 that the considerations made in the Conduit

Missbrauchserfassung im DBA-Recht durch Anwendung von Beneficial-ownership-Konzepten, in *Lang/Schuch/Staringer* (Eds), Die Grenzen der Gestaltungsmöglichkeiten im internationalen Steuerrecht (2009) 169 (176); *see also Vann* in *Lang/Pistone/Schuch/Staringer/Storck* 302: 'To make beneficial ownership correlate with attribution may indeed defeat the purpose of the United Kingdom in introducing the term in the first place if it was in fact because the United Kingdom attributed income to a trustee by its mere receipt.'

948. *See also* the more general considerations (i.e., not limited to the Beneficial Ownership Test) with regard to the Partnership Report in *Lang*, The Application of the OECD Model Tax Convention to Partnerships: a critical analysis of the report prepared by the OECD Committee on Fiscal Affairs (2000) 53 according to whom nothing in the OECD MC 'indicates that it would be of relevance for the entitlement to treaty benefits how the partnership is treated in the State of residence and if the partner is liable to tax "on the income". Therefore, it is not convincing to interpret future tax treaties as suggested by the Commentary [note: as a result of the Partnership Report, the OECD Commentary was changed, *see OECD*, The Application of the OECD Model Tax Convention to Partnerships (1999) 51ff]'.

949. *See also Meindl-Ringler*, Beneficial Ownership in International Tax Law (2016) 56; In this regard, *see also* Art. 1 Mn 13 OECD Commentary 2017: 'Whilst the paragraph [note: Art. 1 (2) OECD MC 2017 on fiscally transparent entities] ensures that the various allocative rules of the Convention are applied to the extent that income of fiscally transparent entities is treated, under domestic law, as income of a resident of a Contracting State, *the paragraph does not prejudge the issue of whether the recipient is the beneficial owner of the relevant income*. Where, for example, a fiscally transparent partnership receives dividends as an agent or nominee for a person who is not a partner, *the fact that the dividend may be considered as income of a resident of a Contracting State under the domestic law of that State will not preclude the State of source from considering that neither the partnership nor the partners are the beneficial owners of the dividend*' (emphasis added); on the relationship between Art. 1(2) OECD MC 2017 and the beneficial ownership test, *see Nikolakakis/Austry/Avery Jones/Baker/Blessing/Danon/Goradia /Hattingh/Inoue/Lüdicke/Maisto/Miyatake/Raad/Vann/Wiman*, Some Reflections on the Proposed Revisions to the OECD Model and Commentaries, and on the Multilateral Instrument, with Respect to Fiscally Transparent Entities – Part 1, BIT 2017, 475 (496ff).

950. *See* sec. 4.2.6.2.

951. *See Lang*, General Report, in *IFA* (Ed.), Cahiers de droit fiscal international, Vol. 89a Double non-taxation (2004) 73 (94f).

952. *OECD*, Double Taxation Conventions and the Use of Conduit Companies (1986) Mn 16.

Companies Report with regard to the Beneficial Ownership Test were incorporated into the OECD Commentary.[953]

4.2.6.2 Content

The former Mn 4 of the Commentary on Article 12 was replaced with the following paragraphs:[954]

> 4. The requirement of beneficial ownership was introduced in paragraph 1 of Article 12 *to clarify how the Article applies in relation to payments made to intermediaries*. It makes plain that the *State of source is not obliged to give up taxing rights over royalty income merely because that income was immediately received by a resident of a State with which the State of source had concluded a convention*. The term 'beneficial owner' *is not used in a narrow technical sense, rather, it should be understood in its context and in light of the object and purposes of the Convention*, including avoiding double taxation and the prevention of fiscal evasion and avoidance.
>
> 4.1 Relief or exemption in respect of an item of income is granted by the State of source to a resident of the other Contracting State to avoid in whole or in part the double taxation that would otherwise arise from the concurrent taxation of that income by the State of residence. Where an item of income is received by a resident of a Contracting State acting in the *capacity of agent or nominee* it would be inconsistent with the object and purpose of the Convention for the State of source to grant relief or exemption merely on account of the status of the immediate recipient of the income as a resident of the other Contracting State. The immediate recipient of the income in this situation qualifies as a resident but *no potential double taxation arises as a consequence of that status since the recipient is not treated as the owner of the income for tax purposes in the State of residence*. It would be *equally inconsistent with the object and purpose of the Convention for the State of source to grant relief or exemption where a resident of a Contracting State, otherwise than through an agency or nominee relationship, simply acts as a conduit for another person who in fact receives the benefit of the income concerned*. For these reasons, the report from the Committee on Fiscal Affairs entitled 'Double Taxation Conventions and the Use of Conduit Companies' concludes that a *conduit company cannot normally be regarded as the beneficial owner if, though the formal owner, it has, as a practical matter, very narrow powers* which render it, *in relation to the income concerned*, a mere fiduciary or administrator acting on account of the interested parties.
>
> 4.2 Subject to other conditions imposed by the Article, the limitation of tax in the State of source remains available when an intermediary, such as an agent or nominee, is interposed between the beneficiary and the payer, in those cases where the beneficial owner is a resident of the other Contracting State (the text of the Model was amended in 1995 to clarify this point, which has been the consistent position of all Member countries). States which wish to make this more explicit are free to do so during bilateral negotiations (emphasis added).

953. *See OECD*, 2002 Reports Related to the OECD Model Tax Convention (2003) 3 and 26ff.
954. *OECD*, 2002 Reports Related to the OECD Model Tax Convention (2003) 28f.

4.2.6.3 *Analysis: Normative Meaning Added with the 2003 Commentary*

As it is rightly pointed out in Article 12 Mn 4 OECD MC 2003, the Beneficial Ownership Test was originally introduced as a clarification.[955] However, the update goes on by stating that beneficial ownership should not be understood in a narrow technical sense but in its context and in light of the object and purposes of the convention. This statement indicates that the term should be interpreted autonomously.[956] Yet, an autonomous interpretation suggests that the beneficial ownership concept itself has a normative meaning and is not merely clarifying. Otherwise, there would be no need to interpret it in any specific way.

The 2003 Commentary even implicitly acknowledges this contradiction when it elaborates on the beneficial ownership status of agents and nominees, on the one hand, and conduit companies on the other hand:[957] Relief from withholding taxes to agents and nominees is denied because the residence state does not attribute income to them,[958] and hence there is no double taxation to avoid. However, there is no reason why the qualification in the source state should be different, that is, why the source state would attribute income to an agent or nominee under its domestic law. Therefore, 'even without a beneficial owner requirement, such agent and nominee would not be able to enjoy treaty benefits'.[959] Conduit companies, on the other hand, are excluded as beneficial owners since they act for another person who, in fact, receives the benefit of the income concerned. Thus, this makes plain that conduit companies are attributed income in the first place,[960] albeit they may not themselves benefit from it eventually (e.g., because they have to forward the received income to somebody else). That is, compared to the merely clarifying exclusion of agents and nominees under the 1977 Commentary, the 2003 Commentary also excludes persons from relief of withholding taxes that would normally be entitled to it.[961]

Therefore, the 2003 Commentary added a normative meaning to the Beneficial Ownership Test that it did not initially have. As this is a new interpretation of the term,[962] it can only have legal relevance for tax treaties that are concluded after the 2003 Commentary update.[963]

955. *See* sec. 4.2.1.3.
956. *De Broe*, International Tax Planning and Prevention of Abuse (2008) 671; *Ng* in *Ecker/Ressler* 537.
957. For similar considerations, *see Vann* in *Lang/Pistone/Schuch/Staringer/Storck* 300.
958. *See* already FN 856.
959. *Yoshimura*, Tax Analysts 2013, 762; *see also Jain*, Effectiveness of the Beneficial Ownership Test in Conduit Company Cases (2013) 210.
960. Otherwise, there would also be a note that there is no risk of double taxation.
961. *See* already the considerations in sec. 4.2.2.3.
962. *See also du Toit*, BIT 2010, 505; different opinion *Gooijer*, Beneficial Owner: Judicial Variety in Interpretation Counteracted by the 2012 OECD Proposals?, Intertax 2014, 204 (209).
963. *See also Gutmann* in *Lang/Pistone/Schuch/Staringer/Storck* 341: '[I]t should be possible for a taxpayer whose quality of beneficial owner is disputed before a court of an OECD country which applies a static interpretation theory of tax treaties (i.e. which believes that a tax treaty should be interpreted by referring to the state of the OECD Model and commentaries at the time when the tax treaty was signed) to argue that the beneficial ownership concept should be

Nonetheless, it is far from clear what the precise normative meaning is that the 2003 Commentary ascribes to beneficial ownership (e.g., how is a conduit company defined;[964] when is the criterion of very narrow powers fulfilled[965]).[966] Indeed, it is hard to pinpoint an exact meaning when not even the OECD seems to be sure about it:[967]

> While it is obvious that the use of the concept excludes bare legal ownership as the criterion for determining availability of treaty benefits *it is less apparent what is intended to be the salient connection with a stream of income in a case where different interests in the income are held by diverse hands who might each be considered, as a matter of general law, to possess some attributes of ownership* (emphasis added).

In the end, however, this - intended?[968] - vagueness invited tax authorities to apply the Beneficial Ownership Test more or less discretionary whenever they saw the need to do so.[969]

4.2.7 2010: CIV Report

4.2.7.1 Background

In 2009, the OECD published a public discussion draft[970] on the granting of treaty benefits with respect to the income of collective investment vehicles (CIVs).[971] In this

interpreted in a restrictive manner, at least until the 2003 change of the Commentary'; on the relevance of the OECD Commentary for the interpretation of DTCs, *see* already FN 821.

964. Also critical in this regard *Lang* in *IFA* 95.
965. In this context, *see Collier*, Clarity, Opacity and Beneficial Ownership, BTR 2011, 684 (690 FN 19) according to whom the 2003 update of the Commentary did not make profound changes to the meaning of beneficial ownership as can be seen from the fact that reference is made not only to 'narrow powers' but also to 'very narrow powers'.
966. *See* already with regard to the Conduit Companies Report, *van Weeghel*, The Improper Use of Tax Treaties: With Particular Reference to the Netherlands and the United States (1998) 73: 'The conclusion is inescapable that the Commentary on the OECD Model Convention '92 and the 1987 report "Double Tax Conventions and the Use of Conduit Companies" do not give clear guidance at all as to the meaning of the term "beneficial owner" where a conduit company is concerned [...] Other than the reference to "very narrow powers", the report does not give any clue.'
967. *OECD*, Restricting the Entitlement to Treaty Benefits (2002) Mn 23; *see also Jiménez*, The 2003 Revision of the OECD Commentaries on the Improper Use of Tax Treaties: A Case for the Declining Effect of the OECD Commentaries?, BIT 2004, 17 (21).
968. *OECD*, Restricting the Entitlement to Treaty Benefits (2002) Mn 22: 'It was noted that any addition to the Commentary had to be drafted in a neutral way so as to avoid inadvertent limitation of the concept.'
969. *See also Vann* in *Lang/Pistone/Schuch/Staringer/Storck* 301.
970. *OECD*, The Granting of Treaty Benefits with Respect to the Income of Collective Investment Vehicles: Public Discussion Draft (2009); as stated on p. 2, 'the Report is a modified version of the Report "Granting of Treaty Benefits with respect to the Income of Collective Investment Vehicles" of the Informal Consultative Group on the Taxation of Collective Investment Vehicles and Procedures for Tax Relief for Cross-Border Investors (ICG) which was released on 12 January 2009'.
971. 'For purposes of this Report, the term "CIV" is limited to funds that are widely-held, hold a diversified portfolio of securities and are subject to investor-protection regulation in the country in which they are established', *see OECD*, The Granting of Treaty Benefits with Respect

context, one of the key questions addressed was whether a CIV can be the beneficial owner of the income it receives.[972] In 2010, the OECD released its final report[973] (CIV Report) and, as a result thereof, the OECD Commentary was updated in the same year.[974]

4.2.7.2 *Content*

The following remarks concerning a CIV's qualification as beneficial owner were added to the OECD Commentary 2010:[975]

> Some countries have questioned whether a CIV, even if it is a 'person' and a 'resident', can qualify as the beneficial owner of the income it receives. Because a 'CIV' [...] must be widely-held, hold a diversified portfolio of securities and be subject to investor-protection regulation in the country in which it is established, such a CIV, or its managers, *often perform significant functions with respect to the investment and management of the assets of the CIV*. Moreover, the position of an investor in a CIV differs substantially, as a legal and economic matter, from the position of an investor who owns the underlying assets, so that it would not be appropriate to treat the investor in such a CIV as the beneficial owner of the income received by the CIV. Accordingly, a vehicle that meets the definition of a widely-held CIV will also be treated as the beneficial owner of the dividends and interest that it receives, *so long as the managers of the CIV have discretionary powers to manage the assets generating such income* (unless an individual who is a resident of that State who would have received the income in the same circumstances would not have been considered to be the beneficial owner thereof) (emphasis added).

4.2.7.3 *Analysis: Relevance of the Functions Performed*

As CIVs are often required by law to distribute all or part of the income (typically dividends and interest)[976] they receive to their investors, they would usually be considered as conduits.[977] As a result, they would not qualify as beneficial owners and,

---

to the Income of Collective Investment Vehicles: Public Discussion Draft (2009) Mn 4; for more details, *see Fibbe*, Changes to the OECD Commentary on Collective Investment Vehicles Proposed by the OECD Committee on Fiscal Affairs, BIT 2010, 138 (139f).

972. *OECD*, The Granting of Treaty Benefits with Respect to the Income of Collective Investment Vehicles: Public Discussion Draft (2009) Mn 31ff.
973. *OECD*, The Granting of Treaty Benefits with Respect to the Income of Collective Investment Vehicles (2010) Mn 31ff.
974. *OECD*, The 2010 Update to the Model Tax Convention (2010) 5f.
975. Art. 1 Mn 6.14 OECD Commentary 2010; *see also* Art. 1 Mn 28 OECD Commentary 2017.
976. *OECD*, The Granting of Treaty Benefits with Respect to the Income of Collective Investment Vehicles (2010) Mn 41.
977. Both under the 2003 Commentary since they act as a conduit for another person who, in fact, receives the benefit of the income concerned (*see* sec. 4.2.6.2) and under the 2014 Commentary since the recipient's right to use and enjoy the income is constrained by a legal obligation to pass on the payment received to another person (*see* sec. 4.2.8.2 [hence typical distribution obligations of CIVs are explicitly exempt in Mn 4.3]); *see also Vann* in *Lang/Pistone/Schuch /Staringer/Storck* 303.

therefore, they could not claim relief from withholding taxes in the source state.[978] At the same time, it would be highly burdensome if CIV investors - as beneficial owners of the income - had to claim treaty benefits individually.[979] Furthermore, if neither a CIV nor its investors could effectively claim treaty benefits, '[i]nvestors who invest through a CIV would be put in a worse position than if they had invested directly'.[980]

For these reasons, the desired policy objective is to grant relief from withholding taxes at the level of the CIV.[981] Consequently, the OECD 'has to twist the beneficial owner concept to make it work appropriately in that context'.[982]

The way the OECD does that is by explaining that the position of an investor who owns the underlying asset is not comparable to the position of an investor in a CIV as, in the latter case, the investor has no right to the underlying asset itself.[983] Instead, the managers of a CIV manage the assets on behalf of the CIV investors, and the CIV investors only have a right to receive an amount equal to the value of their allocable share of the assets. Therefore, 'income from a particular asset generally cannot be traced to a particular investor'.[984] While it can be true that the managers of a CIV 'have practical or legal obligations to distribute the CIV's income in order to qualify for preferential treatment, this obligation does not constrain their ability to vary investments'.[985] For these reasons, a CIV 'should be treated as the beneficial owner of the income it receives, so long as the managers of the CIV have discretionary powers to manage the assets on behalf of the holders of interests in the CIV'.[986]

The OECD relied on the position of *Vogel*[987] to justify the beneficial ownership status of a CIV:[988]

> The 'substance' of the right to receive certain yields has a **dual aspect**. The first is the right to decide whether or not a yield should be realized - i.e., whether the

978. This opinion was apparently also held by different countries, *see OECD*, The Granting of Treaty Benefits with Respect to the Income of Collective Investment Vehicles (2010) Mn 31; *OECD*, Report of the Informal Consultative Group on the Taxation of Collective Investment Vehicles and Procedures for Tax Relief for Cross-Border Investors on the Granting of Treaty Benefits with respect to the Income of Collective Investment Vehicles (2009) Annex 1 Mn 4.
979. *See also OECD*, The Granting of Treaty Benefits with Respect to the Income of Collective Investment Vehicles (2010) Mn 37.
980. *OECD*, The Granting of Treaty Benefits with Respect to the Income of Collective Investment Vehicles (2010) Mn 36.
981. *See also Stevens*, The 2010 CIV-Report: A Comparison with the 1999 Partnership Report, in *Weber/van Weeghel* (Eds), The 2010 OECD Updates: Model Tax Convention and Transfer Pricing Guidelines - A Critical Review (2011) 101 (107).
982. *Vann* in *Lang/Pistone/Schuch/Staringer/Storck* 302.
983. For more details, *see OECD*, The Granting of Treaty Benefits with Respect to the Income of Collective Investment Vehicles (2010) Mn 32ff.
984. *OECD*, The Granting of Treaty Benefits with Respect to the Income of Collective Investment Vehicles (2010) Mn 34.
985. *OECD*, The Granting of Treaty Benefits with Respect to the Income of Collective Investment Vehicles (2010) Mn 33.
986. *OECD*, The Granting of Treaty Benefits with Respect to the Income of Collective Investment Vehicles (2010) Mn 35.
987. *Vogel*, Klaus Vogel on Double Taxation Conventions^3 (1997) Preface to Arts 10-12 Mn 9.
988. *OECD*, Report of the Informal Consultative Group on the Taxation of Collective Investment Vehicles and Procedures for Tax Relief for Cross-Border Investors on the Granting of Treaty Benefits with respect to the Income of Collective Investment Vehicles (2009) Annex 1 Mn 3.

> capital or other assets should be used or made available for use – the second is the right to dispose of the yield. Ownership is merely formal, if the owner is fettered in regard to **both** aspects either in law or in fact. On the other hand, recourse to the treaty is justified – i.e., is not improper – if he who is entitled under private law is free to wield at least **one** of the powers referred to. **Hence, the 'beneficial owner' is he who is free to decide (1) whether or not the capital or other assets should be used or made available for use by others or (2) on how the yields therefrom should be used or (3) both** (emphasis in original).

Since, under this approach, an obligation to forward income alone is not sufficient for disregarding beneficial ownership (second requirement), a CIV is treated as beneficial owner as long as its managers have the ability to vary the CIV's investments (first requirement).[989]

The OECD's conclusions on the beneficial ownership status of CIVs are peculiar in two ways. First, it focuses on assets (e.g., shares) and not on income (e.g., dividends).[990] Second – by contrast to the approach later taken in the 2014 update of the Commentary –[991] it focuses on the investment side (i.e., can the managers of a CIV freely decide on how to invest) and not the distribution side (i.e., is the CIV under an obligation to distribute received income to investors).[992] That is, it 'turns on the functions that the CIV performs'.[993] However, as stated by *Vann*, if this were a 'general test for beneficial ownership, then many agents will not fail the test such as a stockbroking firm running a discretionary account for a client and registering the securities in the name of the firm'.[994]

The 2009 discussion draft on the granting of treaty benefits with respect to the income of CIVs noted that '[a]lthough the Report includes an analysis by WP1 of the application of the "beneficial owner" requirement to the specific case of CIVs, the conclusions with respect to CIVs should not be seen as pre-judging WP1's continuing

989. *OECD*, Report of the Informal Consultative Group on the Taxation of Collective Investment Vehicles and Procedures for Tax Relief for Cross-Border Investors on the Granting of Treaty Benefits with respect to the Income of Collective Investment Vehicles (2009) Annex 1 Mn 3f.
990. *See also Collier*, BTR 2011, 691; different opinion apparently *Tischbirek* in *Vogel/Lehner*, Doppelbesteuerungsabkommen[6] (2015) Vor Art. 10-12 Mn 22.
991. *See* sec. 4.2.8.
992. *See also Avery Jones/Vann/Wheeler*, Response to the 2011 OECD Discussion Draft 'Clarification of the Meaning of "Beneficial Owner" in the OECD Model Tax Convention' (2011) 2 (available at http://www.oecd.org/tax/treaties/48420432.pdf); *Rust* in *Reimer/Rust*, Klaus Vogel on Double Taxation Conventions[4] (2015) Art. 1 FN 75; *Brown*, Fifty Years of Tax Uncertainty: The Problem of International Neutrality for Collective Investment Vehicles, in *Vermeulen* (Ed.), The Tax Treatment of CIVs and REITs (2014) 19 (40); however, *see also Chew*, The Application of Tax Treaties to Collective Investment Vehicles: Beneficial Owner Requirement Explained?, DFI 2015, 2.11 according to whom 'this is too fine a line to draw. After all, a CIV's manager habitually re-invests, which effectively equates the power to decide on investments with the power to deal with the income'.
993. *OECD*, Report of the Informal Consultative Group on the Taxation of Collective Investment Vehicles and Procedures for Tax Relief for Cross-Border Investors on the Granting of Treaty Benefits with respect to the Income of Collective Investment Vehicles (2009) Annex 1 Mn 2; *see also Da Silva*, Granting Tax Treaty Benefits to Collective Investment Vehicles: A Review of the OECD Report and the 2010 Amendments to the Model Tax Convention, Intertax 2011, 195 (201).
994. *Vann* in *Lang/Pistone/Schuch/Staringer/Storck* 303f.

work on the "beneficial owner" requirement more generally'.[995] Therefore, the relevance of the 2010 amendment of the Commentary for interpreting the Beneficial Ownership Test in a non-CIV context is doubtful.[996] However, it would have been advisable if the OECD had considered its conclusions when updating the Commentary in 2014 instead of introducing an additional approach to the concept yet again.

4.2.8 2014: Update of the Commentary – Forwarding Approach

4.2.8.1 Background

Following the 2003 update of the OECD Commentary, a significant increase in court cases on the issue of beneficial ownership could be observed around the world.[997] Often, however, these cases deviate from each other and, in some respects, the differences are substantial.[998]

In an attempt to reach a uniform interpretation of the term, the OECD issued a discussion draft on the 'Clarification of the Meaning of "Beneficial Owner" in the OECD Model Tax Convention'[999] in 2011. The discussion draft received numerous comments[1000] and prompted the OECD to issue a revised discussion draft in 2012.[1001] In 2014, the OECD incorporated the results of this revision project into its Commentary.[1002]

---

995. *OECD*, The Granting of Treaty Benefits with Respect to the Income of Collective Investment Vehicles: Public Discussion Draft (2009) 5; *see also OECD*, Report of the Informal Consultative Group on the Taxation of Collective Investment Vehicles and Procedures for Tax Relief for Cross-Border Investors on the Granting of Treaty Benefits with respect to the Income of Collective Investment Vehicles (2009) Annex 1 Mn 1: '[T]he ICG did not consider some of the more general questions regarding the meaning of the term "beneficial owner", but limited itself to the question of whether a CIV that meets the requirements that it be a "person" and a "resident" should be treated as the beneficial owner of the income it receives.'
996. *See also Collier*, BTR 2011, 692.
997. *See Gooijer*, Intertax 2014, 209ff.
998. For an overview of the case law, *see Verdoner/Offermanns/Huibregtse*, A Cross-Country Perspective on Beneficial Ownership – Part 1, ET 2010, 419 (419ff); *Verdoner/Offermanns /Huibregtse*, A Cross-Country Perspective on Beneficial Ownership – Part 2, ET 2010 465 (465ff).
999. *See OECD*, Clarification of the meaning of 'Beneficial Owner' in the OECD Model Tax Convention – Discussion Draft (2011); it seems that the OECD relied partially on the language of some of the court decisions on beneficial ownership in the discussion draft, *see Duff*, Beneficial Ownership: Recent Trends, in *Lang/Pistone/Schuch/Staringer/Storck* (Eds), Beneficial Ownership: Recent Trends (2013) 1 (5f).
1000. For the comments received on the discussion draft, *see* http://www.oecd.org/tax/treaties/publiccommentsreceivedonthediscussiondraftonthemeaningofbeneficialownerintheoecdmodeltaxconvention.htm.
1001. *OECD*, OECD Model Tax Convention: Revised proposals concerning the meaning of 'beneficial owner' in Articles 10, 11 and 12 (2012); for the comments received on the revised discussion draft, *see* http://www.oecd.org/tax/publiccommentsreceivedontherevisedproposalsconcerningthemeaningofbeneficialownerinarticles1011and12oftheoecdmodeltaxconvention.htm.
1002. *See OECD*, 2014 Update to the OECD Model Tax Convention (2014) Mn 34, 41 and 48; *see also Barret*, The Changes Introduced by the 2014 Update to the OECD Model Tax Convention, BIT 2014, 529 (531f); *Vallada*, Beneficial Ownership under Articles 10, 11 and 12 of the 2014 OECD Model Convention, in *Lang/Pistone/Rust/Staringer/Storck/Schuch* (Eds), The OECD-Model-Convention and its Update 2014 (2015) 25 (35ff).

4.2.8.2 Content

The former Mn 4 to 4.2 of the Commentary on Article 12 were replaced by the following:[1003]

> 4. The requirement of beneficial ownership was introduced in paragraph 1 of Article 12 to clarify how the Article applies in relation to payments made to intermediaries. It makes plain that the State of source is not obliged to give up taxing rights over royalty income merely because that income was paid directly to a resident of a State with which the State of source had concluded a convention. The term 'beneficial owner' is therefore not used in a narrow technical sense (*such as the meaning that it has under the trust law of many common law countries* [1]), rather, it should be understood in its context and in light of the object and purposes of the Convention, including avoiding double taxation and the prevention of fiscal evasion and avoidance.
>
> 4.1 Relief or exemption in respect of an item of income is granted by the State of source to a resident of the other Contracting State to avoid in whole or in part the double taxation that would otherwise arise from the concurrent taxation of that income by the State of residence. Where an item of income is paid to a resident of a Contracting State acting in the capacity of agent or nominee it would be inconsistent with the object and purpose of the Convention for the State of source to grant relief or exemption merely on account of the status of the direct recipient of the income as a resident of the other Contracting State. The direct recipient of the income in this situation qualifies as a resident but no potential double taxation arises as a consequence of that status since the recipient is not treated as the owner of the income for tax purposes in the State of residence.
>
> 4.2 It would be equally inconsistent with the object and purpose of the Convention for the State of source to grant relief or exemption where a resident of a Contracting State, otherwise than through an agency or nominee relationship, simply acts as a conduit for another person who in fact receives the benefit of the income concerned. For these reasons, the report from the Committee on Fiscal Affairs entitled 'Double Taxation Conventions and the Use of Conduit Companies' [2] concludes that a conduit company cannot normally be regarded as the beneficial owner if, though the formal owner, it has, as a practical matter, very narrow powers which render it, in relation to the income concerned, a mere fiduciary or administrator acting on account of the interested parties.
>
> 4.3 In these various examples (agent, nominee, conduit company acting as a fiduciary or administrator), *the direct recipient of the royalties is not the 'beneficial owner' because that recipient's right to use and enjoy the royalties is constrained by a contractual or legal obligation to pass on the payment received to another person. Such an obligation will normally derive from relevant legal documents but may also be found to exist on the basis of facts and circumstances showing that, in substance, the recipient clearly does not have the right to use and enjoy the royalties unconstrained by a contractual or legal obligation to pass on the payment received to another person. This type of obligation would not include contractual or legal obligations that are not dependent on the receipt of the payment by the direct recipient such as an obligation that is not dependent on the receipt of the payment and which the direct recipient has as*

1003. Please note that the related footnotes are not reproduced here for the sake of clarity.

a debtor or as a party to financial transactions, or typical distribution obligations of pension schemes and of collective investment vehicles entitled to treaty benefits under the principles of paragraphs 6.8 to 6.34 of the Commentary on Article 1. Where the recipient of royalties does have the right to use and enjoy the royalties unconstrained by a contractual or legal obligation to pass on the payment received to another person, the recipient is the 'beneficial owner' of these royalties. *It should also be noted that Article 12 refers to the beneficial owner of royalties as opposed to the owner of the right or property in respect of which the royalties are paid, which may be different in some cases.*

4.4 The fact that the recipient of royalties is considered to be the beneficial owner of these royalties does not mean, however, that the provisions of paragraph 1 must automatically be applied. The benefit of these provisions should not be granted in cases of abuse *[...]*. As explained in the section on 'Improper use of the Convention' in the Commentary on Article 1, there are many ways of addressing conduit company and, more generally, treaty shopping situations. These include specific anti-abuse provisions in treaties, general anti-abuse rules and substance-over-form or economic substance approaches. *Whilst the concept of 'beneficial owner' deals with some forms of tax avoidance (i.e. those involving the interposition of a recipient who is obliged to pass on the royalties to someone else), it does not deal with other cases of treaty shopping and must not, therefore, be considered as restricting in any way the application of other approaches to addressing such cases.*

4.5 The above explanations concerning the meaning of 'beneficial owner' make it clear that *the meaning given to this term in the context of the Article must be distinguished from the different meaning that has been given to that term in the context of other instruments* [3] *that concern the determination of the persons (typically the individuals) that exercise ultimate control over entities or assets*. That different meaning of 'beneficial owner' cannot be applied in the context of the Convention. Indeed, that meaning, which refers to natural persons (i.e. individuals), cannot be reconciled with the express wording of subparagraph 2 a) of Article 10, which refers to the situation where a company is the beneficial owner of a dividend. The term 'beneficial owner' was intended to address difficulties arising from the use of the words 'paid to', which are found in paragraph 1 of Articles 10 and 11 and were similarly used in paragraph 1 of Article 12 of the 1977 Model Double Taxation Convention, in relation to dividends, interest and royalties rather than difficulties related to the ownership of the shares, debt-claims, property or rights with respect these dividends, interest or royalties are paid. *For that reason, it would be inappropriate, in the context of these Articles, to consider a meaning developed in order to refer to the individuals who exercise 'ultimate effective control over a legal person or arrangement'.*

4.6 Subject to other conditions imposed by the Article, the exemption from taxation in the State of source remains available when an intermediary, such as an agent or nominee located in a Contracting State *or in a third State,*[1004] is interposed between the beneficiary and the payer, in those cases where the beneficial owner is a resident of the other Contracting State (the text of the Model was amended in 1997 to clarify this point, which has been the consistent position of all Member countries) (emphasis added).

1004. On this issue, *see* already sec. 4.2.3.3.

4.2.8.3 *Analysis: Irrelevance of Substance under the Beneficial Ownership Test*

The update reiterates that beneficial ownership has to be interpreted autonomously.[1005] Furthermore, it makes clear that the meaning of beneficial ownership in tax treaty law must not be confused with the meaning it has in the trust law of many common law countries.[1006] Likewise, the meaning of beneficial ownership for anti-money laundering purposes is irrelevant for the tax treaty concept.[1007]

At the same time, the update provides that - to be the beneficial owner - a recipient of royalties must 'have the right to use and enjoy the royalties unconstrained by a contractual or legal obligation to pass on the payment received to another person' (Forwarding Approach).[1008] However, obligations that are not dependent on the receipt of the payment are not harmful for the qualification as beneficial owner.[1009]

Interestingly, already prior to this addition to the Commentary, various courts had applied this approach. However, how such a harmful obligation to forward a payment can arise was a question of much debate. In general, there are two different lines of reasoning:[1010] First, the legal approach that looks at whether there is a legal obligation to forward a received payment. Second, the broader economic approach where also a factual obligation to forward the income is harmful to beneficial ownership.

For example, in the Canadian *Prévost* case,[1011] the court followed the legal approach. It found that a Netherlands holding company that had no employees and no assets other than the shares of a Canadian subsidiary (Prévost) could still be regarded as the beneficial owner of received dividends since there was 'no predetermined or automatic flow' of these dividends to its shareholders (i.e., it was under no legal

1005. This is even more clear when looking at Art. 10 Mn 12.1 OECD Commentary 2014 which states that 'since the term "beneficial owner" was added to address potential difficulties arising from the use of the words "paid to ... a resident" in paragraph 1, it was intended to be interpreted in this context and *not to refer to any technical meaning that it could have had under the domestic law of a specific country* (in fact, when it was added to the paragraph, the term did not have a precise meaning in the law of many countries)' (emphasis added); *see also* Art. 11 Mn 9.1 OECD Commentary 2014; as stated in sec. 4.2.6.3, this seems to have been already the opinion expressed in the 2003 Commentary.

1006. This was the opinion held by *du Toit*, Beneficial Ownership of Royalties in Bilateral Tax Treaties (1999) 178f and 243; already criticized before the 2014 update by *De Broe*, International Tax Planning and Prevention of Abuse (2008) 679f.

1007. For more details, *see* FN 3 in Art. 12 Mn 4.5 OECD MC 2014; *see also Vann* in *Lang /Pistone/Schuch/Staringer/Storck* 300 according to whom this was the policy asserted in relation to conduit companies in the 2003 Commentary.

1008. *See also Meindl-Ringler*, Beneficial Ownership in International Tax Law (2016) 325ff.

1009. For example, typical distribution obligations of CIVs, *see* Art. 12 Mn 4.3 OECD Commentary 2014; *see also* FN 977.

1010. *See also Wardzynski*, Intertax 2015, 179ff.

1011. Tax Court of Canada, 22. 4. 2008, 2008 TCC 231, Prévost Car Inc. v. Her Majesty the Queen; for more details of the case, *see Arnold*, The Concept of Beneficial Ownership under Canadian Tax Treaties, in *Lang/Pistone/Schuch/Staringer/Storck* (Eds), Beneficial Ownership: Recent Trends (2013) 39 (40ff).

obligation to forward the payment).[1012] Even though a shareholders' agreement between the two shareholders of the Netherlands holding company stipulated that 80 % of the profits of the Netherlands holding company must be distributed, this did not impose any legal obligation on the Netherlands holding company as it was not a party to this agreement.[1013]

By contrast, in the British *Indofood* case,[1014] it is said that the economic approach was applied.[1015] The case revolved around the hypothetical interposition of a subsidiary in the Netherlands between a Mauritian subsidiary and its Indonesian parent company to secure a lower withholding tax rate on interest payments.[1016] The court concluded that 'the meaning to be given to the phrase "beneficial owner" is plainly not to be limited by so technical and legal an approach'.[1017] Rather, '[r]egard is to be had to the substance of the matter'.[1018] The court found that the Netherlands subsidiary would not be the beneficial owner since, in 'practical terms', it would be bound to forward the interest it received and it would therefore be impossible to conceive of any circumstances in which it could derive any benefit from the received interest other than to fund its liability.[1019]

The 2014 update of the Commentary may potentially leave leeway for both the legal and the economic approach.[1020] This is because it is stated that a harmful obligation 'will normally derive from relevant legal documents but may also be found to *exist on the basis of facts and circumstances* showing that, *in substance, the recipient clearly does not have the right to use and enjoy the royalties* unconstrained by a contractual or legal obligation to pass on the payment received to another person' (emphasis added).[1021]

In this context, the following is stated by the OECD in the update document:[1022]

> As regards the sentence referring to obligations that 'may also be found to exist on the basis of facts and circumstances', the Working Party concluded that the sentence was appropriate because *contracts and formal legal obligations may not*

1012. Tax Court of Canada, 22. 4. 2008, 2008 TCC 231, Prévost Car Inc. v. Her Majesty the Queen, Mn 102.
1013. Tax Court of Canada, 22. 4. 2008, 2008 TCC 231, Prévost Car Inc. v. Her Majesty the Queen, Mn 104.
1014. England and Wales Court of Appeal, 2. 3. 2006, A3/2005/2497, Indofood International Finance Ltd. v. JPMorgan Chase Bank NA, London Branch.
1015. *Wardzynski*, Intertax 2015, 185.
1016. For more details of the case, *see Baker*, United Kingdom: Indofood International Finance Ltd v. JP Morgan Chase Bank NA, in *Lang/Pistone/Schuch/Staringer/Storck* (Eds), Beneficial Ownership: Recent Trends (2013) 27 (28ff).
1017. England and Wales Court of Appeal, 2. 3. 2006, A3/2005/2497, Indofood International Finance Ltd. v. JPMorgan Chase Bank NA, London Branch, Mn 44.
1018. England and Wales Court of Appeal, 2. 3. 2006, A3/2005/2497, Indofood International Finance Ltd. v. JPMorgan Chase Bank NA, London Branch, Mn 44.
1019. England and Wales Court of Appeal, 2. 3. 2006, A3/2005/2497, Indofood International Finance Ltd. v. JPMorgan Chase Bank NA, London Branch, Mn 44.
1020. *See also Blum*, International Tax Report 11/2017, 9; *Arnold*, An Introduction to the 2014 Update to the OECD Model, BIT 2014, 526 (527f); *Wardzynski*, Intertax 2015, 189.
1021. Art. 12 Mn 4.3 OECD Commentary 2014; *see also* Art. 10 Mn 12.4 and Art. 11 Mn 10.2 OECD Commentary 2014.
1022. *See* OECD, 2014 Update to the OECD Model Tax Convention (2014) 2.

always reflect reality and this was therefore an area where it was appropriate to look at facts and circumstance (emphasis added).

Indeed, especially in related party transactions, it may occur that contractual arrangements differ from the actual conduct of the parties.[1023] However, as rightly pointed out by some authors,[1024] an obligation to forward a payment can never be 'factual' but must always be based on legal grounds. Only if legal documents are absent or incomplete can the facts and circumstances help to determine that there is a legal obligation to forward the payment. However, 'it is not possible to prove that a person generally should not be considered beneficial owner of a particular income payment on the basis of facts and circumstances'.[1025]

Therefore, the Forwarding Approach applies a formal approach; i.e., it ties to private law ('contractual obligation') or other legal relations ('legal obligation') to assess the beneficial ownership status of a recipient of a payment.[1026] By contrast, the substance of a taxpayer is, in principle, irrelevant.[1027] As *Baker* states, '[i]t is perfectly possible for a holding company to *have real ownership of dividends, and not to be under a binding obligation to pay on the dividends received* to another person, even though the holding company has *no premises, staff or assets* other than the shares that are held' (emphasis added).[1028] Consequently, the Forwarding Approach is also not an activity-based concept.[1029] That is, it is generally not tested whether functions are performed.[1030]

However, this is different with regard to the beneficial ownership status of CIVs for which the functions performed by the CIV (more precisely, the discretionary powers of the managers of the CIV to manage the assets generating the income) are decisive.[1031] For this reason, the 2014 update of the Commentary cannot be classified as a

1023. *See also* OECD TPG 2017 Mn 1.46.
1024. *Lang*, SWI 2012, 228f; *van Raad*, Report on Beneficial ownership under the OECD Model Convention and Commentaries (2011) 3 (available at http://ibdt.org.br/material/arquivos/Atas/jfb_20111020093958.pdf); *see also Danon*, BIT 2018, 34f (with further references in FN 45); *Da Silva*, Evolution of the Beneficial Ownership Concept: More than Half of Century of Uncertainty and What History Can Tell Us, Frontiers of Law in China 2017, 501 (521); *Gutmann* in *Lang/Pistone/Schuch/Staringer/Storck* 343 FN 3; *Vallada* in *Lang/Pistone/Rust/Schuch/Staringer/Storck* 45; different opinion *Baumgartner* in *Reich/Simonek* 133 (with further references in FN 376).
1025. *Van Raad*, Report on Beneficial ownership under the OECD Model Convention and Commentaries (2011) 3.
1026. *See* sec. 1.1; in this context, *see also Zimmer* in *IFA* 28f.
1027. *See also Baker* in *Maisto* 101; *Danon*, Clarification of the Meaning of 'Beneficial Owner' in the OECD Model Tax Convention – Comment on the April 2011 Discussion Draft, BIT 2011, 437 (439); *Perdelwitz*, International Tax Structuring for Holding Activities, in *Cotrut* (Ed.), International Tax Structures in the BEPS Era: An Analysis of Anti-Abuse Measures (2015) 281 (306); *Da Silva*, Frontiers of Law in China 2017, 521; *Chew*, DFI 2015, 3.3.5.1; same opinion already before the 2014 update, *De Broe*, International Tax Planning and Prevention of Abuse (2008) 714.
1028. *Baker* in *Maisto* 101.
1029. *See also Gooijer*, Intertax 2014, 216; *Jain*, Effectiveness of the Beneficial Ownership Test in Conduit Company Cases (2013) 77ff and 207ff.
1030. *See also Monsenego*, ITPJ 2014, 18; accordingly, it is also irrelevant whether a company performs functions through its own employees or whether it outsources functions.
1031. *See* already sec. 4.2.7.3.

mere clarification of the Beneficial Ownership Test but introduces a new dimension. This is notwithstanding the fact that the OECD refers to the update as a clarification[1032] as the wording in the OECD Commentary 2003 ('very narrow powers') can be understood as focusing on either the investment side (as in the case of CIVs) or the distribution side (as under the Forwarding Approach).[1033] Therefore, the Forwarding Approach can only be applied to tax treaties that are concluded after the 2014 Commentary update.[1034]

4.2.9 2017: Update of the OECD MC and the Commentary – PPT as a New Tool to Tackle Conduit Companies

4.2.9.1 Background

Only one year after the latest update of the OECD Commentary on the issue of beneficial ownership, the OECD released its final report on BEPS Action 6.[1035] Against the background that the latest discussion draft on beneficial ownership was issued in 2012 and the BEPS Project was launched in 2013, it is understandable that the BEPS Project did not address beneficial ownership yet again.[1036] On the other hand, however, it is surprising that the final report on BEPS Action 6 suggests introducing a PPT into the OECD MC,[1037] which is supposed to tackle *inter alia* conduit company structures – just like the Beneficial Ownership Test. In 2017, the results of the BEPS Project – and thus the PPT and the comments thereon – were incorporated into the OECD MC and Commentary.[1038]

4.2.9.2 Content[1039]

The newly introduced Article 29(9) OECD MC 2017 – the PPT – has the following wording:

> Notwithstanding the other provisions of this Convention, a benefit under this Convention shall not be granted in respect of an item of income or capital if it is

1032. *See OECD,* OECD Model Tax Convention: Revised proposals concerning the meaning of 'beneficial owner' in Articles 10, 11 and 12 (2012) 16: 'The Working Party considers that the changes are indeed a mere clarification of the existing guidance'; expressed pointedly, *Lang,* BEPS Action 6: Introducing an Antiabuse Rule in Tax Treaties, TNI 2014, 655 (656): '[E]xplicit references to the clarifying character of some rules are even further fueling the suspicion that their actual intention is to bring about substantive change.'
1033. On this issue, *see* already sec. 4.2.7.3.
1034. In a similar direction, *Vallada* in *Lang/Pistone/Rust/Schuch/Staringer/Storck* 35.
1035. *OECD,* Preventing the Granting of Treaty Benefits in Inappropriate Circumstances – Action 6: 2015 Final Report (2015).
1036. *See also* sec. 1.4.
1037. *OECD,* Preventing the Granting of Treaty Benefits in Inappropriate Circumstances – Action 6: 2015 Final Report (2015) 54ff.
1038. *OECD,* 2017 Update to the OECD Model Tax Convention (2017) 21ff and 277ff.
1039. As the purpose of this thesis is not to analyse the PPT but the Beneficial Ownership Test, this section will focus on passages that are of interest with regard to the Beneficial Ownership Test.

> reasonable to conclude, having regard to all relevant facts and circumstances, that *obtaining that benefit was one of the principal purposes of any arrangement* or transaction that resulted directly or indirectly in that benefit, *unless it is established that granting that benefit in these circumstances would be in accordance with the object and purpose of the relevant provisions of this Convention* (emphasis added).

According to Article 29 Mn 175 OECD Commentary 2017, the PPT covers, *inter alia*:

> limitations on the taxing rights of a Contracting State in respect of dividends, interest or royalties arising in that State, and paid to a resident of the other State (*who is the beneficial owner*) under Article 10, 11 or 12 (emphasis added).

Similarly, Article 12 Mn 4.4 OECD Commentary 2017 states:[1040]

> The provisions of Article 29 [...] will apply to prevent abuses, *including treaty-shopping situations where the recipient is the beneficial owner of royalties* (emphasis added).

Furthermore, Article 29 Mn 182 and 187 OECD Commentary 2017 contain 19 examples – many of them dealing with conduit company structures – that illustrate the application of the PPT.

4.2.9.3 *Analysis: Relevance of Substance under the PPT*

As stated above, 'it is remarkable that BEPS Action 6 addresses conduit structures exclusively on the basis of the PPT rule [...] and makes no reference to the beneficial ownership concept [...]'.[1041] This is even more surprising when considering that several of the illustrative examples on the application of the PPT 'seem to be inspired from Court judgments on the "beneficial ownership" clause [...]'.[1042]

In contrast to the Beneficial Ownership Test,[1043] the PPT requires the fulfilment of a subjective element (i.e., obtaining a benefit must have been one of the principal purposes of an arrangement) in addition to an objective element (i.e., granting that benefit in these circumstances is not in accordance with the object and purpose of the relevant provisions of the DTC),[1044] in order to be applied to conduit company cases.[1045]

1040. The same statement concerning dividends and interest can be found in Art. 10 Mn 12.5 and Art. 11 Mn 10.3 OECD Commentary 2017, respectively.
1041. *Danon*, BIT 2018, 31.
1042. *Chand*, The Principal Purpose Test in the Multilateral Convention: An in-depth Analysis, Intertax 2018, 18 (18); for a detailed analysis of the examples and information on which court decisions served as a blueprint, *see Chand*, Intertax 2018, 27ff.
1043. On this issue, *see* already sec. 4.2.4.3.
1044. In this context, *see also Lang*, TNI 2014, 661 according to whom the PPT has no legal relevance as the object and purpose of a provision must always be taken into account when interpreting a treaty; *see also*, *Lang*, The Signalling Function of Article 29(9) of the OECD Model – The 'Principal Purpose Test', BIT 2020, 264 (266) where the author concludes that, for this reason, the subjective element of the PPT loses its significance and, in the end, the PPT merely emphasizes the necessity for purposive interpretation.
1045. *See Danon*, BIT 2018, 44f.

Concerning the subjective element, substance plays a crucial role as it allows a taxpayer to disprove that one of the principal purposes of an arrangement was to obtain a treaty benefit.[1046] In this respect, the OECD refers to the 'Core Commercial Activity' to determine the relevant substance requirement:[1047]

> In particular, *where an arrangement is inextricably linked to a core commercial activity*, and its form has not been driven by considerations of obtaining a benefit, *it is unlikely that its principal purpose will be considered to be to obtain that benefit* (emphasis added).

In order to assess whether a taxpayer undertakes such a Core Commercial Activity, i.e., has the necessary substance under the PPT, the OECD TPG 2017[1048] (in particular the DEMPE Approach) and the Modified Nexus Approach[1049] (or the concept of Core Income Generating Activities) could be suitable instruments.

However, under the Beneficial Ownership Test (Forwarding Approach), the substance of a taxpayer is irrelevant.[1050] Instead, it is only tested whether a taxpayer is under an obligation to forward a received payment (objective element). As a result, it may occur that a structure with an IP Company is regarded as harmful under the Beneficial Ownership Test, whereas, from the perspective of the PPT, it is considered as unproblematic. Section 5.3 will deal in depth with this issue.

Conversely, even if a person is the beneficial owner of a payment, treaty benefits may still be denied under the PPT.[1051] This is somehow surprising when considering that the PPT does not apply when granting a benefit is in accordance with the object and purpose of the relevant provisions of a DTC (objective element). 'After all, the object and purpose of specific antiabuse rules [SAARs; like the Beneficial Ownership Test] is to clearly define the dividing line between those arrangements that convey the envisaged benefit and those that no longer do'.[1052] Therefore, one would suspect that, when a person is the beneficial owner of received royalties, granting an elimination of withholding taxes is in accordance with the object and purpose of Article 12 OECD

1046. *Danon*, BIT 2018, 48.
1047. Art. 29 Mn 181 OECD MC 2017; *see also OECD*, Preventing the Granting of Treaty Benefits in Inappropriate Circumstances – Action 6: 2015 Final Report (2015) 58.
1048. *See* Example G in Art. 29 Mn 182 OECD MC 2017 and Example F in Art. 29 Mn 187 OECD MC 2017 where explicit reference is made to the functions performed, risks assumed, and assets used by a company; *see also Jiménez* in *Dourado* 54: 'In the end, it seems that if the substance required for transfer pricing purposes [...] is located in the residence country, the source country will not be able to use the PPT to refuse treaty benefits'; different *van Weeghel*, A Deconstruction of the Principal Purposes Test, WTJ 2019, 1 (22): 'While there is intuitive appeal to that approach, it seems that the reach of the TP Guidelines and that of the [...] PPT clauses are quite different'; however, according to van Weeghel, the AOA is suitable to cover the substance requirement of the PPT.
1049. *Danon*, Intellectual Property (IP) Income and Tax Treaty Abuse: Relevance of BEPS Actions 5 and 8-10 for the Principal Purpose Test, in *Maisto* (Ed.), Taxation of Intellectual Property under Domestic Law, EU Law and Tax Treaties (2018) 17 (27ff).
1050. *See* already sec. 4.2.8.3.
1051. *See* Art. 29 Mn 175 and Art. 12 Mn 4.4 OECD Commentary 2017 (reproduced in sec. 4.2.9.2).
1052. *Lang*, TNI 2014, 658.

MC.[1053] For this reason, some authors suggest that 'once a purported abusive arrangement passes these SAARs [e.g. the Beneficial Ownership Test], the PPT should only apply to the extent the allegedly abusive behaviour is completely out of the scope of the type(s) of treaty abuse the SAARs intend to counter'.[1054]

4.3 PRELIMINARY CONCLUSIONS

- The Beneficial Ownership Test is concerned with the elimination of withholding taxes on royalties.
- Over the course of its more than 40-year history, the OECD has addressed the issue of beneficial ownership numerous times and in various different publications; often, however, the notion of the concept is not aligned across these publications.
- When the Beneficial Ownership Test was originally introduced into the OECD MC in 1977, it did not have any normative meaning but was only clarificatory.
- The Conduit Companies Report of 1986 intended to turn the Beneficial Ownership Test into a new direction so that it can be applied to conduit company structures; yet, the legal relevance of this report for the interpretation of the Beneficial Ownership Test must seriously be questioned as it goes beyond the understanding of beneficial ownership in the OECD MC and Commentary 1977.
- The 1998 Report on Harmful Tax Competition apparently ascribes a broad anti-abuse meaning - similar to a general anti-avoidance rule - to the Beneficial Ownership Test; however, as such an understanding obviously goes beyond the understanding in the OECD MC and Commentary 1977, it must be disregarded for the interpretation of the Beneficial Ownership Test.
- The 1999 Partnership Report understands the Beneficial Ownership Test as an attribution-of-income rule (i.e., the person that is liable to tax on royalties in the residence state is also their beneficial owner); however, the premise that the tax treatment in the residence state is decisive for the entitlement to treaty benefits in the source state is not convincing and, therefore, the Partnership Report must not be used for the interpretation of the Beneficial Ownership Test.
- In 2003, the considerations of the Conduit Companies Report with regard to the Beneficial Ownership Test were incorporated into the OECD Commentary; however, the exact meaning that this update intended to ascribe to the Beneficial Ownership Test is far from clear.

1053. *See also Blum*, International Tax Report 11/2017, 15: '[A] sound application of the beneficial ownership requirement [...] should render the PPT moot.'
1054. *De Broe/Luts*, BEPS Action 6: Tax Treaty Abuse, Intertax 2015, 122 (133); *see also Danon*, BIT 2018, 38f.

- According to the 2010 amendment of the OECD Commentary, a CIV is the beneficial owner of income it receives as long as its managers have discretionary powers to manage the assets that generate the income; this approach puts an emphasis on the functions that a CIV performs; however, the relevance of this approach for the Beneficial Ownership Test in a non-CIV context is doubtful, especially when considering that the 2014 update of the OECD Commentary does not follow it.
- Since the 2014 update of the OECD Commentary, it is stated that a person is not the beneficial owner when his right to use and enjoy royalties is constrained by a contractual or legal obligation to pass on the payment received to another person (Forwarding Approach); such a harmful forwarding obligation must always be based on legal grounds and can never be factual; consequently, the 2014 update of the OECD Commentary introduces a formal approach as it ties to private law or other legal relations to assess the beneficial ownership status of a recipient of a payment; by contrast, the substance of a taxpayer is irrelevant.
- Contrary to the Beneficial Ownership Test, the PPT also requires the fulfilment of a subjective element (i.e., obtaining a benefit must have been one of the principal purposes of an arrangement); in this context, substance plays a crucial role as it allows a taxpayer to disprove the existence of the subjective element.

CHAPTER 5

Comparison Between DEMPE Approach, Substantial Activity Requirement and Beneficial Ownership

5.1 DEMPE APPROACH AND SUBSTANTIAL ACTIVITY REQUIREMENT

5.1.1 DEMPE Approach and Modified Nexus Approach

At the outset, it has to be highlighted that the DEMPE Approach is broader in subjective and objective terms compared to the Modified Nexus Approach. In subjective terms, it is because the DEMPE Approach considers all of the parties involved in the DEMPE of an intangible,[1055] while the Modified Nexus Approach only focuses on individual entities.[1056] In objective terms, it is because the DEMPE Approach covers the entire life cycle of an intangible (from development to exploitation),[1057] while the Modified Nexus Approach is only concerned with the development or enhancement (and possibly maintenance) of a qualifying IP asset but not its protection[1058] and exploitation.[1059]

1055. *See* sec. 2.5.1.
1056. *See* sec. 3.2.6.6; the stated reason for this is that 'the nexus approach was not designed to disadvantage arrangements where different entities are engaged in activities contributing to the development of IP assets', *see* BEPS Action 5, Mn 31.
1057. *See* sec. 1.3.2.
1058. However, legal protection itself plays a crucial role under the Modified Nexus Approach since, generally, only legally protected IP assets may qualify for preferential tax treatment, *see* sec. 3.2.4; yet, for the extent of the income that may be taxed preferentially (i.e., the nexus ratio) and thus for the question of value creation (substance), it is irrelevant.
1059. *See* sec. 3.2.7.

Both approaches have the common intention of establishing a link between income and the activities necessary to earn it (activity-based concepts).[1060] Consequently, they share the view that the sole provision of capital without the performance of any activities does not create any value (priority of the production factor labour over capital).[1061] Apart from that, however, the way in which a link between activity and income is established varies substantially. In this regard, the DEMPE Approach applies a qualitative approach to define substance, whereas the Modified Nexus Approach applies a quantitative approach.[1062]

Furthermore, the content of this link – i.e., which activities create value – is different under the two concepts. Under the Modified Nexus Approach,[1063] actual R&D activities (operational level) are (primarily) regarded as value-creating, whereas, under the DEMPE Approach, management activities (strategical and tactical level) in the DEMPE of an intangible are regarded as value creating.[1064] On a related note, the issue of risk assumption – crucial under the DEMPE Approach –[1065] is completely irrelevant under the Modified Nexus Approach. As a result, only under the DEMPE Approach will a structure with an IP Principal[1066] that has contract R&D arrangements with related parties in different jurisdiction achieve the intended tax consequences.[1067]

Given the fact that both the DEMPE Approach and the Modified Nexus Approach aim to align taxation and value creation,[1068] it can be concluded that the two concepts have a different understanding of what constitutes value creation. However, a bridge between these two understandings of value creation – activities on the operational level versus activities on the strategical and tactical level – is built by the uplift under the Modified Nexus Approach. The uplift takes into account that 'taxpayers that acquired IP[1069] or outsourced a portion of the R&D to a related party may themselves still be responsible for much of the value creation that contributed to IP income'.[1070]

1060. For the DEMPE Approach, *see* sec. 2.5.5; for the Modified Nexus Approach, *see* sec. 3.2.6.7.
1061. For the DEMPE Approach, *see* sec. 2.5.4.4; for the Modified Nexus Approach, *see* sec. 3.2.6.7; *see also Tavares/Owens*, Asia: Global Tax Policy Post-BEPS and the Perils of the Silk Road, in *Lang/Owens* (Eds), Removing Tax Barriers to China's Belt and Road Initiative (2019) 285 (294 FN 48).
1062. For the DEMPE Approach, *see* sec. 2.5.5; for the Modified Nexus Approach, *see* sec. 3.2.6.7.
1063. *See* sec. 3.2.6.7.
1064. *See* sec. 2.5.2.1.
1065. *See* sec. 2.5.3; in this context, *see also Collier/Andrus*, Transfer Pricing and the Arm's Length Principle After BEPS (2017) Mn 7.55: 'The BEPS Report is quite clear that an entity performing research activities may be entitled to a significant portion of the ultimate return from intangibles, or may be entitled to a relatively small, contract research type, payment for its services depending primarily on the manner in which functions related to the control of risk and the management of development related resources are performed.'
1066. *See* already sec. 1.5.
1067. The Modified Nexus Approach wants to prevent that MNEs outsource R&D to related parties in high-tax jurisdictions and, at the same time, have the corresponding income preferentially taxed in a jurisdiction with a patent box regime, *see* already sec. 3.2.6.7.
1068. *See* sec. 1.6.
1069. Under the Modified Nexus Approach, the activity of acquiring an IP asset is generally regarded as not creating any value (*see* sec. 3.2.6.4); this is different, however, under the DEMPE Approach where, for example, the selection of the most appropriate intangible on the market, the analysis of its potential benefits for an MNE, and the decision to purchase the intangible can be value-creating functions, *see* OECD TPG 2017 Mn 6.49; it is also highlighted that a

The Modified Nexus Approach assumes a correlation between the expenditures of an activity and the value created by it (i.e., the more expensive, the more value created).[1071] This is due to its construction as a quantitative approach in which the facts and circumstances of the individual case are irrelevant.[1072] By contrast, the DEMPE Approach – as a qualitative approach – does not necessarily assume such a correlation.[1073] This becomes particularly clear when one consults the guidance on CCAs where it says that 'measuring current contributions at cost is unlikely to provide a reliable basis for determining the value of the relative contributions of participants, and may lead to non-arm's length results. For development CCAs, the measurement of current contributions at cost [...] will generally not provide a reliable basis for the application of the arm's length principle'.[1074] Similarly, while the OECD TPG state that there is rarely 'any correlation between the cost of developing intangibles and their value or transfer price once developed',[1075] the Modified Nexus Approach regards acquisition costs as 'a proxy for overall expenditures incurred prior to acquisition'.[1076]

At the same time, one has to keep in mind that the DEMPE Approach (more generally, the OECD TPG) feeds into the Modified Nexus Approach. When R&D is outsourced to a related party[1077] or IP is acquired from a related party,[1078] the OECD TPG are necessary for establishing an arm's-length price for the respective expenditures. Therefore, the expenditures for related party outsourcing and for the acquisition of IP from related parties are included in the nexus ratio with arm's-length prices (at

transfer pricing analysis may be more difficult when acquired intangibles serve as a platform for further development; therefore, the importance of the above-mentioned functions may be different in such a case compared to when a fully developed and already exploitable intangible is purchased.

1070. BEPS Action 5, Mn 41; likewise, BEPS Action 5 acknowledges that 'the vast majority of the value of an IP asset rests in both the R&D undertaken to create it and the information necessary to undertake such R&D [...]', *see* BEPS Action 5, Mn 50.

1071. *See* sec. 3.2.6.7.

1072. *See* sec. 1.1.

1073. *See* sec. 2.5.5; in this context, *see also OECD*, Public consultation document: Review of Country-by-Country Reporting (BEPS Action 13) (2020) Mn 125: 'The level of R&D expenditure in a jurisdiction can be an important indicator of the level of substantial activities in that jurisdiction, as well as of the contribution constituent entities are making to value creation within an MNE group'; at the same time, Mn 127 states that the 'presence of R&D activity in a jurisdiction does not necessarily mean that beneficial ownership in any intangibles created by that activity is attributable to that jurisdiction'.

1074. OECD TPG 2017 Mn 8.28.

1075. OECD TPG 2017 Mn 6.142; *see* already the considerations in 3.2.2.

1076. BEPS Action 5, Mn 52; however, since 'taxpayers may have an incentive to undervalue transfers between related parties into IP regimes, any related party acquisitions will require that taxpayers prepare documentation substantiating the arm's length price, including documentation on the overall expenditures that the related party transferor incurred'.

1077. In this context, note BEPS Action 5, Mn 50: 'Where a payment is made through a related party to an unrelated party without any margin, the payment will be included in qualifying expenditures.'

1078. *See* BEPS Action 5, Mn 52: 'In the context of related party acquisitions, the arm's length price must be used to determine acquisition costs.'

value),[1079] whereas a qualifying taxpayer's expenditures for its own R&D activities are only considered at cost.[1080]

5.1.2 Modified Nexus Approach and Core Income Generating Activities

With the resumption of the application of the Substantial Activity Requirement to no or only nominal tax jurisdictions, *Saint-Amans*, director of the OECD Centre for Tax Policy and Administration, proclaimed:[1081]

> *[This action] will ensure that substantial activities must be performed in respect of the same types of mobile business activities, regardless of whether they take place in a preferential regime or in a no or only nominal tax jurisdiction.*

At first glance, this statement suggests that the Modified Nexus Approach and the concept of Core Income Generating Activities are congruent. Indeed, both concepts emphasize conducting R&D (operational level) as substantial activities with regard to qualifying IP assets as under the Modified Nexus Approach.[1082] However, under the Core Income Generating Activities, it is also possible that, in exceptional cases, an entity could perform substantial activities even if it did not conduct R&D.[1083] Substantial activities in this context could be 'conducting the *strategic* decision-making [and] managing and bearing the principal risks relating to the development and subsequent exploitation of the IP asset [...]' (emphasis added).[1084] Therefore, instead of actual R&D activities (operational level), management activities (strategical and tactical level) would then be substantial activities.

However, when foreign related parties are involved in the development and the exploitation of an IP asset (higher-risk scenarios) – like in the case of IP Companies –[1085] there is a presumption that an entity has not performed substantial activities when it did not conduct R&D.[1086] Still, this presumption can be rebutted when an entity demonstrates that 'there was, and historically has been, a high degree of control over the [DEMPE] of the intangible asset, exercised by an adequate number of full-time employees with the necessary qualifications that permanently reside and perform their activities within the jurisdiction'.[1087] Therefore, in this way the DEMPE Approach becomes relevant in determining the Substantial Activity Requirement in no or only nominal tax jurisdictions.

1079. Naturally, this is also true with regard to expenditures for unrelated party outsourcing and expenditures for the acquisition of IP from unrelated parties.
1080. *See also Tavares/Owens*, Human Capital in Value Creation and Post-BEPS Tax Policy: An Outlook, BIT 2015, 590 (593 FN 26).
1081. Statement available at http://www.oecd.org/ctp/oecd-releases-latest-results-on-preferential-regimes-and-moves-to-strengthen-the-level-playing-field-with-zero-tax-jurisdictions.htm.
1082. For the Modified Nexus Approach, *see* sec. 3.2.6.2; for the Core Income Generating Activities, *see* sec. 3.3.3.
1083. *See* sec. 3.3.4.
1084. OECD Resumption, Mn 32.
1085. *See* already sec. 1.5.
1086. *See* sec. 3.3.4.
1087. OECD Resumption, Mn 37.

The situation is different, however, under the Modified Nexus Approach. Although the Modified Nexus Approach is also designed as a rebuttable presumption, it still requires an entity to conduct R&D to a certain extent for a successful rebuttal (i.e., a taxpayer's nexus ratio without the uplift must equal or exceed 25%).[1088] Furthermore, it is doubtful whether the DEMPE Approach can be used to rebut the nexus ratio.[1089]

As already stated above, the uplift emphasizes the importance of management activities (strategical and tactical level) and thereby bridges the understandings of value creation under the Modified Nexus Approach and the DEMPE Approach.[1090] However, since it is not possible by design to apply an uplift under the concept of Core Income Generating Activities,[1091] this could explain why the DEMPE Approach (more precisely, the understanding of value creation under the DEMPE Approach) can come into play by way of the rebuttable presumption.

What is more, contrary to the Modified Nexus Approach,[1092] the concept of Core Income Generating Activities with regard to IP income applies a qualitative approach to determine substance.[1093] As a result, the analysis under the Core Income Generating Activities is more similar to the analysis under the DEMPE Approach (i.e., a correlation between expenditures and value creation need not be the case) than under the Modified Nexus Approach.[1094]

For these reasons, it cannot be said that the Modified Nexus Approach and the concept of Core Income Generating Activities are congruent. On top of that, since the DEMPE Approach must already be applied in order to determine the parties that are entitled to the intangible-related returns, this would mean that an IP Company may not need to fulfil any additional substance requirements under the Core Income Generating Activities (in the case of a successful rebuttal). Consequently, it may be more advantageous to locate an IP Company in a no or only nominal tax jurisdiction than in a jurisdiction with a preferential IP regime.[1095]

As already stated above, the OECD initially also examined a Transfer Pricing Approach to determine the Substantial Activity Requirement with regard to preferential IP regimes.[1096] However, a Transfer Pricing Approach was eventually discarded as it would not have imposed any additional substance requirements than those already provided by the DEMPE Approach.[1097] At the same time, it was apparently not considered, back then, that the chosen Modified Nexus Approach cannot be applied to

1088. *See* sec. 3.2.10; granted, a taxpayer may also achieve a nexus ratio of 25% or above without expenditures for its own R&D activity but only expenditures for outsourcing to unrelated parties.
1089. *See* the considerations in sec. 3.2.10.
1090. *See* sec. 5.1.1
1091. *See* sec. 3.3.2.
1092. *See* sec. 3.2.6.7.
1093. *See* sec. 3.3.3.
1094. *See* sec. 3.3.3.
1095. However, it has to be kept in mind that the rebuttable presumption under the Core Income Generating Activities will be subject to review by the FHTP no later than 2020, *see* FN 813.
1096. *See* sec. 3.2.1.
1097. *See* already sec. 3.2.1, especially FN 479.

no or only nominal tax jurisdictions.[1098] For this reason, an alternative to the Modified Nexus Approach had to be found. As demonstrated, however, the chosen alternative - the concept of Core Income Generating Activities - is not congruent with the Modified Nexus Approach. Yet, from a tax policy perspective, the Substantial Activity Requirement should be defined uniformly for preferential regimes and for no or only nominal tax jurisdictions.

5.2 BENEFICIAL OWNERSHIP (SUBSTANCE PRE-BEPS) VERSUS SUBSTANCE IN THE BEPS PROJECT

Unlike the DEMPE Approach and the Substantial Activity Requirement, the Beneficial Ownership Test (Forwarding Approach) does not set any substance requirements but applies a formal approach.[1099] Likewise, whereas the DEMPE Approach and the Substantial Activity Requirement establish a link between income and activity - albeit the respective link is different under these concepts -[1100] such a link is not tested under the Beneficial Ownership Test (i.e., the Beneficial Ownership Test is not an activity-based concept).[1101] Instead, the Beneficial Ownership Test focuses on the subsequent level and asks about a person's right to use and enjoy a received payment.[1102] This means, unlike under the DEMPE Approach and the Substantial Activity Requirement, it is not tested what a taxpayer contributed to receive a payment but what a taxpayer can do with a received payment.

The situation is different, however, when it comes to the requirements for beneficial ownership for CIVs where the functions performed (more precisely, the discretionary powers to manage the assets that generate income) play a crucial role.[1103] By contrast, the fact that a CIV may have a legal obligation to forward received payments to its investors is not considered as harmful.[1104] This approach to beneficial ownership appears to be similar to the concept of control over risk under the DEMPE Approach ('capability and authority to *decide to take on the risk* [i.e. to make an investment], and to *decide whether and how to respond to the risk* [i.e. to sell an investment] [...]' [emphasis added]).[1105] Furthermore, similarities can also be found

1098. *See* sec. 3.3.2.
1099. *See* sec. 4.2.8.3.
1100. *See* secs 5.1.1 and 5.1.2.
1101. *See* sec. 4.2.8.3.
1102. In this context, *see also* the distinction in *Reimer*, How To Conceptualize Beneficial Ownership, in *Lang/Pistone/Schuch/Staringer/Storck* (Eds), Beneficial Ownership: Recent Trends (2013) 253 (258ff) between prepayment parameters and after-payment parameters.
1103. *See* sec. 4.2.7.3; *see also* the proposed addition to the OECD Commentary in *OECD*, Report of the Informal Consultative Group on the Taxation of Collective Investment Vehicles and Procedures for Tax Relief for Cross-Border Investors on the Granting of Treaty Benefits with respect to the Income of Collective Investment Vehicles (2009) 17 Mn 6.12 where it is stated that the treatment of a CIV as a beneficial owner is 'appropriate because the functions performed by the CIV and its managers are substantially different from those of a nominee, agent or custodian'.
1104. *See* sec. 4.2.7.3.
1105. OECD TPG 2017 Mn 1.67; *see* already sec. 2.5.3.2.

under the concept of Core Income Generating Activities with regard to fund management regimes. In this context, the Core Income Generating Activities could include '*taking decisions on the holding and selling of investments*; calculating risks and reserves; taking decisions on currency or interest fluctuations and hedging positions; and preparing relevant regulatory or other reports for government authorities and investors' (emphasis added).[1106] Therefore, in the context of CIVs, the substance requirements known under the DEMPE Approach or the Substantial Activity Requirement may also be helpful for determining beneficial ownership.

In non-CIV cases, however, this is not the case because, as stated above, the substance of a taxpayer is irrelevant under the Beneficial Ownership Test. A company could perform all of the value-creating activities under the DEMPE Approach or all of the substantial activities under the Substantial Activity Requirement and still be under a harmful obligation to forward income received. Conversely, a company that has outsourced all of its activities can still be the beneficial owner of payments that it receives when it does not have an obligation to forward them.[1107] However, between associated enterprises, the absence of substance under the DEMPE Approach may have an impact on a company's status as beneficial owner:

According to the DEMPE Approach, intangible-related returns - which might often constitute royalties according to Article 12 OECD MC -[1108] have to be attributed to the legal owner of an intangible in a first step. However, since legal ownership alone does not ultimately entitle to any intangible-related returns, the legal owner has to compensate other group companies that made valuable contributions to the DEMPE of the intangible (i.e., effectively pass on received intangible-related returns to them).[1109] Therefore, following the DEMPE Approach, the legal owner may be under a legal obligation to forward received payments.[1110] Concurrently, such a forwarding obligation is harmful to the qualification as a beneficial owner.[1111] Consequently, the source state could levy withholding taxes (provided that the beneficial owner is not resident in the same state as the legal owner receiving the royalties).[1112,1113] At the same time, a

1106. BEPS Action 5, Mn 81; OECD, Harmful Tax Practices - 2017 Progress Report on Preferential Regimes (2017) 41.
1107. *See* sec. 4.2.8.3, especially FN 1030.
1108. *See* sec. 2.3.
1109. *See* sec. 2.4.2.
1110. More precisely, as the DEMPE Approach informs about what independent enterprises would have agreed to (*see* sec. 2.8), the relevant facts and circumstances there may help to establish that a party is under a forwarding obligation according to private law (since the Beneficial Ownership Test applies a formal approach).
1111. *See* sec. 4.2.8.3.
1112. *See* sec. 4.2.3.3.
1113. It is not clear whether the source state may levy withholding taxes on the full payment or only on the amount of the payment that is forwarded; arguing for the latter *Yoshimura*, Tax Analysts 2013, 772f and 780: '[I]f a taxpayer is regarded as not being the beneficial owner regarding certain income or a certain percentage of such income, the taxpayer cannot enjoy treaty benefits only to the extent that it is not considered to be the beneficial owner'; *Meindl-Ringler*, Beneficial Ownership in International Tax Law (2016) 318f: '[I]t may be possible that the person forwarding the income retains a certain spread of the income and that it may be appropriate to qualify that person as the beneficial owner of the spread, making it possible for multiple beneficial owners to exist in regard to the initial income.'

withholding tax reduction based on a DTC between the source state and the state where the company to which royalties are forwarded is resident may not be granted because, from the perspective of the source state, the royalties are not attributed to this company.[1114]

Of course, under the DEMPE Approach, the legal owner of, for example, a patent would regularly use received royalties to compensate other related parties that performed valuable contributions to the DEMPE of the patent by increasing their remuneration for the underlying services and not by simply passing on part of the royalties. Effectively, however, the legal owner would still forward a received payment albeit in a different form (i.e., service fee instead of a royalty). In this regard, it is left unanswered by the Commentary whether a change in the identity of the income influences the qualification as a beneficial owner.[1115] Case law[1116] and scholarly opinion[1117] seem to be of the opinion that such a change of the character of the payment does not affect the Beneficial Ownership Test (i.e., same outcome as if the payment was forwarded as the same character).

However, as legal obligations 'that are not dependent on the receipt of the payment by the direct recipient' do not harm one's status as beneficial owner,[1118] one could ask whether such a forwarding obligation according to the DEMPE Approach does fall under this exception. Unfortunately, with the exception of a few inconclusive examples,[1119] the OECD Commentary does not provide further details on when an

1114. On this issue, *see* sec. 4.2.3.3.
1115. *See also* the comment of the Capital Markets Tax Committee of Asia (CMTC) Mn 3.9 (available at http://www.oecd.org/tax/treaties/48413629.pdf) on the 2011 Discussion Draft (OECD, Clarification of the Meaning of 'Beneficial Owner' in the OECD Model Tax Convention [2011]) that highlighted this issue: 'To clarify what constitutes a payment in this context, the Commentary might usefully include examples which demonstrate the necessary connection required for there to be a particular amount "passed on", including for example, *where the nature of the amount received changes before it is paid. For example, a payment under a Transfer Pricing Agreement (because a function that contributed to the receipt of the relevant amount is based in another location) should not be considered as changing the beneficial owner*' (emphasis added); likewise, the comment of the United States Council for International Business (USCIB) 4 (available at http://www.oecd.org/tax/treaties/48414129.pdf): 'It is assumed, but *the Discussion Draft should make clear, that payments under transfer pricing requirements do not affect beneficial ownership*' (emphasis added); however, the OECD did not specifically address these comments, *see OECD*, OECD Model Tax Convention: Revised Proposals Concerning the Meaning of 'Beneficial Owner' in Articles 10, 11 and 12 (2012) Mn 17, 31 and 32.
1116. *See*, for example, the Danish HHU case, Østre Landsret (High Court of Eastern Denmark), 20. 12. 2011, B-2152-10, where a company forwarded received interest in the form of a group contribution; for more details of this case, *see Bundgaard*, The Notion of Beneficial Ownership in Danish Tax Law: The Creation of a New Legal Order with Uncertainty as a Companion, in *Lang/Pistone/Schuch/Staringer/Storck* (Eds), Beneficial Ownership: Recent Trends (2013) 91 (101ff); for further case law, *see Pamperl*, Auswirkungen einer Verpflichtung zur Weiterleitung passiver Einkünfte auf eine DBA-rechtliche Quellensteuerreduktion, SWI 2013, 403 (405f).
1117. *Arnold*, Tax Treaty News, BIT 2011, 367 (372); *Bernstein*, The 2014 OECD Update on Beneficial Ownership, TNI 2015, 345 (346).
1118. *See* sec. 4.2.8.3.
1119. *See* sec. 4.2.8.2.

obligation can be considered to be dependent on the receipt of a payment.[1120] This may be due to the fact that '[d]etermining the more precise requirements for such an interconnectivity is not easy'.[1121] According to *Baumgartner*, the following two factors could be used in this context:[1122] First, the receipt of the payment is dependent on the obligation to forward the payment. Second, the obligation to forward the payment is dependent on the receipt of the payment.

Formulated differently, on the one hand, it has to be examined whether the payment would not have been received if there had not been an obligation to forward the payment.[1123] This is the case in the above-mentioned scenario because intangible-related returns would not have been generated (or, at least, not to the same extent) if valuable contributions to the DEMPE of the intangible had not been performed by the group company to which (part of) the payment is forwarded.

On the other hand, it has to be examined whether the obligation to forward a payment only exists if income is actually generated. Again, this is the case in the above-mentioned scenario because intangible-related returns are only to be forwarded if intangible-related returns are, in fact, realized.[1124]

As a consequence, the absence of substance under the DEMPE Approach - i.e., when the legal owner does not perform all of the valuable contributions to the DEMPE of an intangible - could result in the denial of beneficial ownership of received royalties. However, according to *Baumgartner*, the qualification as a beneficial owner shall ultimately not be denied when only part of the received income is forwarded but not all of it (which would be the case when a company has a certain degree of substance under the DEMPE Approach).[1125] Although this solution may seem appropriate, it is not undisputed.[1126]

1120. *See also Collier*, Beneficial owner proposals: Not so beneficial, International Tax Review 2013, 10 (11).

1121. *Meindl-Ringler*, Beneficial Ownership in International Tax Law (2016) 329; *see* already *Gassner/Lang*, Treaty Shopping, in *Gassner/Lang/Lechner* (Eds), Aktuelle Entwicklungen im internationalen Steuerrecht: Das neue Musterabkommen der OECD (1994) 43 (52) who state that it is difficult to establish a connection between a received and a forwarded payment.

1122. *Baumgartner* in *Reich/Simonek* 139ff.

1123. In this context, *see also* Art. 12 (5) DTC USA – Japan (2003): 'A resident of a Contracting State shall *not be considered the beneficial owner of royalties in respect of the use of intangible property if such royalties would not have been paid to the resident unless the resident pays royalties in respect of the same intangible property to a person*: (a) that is not entitled to benefits with respect to royalties arising in the other Contracting State which are equivalent to, or more favorable than, those available under this Convention to a resident of the first-mentioned Contracting State; and (b) that is not a resident of either Contracting State' (emphasis added).

1124. In principle, a distinction should also be made between anticipated (or *ex ante*) remuneration and actual (or *ex post*) remuneration under the DEMPE Approach, *see* OECD TPG 2017 Mn 6.44ff and 6.69ff.

1125. *Baumgartner* in *Reich/Simonek* 142ff; in this context, *see also* the Canadian Velcro Case, Tax Court of Canada, 24. 2. 2012, 2012 TCC 57, Velcro Canada Inc. v. Her Majesty the Queen, Mn 43; for more details of this case, *see Arnold* in *Lang/Pistone/Schuch/Staringer/Storck* 44ff.

1126. *See*, for example, the decision by the Swiss Federal Supreme Court, 16. 12. 2019, 2C_209 /2017, A. Sàrl v. Eidgenössische Steuerverwaltung, 3.3.

5.3 BENEFICIAL OWNERSHIP AND THE PPT: CHANGED PERCEPTION ON THE RELEVANCE OF SUBSTANCE WITH THE BEPS PROJECT

As stated above, the substance of a taxpayer is, in principle, irrelevant under the Beneficial Ownership Test (Forwarding Approach).[1127] However, in interplay with the DEMPE Approach, the absence of substance may have an impact on the Beneficial Ownership Test:[1128] A legal owner that does not perform all of the valuable contributions to the DEMPE of an intangible is under a legal obligation to forward part of the received intangible-related returns to other group companies that made valuable contributions to the DEMPE of the intangible. At the same time, such a forwarding obligation could be harmful to the legal owner's status as a beneficial owner. Furthermore, it is doubtful whether such a forwarding obligation according to the DEMPE Approach falls under the exception of an obligation that does not depend on the receipt of the payment by the direct recipient.

However, it could be argued that this exception will generally apply when the legal owner performed all of the valuable contributions with regard to the DEMPE of an intangible (i.e., the legal owner can ultimately retain all the intangible-related returns). Stated differently, the DEMPE Approach establishes a link between activity and income, while the Beneficial Ownership Test establishes a link between two payment flows (i.e., a forwarded payment[1129] must depend on the receipt of a payment).[1130] If there is no link between two payment flows, that is, an obligation does not depend on the receipt of a payment, the Beneficial Ownership Test is satisfied. The argumentation would now be that a strong link between activity and income can be used to establish that there is no link between a received payment and a forwarded payment (i.e., the link between activity and income could disconnect the link between two payment flows). The reasoning behind this seems intuitively logical: If a company has performed all of the activities that lead to income, it should also be able to harmlessly decide how to apply this income.[1131]

However, examples are conceivable - especially with IP Companies -[1132] that cast doubt on the general validity of this statement. Let us assume that a subsidiary

---

1127. *See* secs 4.2.8.3 and 5.2.

1128. *See* sec. 5.2.

1129. In this context, *see Meindl-Ringler*, Beneficial Ownership in International Tax Law (2016) 328 on the issue of 'whether the income must be actually forwarded or whether the mere obligation to forward the income should be sufficient'.

1130. On an approach to determine this interdependency, *see* sec. 5.2.

1131. *See also OECD*, Double Taxation Conventions and the Use of Conduit Companies (1986) Mn 9 where it is stated that 'bona fide transactions do not fall within the scope of this report, for they clearly involve no improper use of tax treaties. This is, generally speaking, true *in all cases in which the assets or rights giving rise to income for which treaty benefits are claimed are effectively connected to activities* like producing, rendering of services or trading in the market of [the residence state]' (emphasis added).

1132. Furthermore, similar problems are conceivable with regard to cash pools; for case law on the issue of beneficial ownership in a cash pool, *see Tetlak*, Poland: Beneficial Ownership of

successfully develops a patent that it licenses to a related IP Company (the parent of the group) which then – without further developing the patent – grants a licence to this patent to related operating companies.[1133] According to the DEMPE Approach, a patent and a licence to it are two distinct intangibles. As a consequence, there are different legal owners, and different functional analyses – one with regard to the patent and one with regard to the licence – have to be carried out.[1134]

Concerning the licence, the IP Company does not assume any development risk as the respective patent has already been successfully developed. However, the IP Company assumes risks in terms of the acquisition and exploitation of the licence rights. Important functions performed by the IP Company in this case are 'those necessary to select the most appropriate intangible on the market, to analyse its potential benefits [...] and the decision to take on the risk-bearing opportunity through [licensing] the intangible'.[1135] Consequently, if these functions are performed by the IP Company, it will be entitled to all intangible-related returns generated via the licence. At the same time, however, the IP Company has to compensate the subsidiary that provided the patent in the first place. Therefore, a bulk of the received royalties would effectively be passed on to the subsidiary. As a result, it is questionable whether the IP Company – although it performs all of the valuable contributions with regard to the licence according to the DEMPE Approach – can be regarded as the beneficial owner of the royalties it has to forward in such a case.[1136] Applying the same approach as presented above to determine the interdependency between two payments,[1137] this would likely be considered as a harmful obligation to forward a payment (and not an obligation that is independent of the receipt of a payment).

In this case, it is interesting to take a look at the PPT. If, for example, the state of the subsidiary that developed the patent has not concluded a DTC with a state in which operating group companies that receive a licence from the IP Company are active, a tax advantage could result by structuring the transactions via the IP Company (if a more favourable DTC exists). However, according to the OECD Commentary, the PPT is not applicable provided the IP Company is 'conforming to the standard commercial organisation and behaviour of the group in the way that it structures its licensing and sub-licensing activities'. That is, 'assuming the same structure is employed with

---

Interest in the Context of Cash Pooling, in *Kemmeren/Essers/Smit/Lang/Pistone/Schuch /Staringer/Storck/Owens/Rust* (Eds), Tax Treaty Case Law around the Globe 2016 (2017) 275 (275ff).

1133. *See* Figure 1.2 in sec. 1.5.

1134. *See* sec. 2.4.2.

1135. OECD TPG 2017 Mn 6.49; granted, this example concerns the purchase of an intangible from an unrelated company; however, similar considerations may also apply in the scenario presented above.

1136. In this context, *see also* the comment to the 2011 Discussion Draft from IFA Grupo Mexicano, A.C, 2 (available at http://www.oecd.org/tax/treaties/48504135.pdf): '[E]ntities holding royalty rights of a given group [...] should be an exception to the general definition of "Beneficial Owner", since the nature of the activities of these entities is more a combination of an economic and legal approach, which per se should provide enough substance to the structure as to prove the entitlement of said entities to tax treaty benefits, considering that there are clear business reasons different than tax for their existence within a group of entities.'

1137. *See* sec. 5.2.

respect to other subsidiaries carrying out similar activities in countries which have treaties which offer similar or more favourable benefits, [such an] arrangement [...] does not constitute a conduit arrangement'.[1138]

This example shows that – unlike the Beneficial Ownership Test – the 'PPT rule is not just triggered because of the existence of an interdependence between two income streams [...]'.[1139] Instead, the PPT requires the fulfilment of not only an objective element but also a subjective element in order to be applicable in conduit company cases.[1140] In other words, the Beneficial Ownership Test focuses solely on whether a forwarding obligation exists with regard to a received payment (objective element), whereas the motives behind a chosen structure are irrelevant (subjective element).[1141] However, precisely this subjective element under the PPT is an essential element of the BEPS Project as it emphasizes the relevance of substance of a taxpayer.[1142]

The OECD has dealt extensively with the issue of substance (i.e., aligning taxation and value creation) in the BEPS Project.[1143] Of course, as this thesis has shown, there is (still) no universal definition of substance (or value creation, respectively). However, it is certainly fair to speak of an existing consensus in the BEPS Project that substance shall have a crucial meaning in international tax law.[1144] Conversely, the Beneficial Ownership Test (Forwarding Approach) – a concept from the pre-BEPS era – completely ignores this factor.[1145] As a result, the Beneficial Ownership Test appears alien in a post-BEPS world.

5.4 PROPOSED SOLUTION: BENEFICIAL OWNERSHIP WITHOUT NORMATIVE MEANING AND DELETION FROM THE OECD MC

As the above-mentioned case with the IP Company shows,[1146] it is possible that treaty benefits are denied under the Beneficial Ownership Test whereas, under the PPT, the same situation is considered as unproblematic.[1147] This outcome, however, is undesirable with regard to the overall policy of the BEPS Project that emphasized the vital importance of substance in international tax law – a factor irrelevant under the Beneficial Ownership Test. Similarly, *Danon* argues that 'the outcome of BEPS Action

1138. *See* Art. 29 Mn 187 OECD MC 2017 (Example E).
1139. *Danon*, BIT 2018, 50.
1140. *See* sec. 4.2.9.3.
1141. *Danon*, BIT 2018, 55; for this reason, *Gutmann* advocated for including a subjective element in the Beneficial Ownership Test in order to avoid that treaty benefits are denied in bona fide cases; *see* sec. 4.2.4.3.
1142. With regard to the PPT, the OECD uses the concept of the 'Core Commercial Activity' to determine the relevant substance requirement; for more details, *see* sec. 4.2.9.3.
1143. *See* sec. 1.3.1.
1144. *OECD*, Explanatory Statement – 2015 Final Reports (2015) Mn 22: 'With the adoption of the BEPS package, OECD and G20 countries, as well as all developing countries that have participated in its development, will lay the foundations of a modern international tax framework under which profits are taxed where economic activity and value creation occurs.'
1145. *See* sec. 4.2.8.3.
1146. *See* sec. 5.3.
1147. *See also Danon*, BIT 2018, 55.

6 expresses a consensus as regards the way to address conduit situations (through a PPT rule)'.[1148] For this reason, he concludes that 'conduit structures must now be tackled on the basis of a PPT rule [...]' and not the Beneficial Ownership Test.[1149] The author subscribes to this conclusion.

However, also regarding the situation prior to the BEPS Project, one may ask whether the Beneficial Ownership Test is at all a suitable means for addressing conduit companies. As has been shown, when the concept was initially introduced in the OECD MC in 1977, it did not have any normative meaning and was therefore incapable of tackling conduit companies.[1150] Furthermore, while the 2003 Commentary update may have mentioned conduit companies in the context of the Beneficial Ownership Test, it was anything but clear under which conditions it should be applied.[1151] Even the latest content revision of the OECD Commentary on the Beneficial Ownership Test (Forwarding Approach) in 2014 still left open many ambiguities, most specifically on the issue of when a forwarding obligation is dependent on the receipt of a payment.[1152] In fact, the 'use of the terms "related"/"unrelated" [payments] without any explanation relocates the discussion on the beneficial owner test but does not solve it'.[1153] At the same time, the Commentary is also inconsistent as it uses a different approach to determine the beneficial ownership status of CIVs.[1154] For these reasons, one may rightfully question whether the Commentary is at all a suitable means that should be considered when interpreting the Beneficial Ownership Test.

On top of that, it has to be kept in mind that '[i]n addition to the OECD Model and the Commentary, other historical, teleological and systematic aspects, as well as the wording of the convention itself, have to be taken into account. Which arguments are more convincing is to be evaluated on a case-by-case basis'.[1155] From a systematic standpoint, one may ask why 'treaty partners [would] want to avoid abusive situations under Articles 10, 11 and 12 and gladly allow similar abuses under other articles'?[1156] In particular, the absence of the Beneficial Ownership Test in Article 13 OECD MC can be questioned.[1157] Indeed, if the Beneficial Ownership Test was really an additional requirement for the application of the rules on passive income but irrelevant for capital gains, this could lead to odd results. Taxpayers may not be able to claim a reduction of

1148. *Danon*, BIT 2018, 55.
1149. *Danon*, BIT 2018, 55.
1150. *See* sec. 4.2.1.3.
1151. *See* sec. 4.2.6.3.
1152. *See* secs 4.2.8.3 and 5.2.
1153. *Collier*, International Tax Review 2013, 11.
1154. *See* secs 4.2.8.3 and 5.2.
1155. *Lang*, Introduction to the Law of Double Taxation Conventions (2013) Mn 84.
1156. *See* Mooji's comment in *Walser* in *IFA* 32.
1157. *See also Lang* in *The Chamber of Tax Consultants* 601; in this context, *see* the situation in Russia where the Beneficial Ownership Test is also applied to income from capital gains, *see Tasalov*, Identifying Conduit Companies: A Russian Perspective on the Beneficial Ownership Concept, ET 2020, 536 (537); on considerations concerning the Beneficial Ownership Test in other treaty articles, *see Navisotschnigg* in *Lang/Pistone/Rust/Schuch/Staringer* 91; *Baker* in *United Nations Economic and Social Council*, Note by the Coordinator of the Subcommittee on Improper Use of treaties: Proposed amendments – Addendum: Progress Report of Subcommittee on Improper Use of Tax Treaties: Beneficial Ownership (2008) Mn 30ff.

withholding taxes according to Article 10 OECD MC because they would not be the beneficial owner of the dividends but, at the same time, withholding taxes would be completely eliminated according to Article 13(5) of the OECD MC 2017 if they were to sell the respective participation.[1158] Instead, a convincing argument why the Beneficial Ownership Test is only enshrined in Articles 10-12 OECD MC is that these articles cover the 'type of income which can be transferred to other taxpayers most easily'.[1159] However, 'the usage of the term "beneficial ownership" makes it clear for all other tax treaty provisions as well that tax treaty terms have to be interpreted applying an economic approach'.[1160]

Therefore, it would be best to simply understand the Beneficial Ownership Test as a 'mere indication that one has to apply an economic - and not a formal - approach in interpreting tax treaties'.[1161] As such, the Beneficial Ownership Test does not have any normative meaning but is only a positivist interpretation rule. This understanding would also be consistent with the history of origin of the Beneficial Ownership Test when it was first introduced into the OECD MC.[1162]

At the same time, understanding the Beneficial Ownership Test as a positivist interpretation rule also presents certain difficulties. Stated in the words of *Lang* - albeit in a different context - 'such a rule is not merely superfluous but also detrimental to legal culture', and 'the mere existence of this rule will cause uncertainty, and individual tax administrations and courts will not be deterred from using it as a basis for the denial of treaty benefits'.[1163] This is exactly what happened with the Beneficial Ownership Test. As a result, 'courts in different jurisdictions have already established a line of jurisprudence on the term and probably may not deviate from it without profound reason, that is, only a further amendment of the OECD Commentary'.[1164] Therefore, the best solution would be that the OECD removes the Beneficial Ownership Test from the MC with its next update. This would also be best in line with the outcomes of BEPS Project.[1165]

1158. From an economic perspective, the present value of a share is equivalent to the discounted estimated future dividends (according to the Dividend Discount Model), *see Geyer/Hanke /Littich/Nettekoven*, Grundlagen der Finanzierung (2015) 190ff.
1159. *Lang* in *The Chamber of Tax Consultants* 601.
1160. *Lang* in *The Chamber of Tax Consultants* 601; for a similar opinion, *see* Mooji's comment in *Walser* in *IFA* 32.
1161. *Lang* in *The Chamber of Tax Consultants* 601.
1162. *See* sec. 4.2.1.3.
1163. *See Lang*, TNI 2014, 663 who refers to the PPT with this quote; on *Lang's* position regarding the PPT, *see* FN 1044.
1164. *Navisotschnigg* in *Lang/Pistone/Rust/Schuch/Staringer* 116.
1165. *See also Danon*, The Beneficial Ownership Limitation in Articles 10, 11 and 12 OECD Model and Conduit Companies in Pre- and Post-BEPS Tax Treaty Policy: Do We (Still) Need It? in *Maisto* (Ed.), Current Tax Treaty Issues: 50th Anniversary of the International Tax Group (2020) 585 (660); *Jiménez*, BIT 2020, 212: 'If before the OECD/G20 BEPS Project, there were relevant reasons to get rid of the concept of beneficial ownership, after the Project, this perception is even stronger not only due to the new article 29(9) of the OECD Model (2017), but also because there is a third element for confusion - the value creation transfer pricing framework. This situation is something that should be taken into account if the OECD is serious in following its work on legal certainty.'

5.5 EXCURSUS: NEW DIRECTION OF THE OECD WITH REGARD TO SUBSTANCE?[1166]

The BEPS Project introduced a variety of new substance requirements in the field of intangibles.[1167] As a result, MNEs have taken steps that are 'aimed at aligning their corporate structures with their real economic activity, either by reconsidering their transfer pricing positions and/or by relocating valuable assets, such as intangibles, in jurisdictions where substantial economic activities take place'.[1168] Overall, the measures developed in the BEPS Project seem to be well suited to limit the profit shifting via intangibles.[1169]

However, despite these extensive changes just recently, the OECD still appears to see the need for further revisions. At the moment, fundamental changes to the international tax framework are being discussed in order to master the tax challenges arising from digitalization.[1170] In short, the OECD examines proposals involving two pillars:[1171]

- Pillar One focuses on the allocation of taxing rights, and seeks to undertake a coherent and concurrent review of the profit allocation and nexus rules;[[1172]]
- Pillar Two focuses on the remaining BEPS issues and seeks to develop rules that would provide jurisdictions with a right to 'tax back' where other jurisdictions have not exercised their primary taxing rights or the payment is otherwise subject to low levels of effective taxation.[[1173]]

With regard to Pillar One, the intention is to modify current nexus and profit allocation rules (i.e., transfer pricing rules) to allocate more profits and hence tax revenue to market jurisdictions.[1174] Effectively, this would entail a reallocation of taxing rights between residence state and source state beyond the arm's-length principle.[1175] However, this is exactly what the OECD did not want to do with the BEPS Project.[1176]

1166. This chapter is based on information that was available as of 1 March 2021.
1167. *See* already sec. 1.3.
1168. *OECD*, Tax Challenges Arising from Digitalisation – Interim Report 2018 (2018) Mn 253; *see also OECD*, Addressing the Tax Challenges of the Digitalisation of the Economy (2019) Mn 3.
1169. Expressly, the two leading figures of the BEPS Project, *Saint-Amans/Russo*, BIT 2016, 240: 'Sand, if not stones, has been thrown into the wheels of common and insidious BEPS planning structures [...] Once the various BEPS measures are implemented, these structures will no longer be effective.'
1170. *See OECD*, Addressing the Tax Challenges of the Digitalisation of the Economy – Policy Note (2019).
1171. *OECD*, Programme of Work to Develop a Consensus Solution to the Tax Challenges Arising from the Digitalisation of the Economy (2019) Mn 7.
1172. *See OECD*, Secretariat Proposal for a 'Unified Approach' under Pillar One (2019); *OECD*, Tax Challenges Arising from Digitalisation – Report on Pillar One Blueprint (2020).
1173. *See OECD*, Global Anti-Base Erosion Proposal ('GloBE') – Pillar Two (2019); *OECD*, Tax Challenges Arising from Digitalisation – Report on Pillar Two Blueprint (2020).
1174. *See OECD*, Programme of Work to Develop a Consensus Solution to the Tax Challenges Arising from the Digitalisation of the Economy (2019) Mn 26.
1175. *See OECD*, Secretariat Proposal for a 'Unified Approach' under Pillar One (2019) Mn 15.
1176. *OECD*, Action Plan on Base Erosion and Profit Shifting (2013) 11: 'While actions to address BEPS will restore both source and residence taxation in a number of cases where cross-border

Furthermore, also with Pillar Two, the OECD is contemplating an about-face from fundamental values of the BEPS Project. Regarding the BEPS Project, it was stated that '[n]o or low taxation is not per se a cause of concern, but it becomes so when it is associated with practices that artificially segregate taxable income from the activities that generate it'.[1177] By contrast, the current proposal of an income inclusion rule under Pillar 2 intends to ensure that the income of an 'MNE group is subject to tax at a minimum rate thereby reducing the incentive to allocate income for tax reasons to low taxed entities'.[1178] It is not clear yet to what extent this proposal will take substance – one of the fundamental pillars of the BEPS Project –[1179] into consideration. In this regard, it is stated that 'substance based carve-outs would undermine the policy intent and effectiveness of the [...] proposal'.[1180] However, given that the OECD has only recently introduced comprehensive new substance requirements and that MNEs have already adapted their structures accordingly, it would be unfortunate to 'dilute' these new substance requirements only a short time later.[1181]

Last, but not least, the OECD examines the insertion of a subject-to-tax rule that would deny 'treaty benefits on certain items of income where the payment is not subject to tax at a minimum rate'.[1182] This comes full circle to the Beneficial Ownership Test because a subject-to-tax rule was originally proposed as an alternative to it.[1183] However, a subject-to-tax rule was found to 'be contrary to the spirit and general economy of the Draft Convention' and, eventually, the Beneficial Ownership Test was

income would otherwise go untaxed or would be taxed at very low rates, these actions are not directly aimed at changing the existing international standards on the allocation of taxing rights on cross-border income.'

1177. *OECD*, Action Plan on Base Erosion and Profit Shifting (2013) 10; *see* already sec. 1.3.3.

1178. *OECD*, Statement by the OECD/G20 Inclusive Framework on BEPS on the Two-Pillar Approach to Address the Tax Challenges Arising from the Digitalisation of the Economy (2020) Annex 2 Mn 8; by contrast, *see OECD*, Resumption of Application of Substantial Activities Factor to No or only Nominal Tax Jurisdictions (2018) Mn 20: 'However, this does not suggest that the absence of a corporate tax rate, or any particular level of corporate income tax is in itself harmful'; *see also OECD*, Measuring and Monitoring BEPS – Action 11: 2015 Final Report (2015) Mn 117: 'MNEs taking advantage of differences in countries' tax rates does not amount to BEPS on its own.'

1179. *See* sec. 1.3.1.

1180. *OECD*, Statement by the OECD/G20 Inclusive Framework on BEPS on the Two-Pillar Approach to Address the Tax Challenges Arising from the Digitalisation of the Economy (2020) Annex 2 Mn 12.

1181. *See also Buriak/Riedl*, Global Transfer Pricing Conference 2020: Transfer Pricing Developments around the World, ITPJ 2020, 239 (240) where it was mentioned that 'there are still difficulties with the implementation of certain regulations and concepts introduced in the past, including those in the OECD Transfer Pricing Guidelines for Multinational Enterprises and Tax Administrations 2017. Hence, further revision of these regulations and concepts is questionable'; for a different view, *see Englisch/Becker*, International Effective Minimum Taxation – The GLOBE Proposal, WTJ 2019, 483 (491f).

1182. *OECD*, Statement by the OECD/G20 Inclusive Framework on BEPS on the Two-Pillar Approach to Address the Tax Challenges Arising from the Digitalisation of the Economy (2020) Annex 2 Mn 18.

1183. *OECD*, Preliminary Report on suggested amendments to Articles 11 and 12 of the Draft Convention, relating to interest and royalties respectively, FC/WP27(68)1 (1968) 14; *see* already sec. 4.2.1.1.

introduced into the OECD MC 1977.[1184] Looking back on the more than 40-year history of the Beneficial Ownership Test and the associated uncertainty in its application, it can hardly be called a success story. It remains to be seen whether the same will one day also be said about these newly conceived concepts in the case that they will actually be implemented.

5.6 PRELIMINARY CONCLUSIONS

- The DEMPE Approach and the Substantial Activity Requirement – i.e., the Modified Nexus Approach for preferential IP regimes and the Core Income Generating Activities for IP income in no or only nominal tax jurisdictions – have the common aim to align taxation and value creation.
- When it comes to the DEMPE Approach and the Modified Nexus Approach, their understanding of value creation diverges; under the DEMPE Approach, management activities (strategical and tactical level) are considered as value creating, whereas, under the Modified Nexus Approach, actual R&D activities (operational level) are considered as value creating; however, the uplift under the Modified Nexus Approach bridges these two understandings of value creation to a certain extent; furthermore, since both approaches are activity-based concepts, they have in common that the sole provision of capital without the performance of any activities is not considered as value creating (priority of the production factor labour over capital).
- From a conceptual point of view, the Modified Nexus Approach is a quantitative approach for determining substance, and it assumes a correlation between the expenditures of an activity and the value created by it; by contrast, the DEMPE Approach – as a qualitative approach – does not necessarily assume such a correlation.
- At the same time, one has to keep in mind that the DEMPE Approach feeds into the Modified Nexus Approach as expenditures for related party outsourcing and for the acquisition of IP from related parties are included in the nexus ratio with arm's-length prices (at value).
- When it comes to the Modified Nexus Approach and the Core Income Generating Activities, their understanding of value creation appears prima facie congruent as both concepts emphasize the relevance of conducting R&D (operational level).
- However, the concept of Core Income Generating Activities is designed as a rebuttable presumption; in this way, the DEMPE Approach can come into play; as a result, management activities (strategical and tactical level) instead of actual R&D activities (operational level) become relevant.
- The situation is different under the Modified Nexus Approach; although it is also designed as a rebuttable presumption, it still requires an entity to conduct

1184. OECD, Report on suggested amendments to Articles 11 and 12 of the Draft Convention, relating to interest and royalties respectively, FC/WP27(70)1 (1970) 13.

R&D to a certain extent for a successful rebuttal; furthermore, it is doubtful whether the DEMPE Approach can be used to rebut the nexus ratio.

- This difference between the two concepts can be explained by the possibility of an uplift under the Modified Nexus Approach which emphasizes the importance of management activities (strategical and tactical level); since it is, by design, not possible to apply an uplift under the concept of Core Income Generating Activities, this could explain why the DEMPE Approach (more precisely, the understanding of value creation under the DEMPE Approach) can eventually come into play.
- From a conceptual point of view, the concept of Core Income Generating Activities with regard to IP income applies a qualitative approach to determine substance; as a result, the analysis under the Core Income Generating Activities is more similar to the analysis under the DEMPE Approach than under the Modified Nexus Approach.
- The Beneficial Ownership Test (Forwarding Approach) - unlike the DEMPE Approach and the Substantial Activity Requirement - does not set any substance requirements but applies a formal approach; contrary to the DEMPE Approach and the Substantial Activity Requirement, the Beneficial Ownership Test does not test what a taxpayer contributed to receive a payment (i.e., it is not an activity-based concept) but what a taxpayer can do with a received payment.
- However, since it is unclear in the OECD Commentary when a forwarding obligation is dependent on the receipt of a payment, it could be argued that the absence of substance under the DEMPE Approach could lead to the denial of beneficial ownership of received royalties.
- Contrary to the Beneficial Ownership Test, the PPT is not simply applicable because there is an interdependence between two income streams; rather, the PPT also requires the fulfilment of a subjective element; in light of the BEPS Project, this subjective element is essential as it emphasizes the relevance of substance of a taxpayer; since the Beneficial Ownership Test completely neglects the factor substance, it appears alien in a post-BEPS world; furthermore, the application of the Beneficial Ownership Test and the PPT may lead to different results.
- This discrepancy between the Beneficial Ownership Test and the PPT can be overcome with a proper interpretation of the Beneficial Ownership Test; the Beneficial Ownership Test is a positivist interpretation rule and, as such, does not have any normative meaning; it merely indicates that DTCs have to be interpreted by applying an economic approach.
- Still, since courts in different jurisdictions have already established a line of jurisprudence on the term from which they may not deviate without reason, it is advisable to remove the Beneficial Ownership Test from the MC; this would also be the best solution with regard to the outcomes of the BEPS Project.
- Currently, the OECD is discussing further revisions to the international tax framework in order to master the tax challenges arising from digitalization; in

this context, a departure from fundamental values of the BEPS Project is looming; at the moment, it is not clear which role substance will play in this future environment; however, given that the OECD has only recently introduced comprehensive new substance requirements and that MNEs have already adapted their structures accordingly, it would be regrettable to abandon these new substance requirements only a short time later.

CHAPTER 6
Conclusions

Setting the scene

- Tax provisions tie to either the (legal) form or the (economic) substance of an action; that is, some tax provisions use private law concepts and connect tax consequences to them, whereas others use own tax concepts that are independent from private law.
- When a provision does not tie to the form but rather to the substance of an action, there are essentially two ways that the substance requirement can be formulated: On the one hand, concrete criteria can be used for which fulfilment can be objectively assessed (quantitative approach); on the other hand, a provision can contain abstract – albeit very detailed – criteria that may only provide indications to assess when the substance requirement is fulfilled (qualitative approach).
- MNEs often centralize their intangibles in an own legal entity (IP Company); on the one hand, this is done for business reasons; on the other hand, tax considerations may also play an important role due to the high-profit potential associated with intangibles; therefore, IP Companies are often established in jurisdictions that offer a preferential IP regime or in low or no tax jurisdictions.
- In order to sustain such a structure, an IP Company must have the necessary substance to:
  - retain the intangible-related returns (DEMPE Approach);
  - qualify for preferential taxation/no or only nominal taxation of the income from the IP asset (Substantial Activity Requirement – Modified Nexus Approach or Core Income Generating Activities, respectively);
  - collect royalties free from withholding taxes (Beneficial Ownership Test).
- As the DEMPE Approach and the Substantial Activity Requirement both aim to align taxation with value creation (value creation as substance), this thesis examined whether both concepts share the same understanding of value creation; additionally, since there are two concepts used to determine the

Substantial Activity Requirement, i.e., the Modified Nexus Approach for preferential IP regimes and the Core Income Generating Activities for IP income in no or only nominal tax jurisdictions, this thesis analysed whether these concepts are congruent.

- Furthermore, since the OECD did not address the Beneficial Ownership Test in the BEPS Project, this thesis analysed how substance was defined in the pre-BEPS era (i.e., in the Beneficial Ownership Test) compared to how substance was defined in the BEPS Project (DEMPE Approach and Substantial Activity Requirement); additionally, since, with the BEPS Project, the OECD introduced a PPT that targets the same structures as the Beneficial Ownership Test, this thesis examined whether both concepts share the same underlying values or whether the BEPS Project changed the perception of substance in this area and, as a consequence, diverging results between these concepts are possible.

Substance in the area of Transfer Pricing – DEMPE Approach

- Contractual arrangements between associated enterprises form the starting point of the transfer pricing analysis; ultimately, however, the actual conduct of the parties is decisive; therefore, the expected substance from a taxpayer is the same notwithstanding whether contractual arrangements exist.
- The legal owner of an intangible is considered as the owner of that intangible for transfer pricing purposes; however, legal ownership alone does not ultimately grant entitlement to any intangible-related returns; still, the identification of the legal owner of an intangible is important because income should initially be attributed to the legal owner; in a second step, the legal owner has to compensate other associated enterprises corresponding to the value created by them with regard to the DEMPE of the intangible.
- When strictly referring to the DEMPE Approach, terms like economic ownership or beneficial ownership should be avoided since the OECD deliberately did not use them and, otherwise, confusion might ensue; of course, this does not mean that there cannot be an overlap between these concepts and the DEMPE Approach.
- In order to retain all of the intangible-related returns, the legal owner must
  - perform the important DEMPE functions through its own personnel;
  - have control over risks related to the DEMPE of the intangible;
  - have the financial capacity to assume risks related to the DEMPE of the intangible; and
  - provide the necessary funding for the DEMPE of the intangible.
- Important functions are such that usually make a significant contribution to intangible value; although it always depends on the facts and circumstances which functions are important functions in a specific case, it can generally be said that important functions concern management activities in the DEMPE of an intangible (activities on the strategical and tactical level); consequently, the

DEMPE Approach expects a company to have employees with certain managerial skills.

- Other normal functions, like operational R&D activity, can be outsourced; however, it is expected that the legal owner controls the performance of the outsourced normal functions in this case; to assess whether this is the case, the same substance requirements as those for determining control over risk apply; if the legal owner controls outsourced normal functions, he regularly does not have to share the intangible-related returns but only has to compensate the service provider at arm's length.
- The legal owner must assume economically significant risks associated with the DEMPE of an intangible; it is not determinative who contractually assumes a risk; instead, risk assumption requires control over risk and financial capacity to assume the risk.
- Control over risk includes the capability and authority to decide to take on a risk and to decide whether and how to respond to a risk (decision-making functions).
- The capability to perform decision-making functions requires that decision makers in a company have competence and experience in the area of the particular risk for which the decision is being made and that they have an understanding of the impact of their decision on the business; therefore, decision makers should be competent persons in the sense that they have the relevant technical or scientific skills in the field in which a decision is taken; furthermore, in line with the evaluations under important functions, control over risk requires a company to perform the strategical and tactical risk management, whereas the operational risk management can be outsourced.
- The authority to perform decision-making functions concerns the actual performance of a decision-making function; the focus is on the decision-making of the parties to a transaction in relation to the specific risk arising from a transaction, whereas the setting of general policies in an MNE with regard to the assumption of risk is not decisive; likewise, merely formally approving decisions that were effectively made in other locations is insufficient.
- Financial capacity to assume risk concerns the access to funding to bear the consequences of the risk if it materializes; in addition to available assets, it also takes into account the options realistically available to access additional liquidity from external sources; in this regard, financial capacity to assume risk considers the functionality of a company – the higher the functionality of a company, the easier it has access to funding; however, since the functionality of a company is already tested when it comes to control over risk, the requirement of financial capacity to assume risk is only a secondary issue.
- The legal owner must provide the funding for the DEMPE of an intangible; in this context, it is distinguished between three different scenarios: Provision of funding and control over operational risks, provision of funding and control over financial risks, and mere provision of funding.

- In order to retain all of the intangible-related returns, the legal owner must provide funding and exercise control over risks that are linked to the operational activities for which the funding is used (operational risks); this means that, in the case of a contract R&D arrangement, the principal must have control over the development risk; with respect to the necessary substance requirements, reference can be made to the substance requirements with regard to important functions and control over risk.
- By contrast, the provision of funding together with control over the risk linked to the funding (financial risk) but not control over the operational risk only entitles to a risk-adjusted return; control over financial risks expects a taxpayer to have the capability and authority to evaluate a potential project for which funding is provided from a financial perspective; unlike control over operational risk, control over financial risk does generally not require an active involvement in the development of the intangible; as a consequence, control over the financial risk requires knowledge about the funding itself (focus on financial skills), whereas control over the operational risk (in particular, the development risk) requires knowledge in the field for which funding is provided (focus on technical or scientific skills).
- The mere provision of funding without control over the operational risk or even the financial risk only entitles to a risk-free return; therefore, funding alone is not considered as creating any value under the DEMPE Approach (i.e., it is not considered as relevant substance); funding always has to be undertaken together with other relevant economic activities (i.e., the performance of important functions or the control over operational risks) to have an impact on the allocation of intangible-related returns.
- For this reason, the DEMPE Approach is an activity-based concept (i.e., profits are allocated to the economic activities that generate them); it focuses on functions - more precisely, important functions and decision-making functions - that people perform; the intended purpose of emphasizing the importance of people functions under Article 9 OECD MC is to prevent tax planning that separates functions from risks and assets; cash box companies - capital-rich companies with few, if any, employees and little or no economic activity often resident in low or no tax jurisdictions - that only contractually assume risks and provide funding are unwanted.
- In short, value creation under the DEMPE Approach concerns people functions on the strategical and tactical level (management activities); to be solely entitled to all of the intangible-related returns, the legal owner must have the internal competencies; that is, they must not be outsourced for performing important functions and decision-making functions and for actually performing these functions; by contrast, external factors (e.g., market-specific characteristics) are not considered as value-creating factors under the DEMPE Approach (i.e., they are not considered as substance of a company); nevertheless, they have to be considered as comparability factors when performing a comparability analysis; as a result, it is possible that associated enterprises

resident in different countries may receive a different remuneration even though they have the same level of substance.

- The DEMPE Approach is a qualitative approach for defining substance as it only provides abstract criteria ('important functions') for assessing whether the relevant substance requirements are met; although the DEMPE Approach provides illustrative examples of important functions, which functions are important functions always has to be assessed on the basis of the relevant facts and circumstances.
- Since operational R&D activities can, in principle, harmlessly be outsourced under the DEMPE Approach, a structure with a typical IP Principal is still possible; yet, with the focus being on people functions - and where these functions are performed - MNEs have to ensure that competent personnel with decision-making authority is located in the jurisdiction of the IP Company; the DEMPE Approach may therefore have the unintended consequence that MNEs will shift not only profits but also people - and, attached with them, profit-potential - from high-tax jurisdictions to low-tax jurisdictions.
- The arm's-length principle is generally a neutral concept that intends to put related parties and unrelated parties on an equal footing; however, the requirement of control over risk and the insignificance of the provision of funding for an entitlement to intangible-related returns move the arm's-length principle into the direction of an anti-abuse rule; as these presumptions are not necessarily in line with how independent parties behave in comparable transactions, they may strain the arm's-length principle beyond its limits; however, empirical evidence of third-party behaviour should always be able to disprove these hypothetical assumptions; in any event, it should be ensured that related parties need not have more substance than unrelated parties in the same or similar circumstances.
- The DEMPE Approach is not a mere clarification but a new concept for the allocation of intangible-related returns; consequently, the DEMPE Approach can only be applied to tax treaties that are concluded after its introduction.

Substance in the area of Harmful Tax Practices – Substantial Activity Requirement

- Compared to the broad definition of intangibles under the OECD TPG 2017, the substantive scope of the Modified Nexus Approach is rather narrow as it generally only encompasses trade intangibles that are legally protected.
- A qualifying taxpayer has to be the legal owner or an exclusive licensee of a qualifying IP asset to receive preferential tax treatment under the Modified Nexus Approach.
- The Modified Nexus Approach applies a formula to determine how much of the income that a qualifying taxpayer receives from a qualifying IP asset may be taxed preferentially; according to this formula, expenditures are a proxy for substantial activities; the ratio of qualifying expenditures to overall expenditures (nexus ratio) is used to determine the value creation and hence the

substance of a taxpayer in the development of a qualifying IP asset; qualifying expenditures are such where it is assumed that the underlying activity of the taxpayer that caused the respective expenditures created value; overall expenditures also include additional expenditure items for which it is assumed that the underlying value-creating activity was not directly performed by the taxpayer itself.

- The legal owner of a qualifying IP asset is expected to incur expenditures only for its own actual R&D activity and for outsourcing R&D to unrelated parties; by contrast, outsourcing to related parties and the acquisition of IP is generally harmful (i.e., included in overall expenditures but not in qualifying expenditures); however, unless a taxpayer's expenditures for outsourcing to related parties and the acquisition of IP do not exceed his expenditures for its own actual R&D activity and for outsourcing R&D to unrelated parties by more than 30% (uplift), the overall IP income may be taxed preferentially.
- According to the Modified Nexus Approach, value is primarily created by the performance of activities on the operational level (day-to-day activities); however, it is also acknowledged that activities on the strategical and tactical level (management activities) play an important role in creating value for an IP asset; in this regard, the uplift functions as a bridge between these two understandings of value creation.
- By contrast, mere capital contribution is not regarded as creating value; therefore, the Modified Nexus Approach is an activity-based concept (link between expenditures that serve as a proxy for activity and income).
- The Modified Nexus Approach is a quantitative approach for defining substance as the fulfilment of the relevant criteria (i.e., distinguishing expenditures incurred in qualifying expenditures and overall expenditures) can be objectively assessed; the Modified Nexus Approach operates under the assumption that the significance of an activity for the creation of value is reflected in the expenditures incurred in the performance of said activity and, hence, it does not depend on the relevant facts and circumstances which activity has actually created more value.
- When establishing an IP Company, MNEs have to make sure that they locate people that perform operational R&D activities in the jurisdiction of the IP Company; an IP Company that is only responsible for the management of the R&D process while the operational R&D activities are performed by related parties in a different jurisdiction will not be able to claim preferential tax treatment.
- In exceptional circumstances, it is possible to rebut the nexus ratio; however, the requirements for a successful rebuttal are anything but clear.
- The requirement of Core Income Generating Activities with regard to IP income earned in a no or only nominal tax jurisdiction is met when an entity conducts R&D rather than simply acquiring or outsourcing it; therefore, the concept of Core Income Generating Activities is also an activity-based concept

(link between activity and income); however, unlike the Modified Nexus Approach, it applies a qualitative approach to define substance.
- Furthermore, while the Modified Nexus Approach has a rather narrow definition of a qualifying IP asset, the concept of Core Income Generating Activities has a broader scope that also encompasses marketing intangibles; with regard to marketing intangibles, the Core Income Generating Activities would be branding, marketing, and distribution.
- In exceptional circumstances, an entity may demonstrate that it performed the Core Income Generating Activities even if it did not conduct R&D or branding, marketing, and distribution, respectively; in this regard, the substance requirements under the DEMPE Approach may be used to provide evidence of Core Income Generating Activities.

Beneficial Ownership

- Over the course of its more than 40-year history, the OECD has addressed the issue of beneficial ownership numerous times and in various different publications; often, however, the notion of the concept is not aligned across these publications; for this reason, knowledge of the historical evolution of the Beneficial Ownership Test is essential for comprehending the different views often expressed on it.
- When the Beneficial Ownership Test was originally introduced into the OECD MC in 1977, it did not have any normative meaning but was only clarificatory.
- The Conduit Companies Report of 1986 intended to turn the Beneficial Ownership Test towards a new direction so that it can be applied to conduit company structures; yet, the legal relevance of this report for the interpretation of the Beneficial Ownership Test must seriously be questioned as it goes beyond the understanding of beneficial ownership in the OECD MC and Commentary 1977.
- The 1998 Report on Harmful Tax Competition apparently ascribes a broad anti-abuse meaning - similar to a general anti-avoidance rule - to the Beneficial Ownership Test; however, as such an understanding obviously goes beyond the understanding in the OECD MC and Commentary 1977, it must be disregarded for the interpretation of the Beneficial Ownership Test.
- The 1999 Partnership Report understands the Beneficial Ownership Test as an attribution-of-income rule (i.e., the person that is liable to tax on royalties in the residence state is also their beneficial owner); however, the premise that the tax treatment in the residence state is decisive for the entitlement to treaty benefits in the source state is not convincing and, therefore, the Partnership Report must not be used for the interpretation of the Beneficial Ownership Test.
- In 2003, the considerations of the Conduit Companies Report with regard to the Beneficial Ownership Test were incorporated into the OECD Commentary;

however, the exact meaning that this update intended to ascribe to the Beneficial Ownership Test is far from clear.

- According to the 2010 amendment of the OECD Commentary, a CIV is the beneficial owner of income that it receives as long as its managers have discretionary powers to manage the assets that generate the income; this approach puts an emphasis on the functions that a CIV performs; however, the relevance of this approach for the Beneficial Ownership Test in a non-CIV context is doubtful, especially when considering that the 2014 update of the OECD Commentary does not follow it.
- Since the 2014 update of the OECD Commentary, it is stated that a person is not the beneficial owner when its right to use and enjoy royalties is constrained by a contractual or legal obligation to pass on the payment received to another person (Forwarding Approach); such a harmful forwarding obligation must always be based on legal grounds and can never be factual; consequently, the 2014 update of the OECD Commentary introduces a formal approach as it ties to private law or other legal relations for assessing the beneficial ownership status of a recipient of a payment; by contrast, the substance of a taxpayer is irrelevant.
- Contrary to the Beneficial Ownership Test, the PPT also requires the fulfilment of a subjective element (i.e., obtaining a benefit must have been one of the principal purposes of an arrangement); in this context, substance plays a crucial role as it allows a taxpayer to disprove the existence of the subjective element.

Comparison between DEMPE Approach, Substantial Activity Requirement and Beneficial Ownership

- The DEMPE Approach and the Substantial Activity Requirement – i.e., the Modified Nexus Approach for preferential IP regimes and the Core Income Generating Activities for IP income in no or only nominal tax jurisdictions – have the common aim to align taxation and value creation.
- When it comes to the DEMPE Approach and the Modified Nexus Approach, their understanding of value creation differs substantially; under the DEMPE Approach, management activities (strategical and tactical level) are considered as value creating, whereas, under the Modified Nexus Approach, actual R&D activities (operational level) are considered as value creating; however, the uplift under the Modified Nexus Approach bridges these two understandings of value creation to a certain extent; furthermore, since both approaches are activity-based concepts, they have in common that the sole provision of capital without the performance of any activities is not considered as value creating (priority of the production factor labour over capital).
- From a conceptual point of view, the Modified Nexus Approach is a quantitative approach for determining substance, and it assumes a correlation between the expenditures of an activity and the value created by it; by contrast, the

DEMPE Approach – as a qualitative approach – does not necessarily assume such a correlation.

- At the same time, one has to keep in mind that the DEMPE Approach feeds into the Modified Nexus Approach as expenditures for related party outsourcing and for the acquisition of IP from related parties are included in the nexus ratio with arm's-length prices (at value).
- When it comes to the Modified Nexus Approach and the Core Income Generating Activities, their understanding of value creation appears prima facie congruent as both concepts emphasize the relevance of conducting R&D (operational level).
- However, the concept of Core Income Generating Activities is designed as a rebuttable presumption; in this way, the DEMPE Approach can come into play; as a result, management activities (strategical and tactical level) instead of actual R&D activities (operational level) become relevant.
- The situation is different under the Modified Nexus Approach; although it is also designed as a rebuttable presumption, it still requires an entity to conduct R&D to a certain extent for a successful rebuttal; furthermore, it is doubtful whether the DEMPE Approach can be used to rebut the nexus ratio.
- This difference between the two concepts can be explained by the possibility of an uplift under the Modified Nexus Approach which emphasizes the importance of management activities (strategical and tactical level); since it is, by design, not possible to apply an uplift under the concept of Core Income Generating Activities, this could explain why the DEMPE Approach (more precisely, the understanding of value creation under the DEMPE Approach) can eventually come into play.
- From a conceptual point of view, the concept of Core Income Generating Activities with regard to IP income applies a qualitative approach for determining substance; as a result, the analysis under the Core Income Generating Activities is more similar to the analysis under the DEMPE Approach than under the Modified Nexus Approach.
- The Beneficial Ownership Test (Forwarding Approach) – unlike the DEMPE Approach and the Substantial Activity Requirement – does not set any substance requirements but applies a formal approach; contrary to the DEMPE Approach and the Substantial Activity Requirement, the Beneficial Ownership Test does not test what a taxpayer contributed for receiving a payment (i.e., it is not an activity-based concept) but what a taxpayer can do with a received payment.
- However, since it is unclear in the OECD Commentary when a forwarding obligation is dependent on the receipt of a payment, it could be argued that the absence of substance under the DEMPE Approach could lead to the denial of beneficial ownership of received royalties.
- Contrary to the Beneficial Ownership Test, the PPT is not simply applicable because there is an interdependence between two income streams; rather, the PPT also requires the fulfilment of a subjective element; in light of the BEPS

Project, this subjective element is essential as it emphasizes the relevance of substance of a taxpayer; since the Beneficial Ownership Test completely neglects the factor substance, it appears alien in a post-BEPS world; furthermore, the application of the Beneficial Ownership Test and the PPT may lead to different results.

- This discrepancy between the Beneficial Ownership Test and the PPT can be overcome by a proper interpretation of the Beneficial Ownership Test; the Beneficial Ownership Test is a positivist interpretation rule and, as such, does not have any normative meaning; it merely indicates that DTCs have to be interpreted by applying an economic approach.
- Still, since courts in different jurisdictions have already established a line of jurisprudence on the term from which they may not deviate without reason, it is advisable to remove the Beneficial Ownership Test from the MC; this would also be the best solution with regard to the outcomes of the BEPS Project.

Bibliography

Journals

Andresen, Comments on Professor Schoueri's Lecture 'Arm's Length: Beyond the Guidelines of the OECD', BIT 2015, 717.

Arginelli, Innovation through R&D Tax Incentives: Ideas for a Fair and Transparent Tax Policy, WTJ 2015, 3.

Arnold, Tax Treaties and Tax Avoidance: The 2003 Revisions to the Commentary to the OECD Model, BIT 2004, 244.

Arnold, Tax Treaty News, BIT 2008, 263.

Arnold, Tax Treaty News, BIT 2010, 306.

Arnold, Tax Treaty News, BIT 2011, 367.

Arnold, Tax Treaty News, BIT 2011, 555.

Arnold, An Introduction to the 2014 Update to the OECD Model, BIT 2014, 526.

Avery Jones, The United Kingdom's Influence on the OECD Model Tax Convention, BTR 2011, 653 (677ff).

Avery Jones/De Broe/Ellis/van Raad/Le Gall/Goldberg/Killius/Maisto/Miyatake/Torrione /Vann/Ward/Wiman, The Origins of Concepts and Expressions Used in the OECD Model and Their Adoption by States, BIT 2006, 220.

Bañuelos, The Nexus Approach and Its Compatibility With EU Law, Journal of International Taxation 2016, 28.

Barret, The Changes Introduced by the 2014 Update to the OECD Model Tax Convention, BIT 2014, 529.

Bärsch/Luckhaupt/Schulz, Bestimmung angemessener Verrechnungspreise im Zusammenhang mit immateriellen Vermögenswerten – Eine kritische Analyse der überarbeiteten OECD-Verrechnungspreisleitlinien, Ubg 2014, 37.

Becker, Der OECD-Bericht zu Maßnahme 5 des BEPS-Aktionsplans, IStR 2014, 704.

Becker/Englisch, Taxing Where Value Is Created: What's 'User Involvement' Got to Do with It?, Intertax 2019, 161.

Bernstein, The 2014 OECD Update on Beneficial Ownership, TNI 2015, 345.

Bilaney, Understanding Risk in the Era of the OECD/G20 Base Erosion and Profit Shifting Initiative, BIT 2016, 576.

Blum, Treaty shopping and prevention in a post-BEPS world, International Tax Report 11/2017, 1.

Boidman/Kandev, BEPS: A Spent Force or Radical Change?, TNI 2015, 837.

Boivin/Vollenweider, Patentbox und KMU – Bloss eine gute Absicht?, Expert Focus 2016, 841.

Broemel, Konzerninterne Auftragsforschungsverhältnisse im Spannungsfeld aktueller Entwicklungen bei der Zurechnung von immateriellen Wirtschaftsgütern, IStR 2013, 249.

Brülisauer, The substance-based approach in tax law – 'A' Swiss perspective in the context of 'BEPS', ASA 2014/2015, 811.

Buriak/Riedl, Global Transfer Pricing Conference 2020: Transfer Pricing Developments around the World, ITPJ 2020, 239.

Castro, The Concept of Beneficial Owner in Tax Treaties: Separating the Wheat from the Chaff Through Case Law Method Internationally, International Tax Journal 2013, 21.

Chand, The Principal Purpose Test in the Multilateral Convention: An in-depth Analysis, Intertax 2018, 18.

Chand/Malek, The relevant economic activity test and its impact on the international corporate tax policy framework, BTR 2019, 394.

Chew, The Application of Tax Treaties to Collective Investment Vehicles: Beneficial Owner Requirement Explained?, DFI 2015, 2.

Collier, Clarity, Opacity and Beneficial Ownership, BTR 2011, 684.

Collier, Beneficial owner proposals: Not so beneficial, International Tax Review 2013, 10.

Collier/Dykes, The Virus in the ALP, BIT 2020, 702.

Colling Russo/Karnath, Intercompany Licensing of Intangibles – A Comparative Global Outlook, ITPJ 2019, 381.

Creed, Steuergestaltungen über Lizenz- bzw. Patentboxen – Ein Auslaufmodell?, GRUR-Prax 2014, 346.

Danon, Clarification of the Meaning of 'Beneficial Owner' in the OECD Model Tax Convention – Comment on the April 2011 Discussion Draft, BIT 2011, 437.

Danon, Will nexus based patent boxes be internationally safe?, ASA 2015, 171.

Danon, Treaty Abuse in the Post-BEPS World: Analysis of the Policy Shift and Impact of the Principle Purpose Test for MNE Groups, BIT 2018, 31.

Danon/Salomé, The BEPS Multilateral Instrument: General overview and focus on treaty abuse, IFF 2017, 197.

Das, The Concept of Value Creation: Is It Relevant for the Allocation of Taxing Rights?, BIT 2020, 134.

Dawid/Ebering, Eckpunkte des Scoping Document der OECD vom 25.1.2011, IWB 2011, 490.

Dawid/Schwerdt/Stumpf, Überblick und Einschätzung des OECD-Papiers zum BEPS-Aktionspunkt 8, IWB 2014, 910.

Da Silva, Granting Tax Treaty Benefits to Collective Investment Vehicles: A Review of the OECD Report and the 2010 Amendments to the Model Tax Convention, Intertax 2011, 195.
Da Silva, Evolution of the Beneficial Ownership Concept: More than Half of Century of Uncertainty and What History Can Tell Us, Frontiers of Law in China 2017, 501.
De Baets, Risk Assumption under the Authorised OECD Approach and the 2017 OECD Transfer Pricing Guidelines, TPI 2018, 243.
De Broe/Luts, BEPS Action 6: Tax Treaty Abuse, Intertax 2015, 122.
De Lange/Lankhorst/Hafkenscheid, (Non-)Recognition of Transactions between Associated Enterprises: On Behaving in a Commercially Rational Manner, Decision-Making Traps and BEPS, ITPJ 2015, 85.
Ditz/Pinkernell/Quilitzsch, BEPS-Reformvorschläge zu Lizenzgebühren und Verrechnungspreisen bei immateriellen Wirtschaftsgütern aus Sicht der Beratungspraxis, IStR 2014, 45.
Du Toit, The Evolution of the Term 'Beneficial Ownership' in Relation to International Taxation over the Past 45 Years, BIT 2010, 500.
Dziurdź/Huisman/Kollmann/Spies/Turić, Tagungsbericht zum IFA-Kongress 2015 in Basel, ÖStZ 2016, 32.
Eigelshoven/Ebering/Schmidtke, Der OECD Diskussionsentwurf vom 6. 6. 2012, IWB 2012, 487.
Englisch/Becker, International Effective Minimum Taxation – The GLOBE Proposal, WTJ 2019, 483.
Evers/Miller/Spengel, Intellectual property box regimes: effective tax rates and tax policy considerations, International Tax and Public Finance 2015, 502.
Eynatten/De Haen/Hostyn, The Concept of 'Beneficial Owner' under Belgian Tax Law: Legal Interpretation is Maintained, Intertax 2003, 523.
Fehling/Schmid, BEPS und die EU: Was ist die 'europäische Dimension' von BEPS? – Das Beispiel grenzüberschreitender Lizenzzahlungen, IStR 2015, 493.
Fensby, The Dangers Posed by the OECD's Approach to Preferential Tax Regimes, TNI 2018, 953
Fibbe, Changes to the OECD Commentary on Collective Investment Vehicles Proposed by the OECD Committee on Fiscal Affairs, BIT 2010, 138.
Finley, OECD Forum to Scrutinize Tax Havens' Substance Requirements, TNI 2018, 821.
Finley, OECD Issues Information Exchange Rules For No-Tax Jurisdictions, TNI 2019, 454.
Gentsch/Matteotti/Roth, Aufwandseitige Förderung von Forschung und Entwicklung: Vorschlag für eine verfassungskonforme und standortfördernde Ausgestaltung von Art. 25a Abs. 2 E-StHG, Expert Focus 2015, 1058.
Gibert/Ouamrane, Beneficial Ownership – A French Perspective, ET 2008, 2.
Gooijer, Beneficial Owner: Judicial Variety in Interpretation Counteracted by the 2012 OECD Proposals?, Intertax 2014, 204.
Gosch, Sperrwirkungen – Nationales Recht und Abkommensrecht, allgemeines und spezielles Recht im Widerstreit, ISR 2018, 289.

Groß, Anpassung der Ergebnisse von Verrechnungspreisen an die Wertschöpfung - Der G20/OECD-Abschlussbericht zu den Maßnahmen 8-10 des BEPS-Aktionsplans, IStR 2016, 233.

Gupta, Modifying the Modified Nexus Approach—Behind Closed Doors, TNI 2015, 1128.

Hafkenscheid, The BEPS Report on Risk Allocation: Not So Functional, ITPJ 2017, 19.

Hattingh, The Relevance of BEPS Materials for Tax Treaty Interpretation, BIT 2020, 179.

Haumer, Rechtliches versus wirtschaftliches Eigentum bei immateriellen Wirtschaftsgütern, SWI 2016, 484.

Hausmann, Die Patentbox und zusätzliche F&E-Abzüge im Rahmen der Steuervorlage 17, Expert Focus 2018, 506.

Hausmann/Roth/Meyer-Nandi, Die Patentbox als Steuerplanungsmodell für KMU, Expert Focus 2016, 189.

Hausmann/Widler/Spillmann, Gesamtüberblick über die Patentbox, Expert Focus 2016, 821.

Heggmair, The New Interpretation of the Arm's Length Principle: A Post-BEPS Evaluation, ITPJ 2017, 263.

Herbert/Luckhaupt, Bestimmung von Verrechnungspreisen für immaterielle Wirtschaftsgüter - zum Diskussionsentwurf der OECD, Ubg 2012, 672.

Helderman/Sporken, Revision of the Special Considerations for Intangibles in Chapter VI of the OECD Transfer Pricing Guidelines and Related Provisions, ITPJ 2012, 383.

Helderman/Sporken/Okten/Kanter, A New Era in Determining Arm's Length Compensation for Intangibles? A Comparative Overview of Existing and Possible Future Transfer Pricing Principles, ITPJ 2013, 359.

Helderman/Sporken/Okten, The Revised OECD Discussion Draft on Transfer Pricing Aspects of Intangibles, ITPJ 2014, 3.

Hey, 'Taxation Where Value is Created' and the OECD/G20 Base Erosion and Profit Shifting Initiative, BIT 2018, 203.

Hinny, Steuerliche Behandlung von Immaterialgüterrechten gemäss Unternehmenssteuerreform III, IFF 2016, 192.

Holinski/Schwarz/Stein, Namensnutzung im Konzern - Implikationen für die Praxis durch die neue BFH-Rechtsprechung, Der Konzern 2016, 316.

Hoor, The Revised OECD Transfer Pricing Guidance on Intangibles: A Critical Analysis, TNI 2018, 529.

Huibregtse/Peeters/Verdoner/Carey, IP companies and substance: no-fly zones? TPIJ 2011, 4.

Jiménez, The 2003 Revision of the OECD Commentaries on the Improper Use of Tax Treaties: A Case for the Declining Effect of the OECD Commentaries?, BIT 2004, 17.

Jiménez, Beneficial Ownership: Current Trends, WTJ 2010, 35.

Jiménez, Value Creation: A Guiding Light for the Interpretation of Tax Treaties?, BIT 2020, 197.

Johnston, Tax Havens Make the Grade On OECD Substance Requirements, TNI 2019, 445.

Koch, Die neue OECD-Definition immaterieller Werte für Verrechnungspreiszwecke – hat die OECD ihre selbst gesteckten Ziele erreicht?, IStR 2015, 199.

Koch, BEPS und Intangibles oder die Grenzen des Fremdvergleichsgrundsatzes, IStR 2016, 881.

Koch, Patentbox und steuerliche Förderung von Forschung und Entwicklung, Expert Focus 2016, 828.

Koch/Küttel/Trüssel, Die Schweizer Patentbox, TPI 2018, 154.

Kofler, The BEPS Action Plan and Transfer Pricing: The Arm's Length Standard Under Pressure?, BTR 2013, 646.

Kofler, Die 'Sperrwirkung' des Art 9 OECD-MA, TPI 2017, 70.

Kofler/Verlinden, Unlimited Adjustments: Some Reflections on Transfer Pricing, General Anti-Avoidance and Controlled Foreign Company Rules, and the 'Saving Clause', BIT 2020, 269.

Kramer, Germany's New Royalties Barrier Rule: Preventing Tax Evasion By Limiting Deductibility in Specified Cases, TNI 2017, 879.

Kroppen/Eigelshoven, Verrechnungspreise im Wandel, TPI 2019, 2.

Kroppen/Rasch, Immaterielle Vermögenswerte – Neudefinition des Fremdvergleichsgrundsatzes? – Die finalen Aktionspunkte 8-10 der BEPS-Initiative, IWB 2015, 828.

Lang, 'Treaty Shopping' – Der Mißbrauch von Doppelbesteuerungsabkommen, SWI 1991, 55.

Lang, Later Commentaries of the OECD Committee on Fiscal Affairs, Not to Affect the Interpretation of Previously Concluded Tax Treaties, Intertax 1997, 7.

Lang, Personengesellschaften im DBA-Recht, SWI 2000, 60.

Lang, VwGH zur Verweigerung der Abkommensberechtigung, SWI 2000, 423.

Lang, CFC Regulations and Double Taxation Treaties, BIT 2003, 51.

Lang, Kommunalsteuer und DBA, SWI 2005, 16.

Lang, Wer hat das Sagen im Steuerrecht?, ÖStZ 2006, 203.

Lang, Schweizer Grundsatzurteil zum Beneficial Owner nach DBA-Recht, SWI 2012, 226.

Lang, BEPS Action 6: Introducing an Antiabuse Rule in Tax Treaties, TNI 2014, 655.

Lang, Einkünftezurechnung im Lichte des Entwurfs zu Art 1 Abs 2 OECD-MA, SWI 2015, 153.

Lang, The Signalling Function of Article 29(9) of the OECD Model – The 'Principal Purpose Test', BIT 2020, 264.

Lang/Brugger, The role of the OECD Commentary in tax treaty interpretation, Australian Tax Forum 2008, 95.

Langer, Die Weiterentwicklung der OECD-Verrechnungspreisleitlinien nach dem BEPS-Projekt, TPI 2017, 78.

Larking, A Matter of Substance, TNI 2018, 329.

Larking, Navigating the EU-OECD Harmful Tax Competition Jungle, TNI 2019, 501.

Luts, Compatibility of IP Box Regimes with EU State Aid Rules and Code of Conduct, EC Tax Review 2014, 258.
Mang, The (In)Compatibility of IP Box Regimes with EU Law, the Code of Conduct and the BEPS Initiatives, ET 2015, 78.
Mansori/Sanschagrin, Assessing Value Creation for Transfer Pricing, TNI 2016, 1123.
Matteotti, Fairness im Steuerrecht: Schlaglichter auf Anspruch und Wirklichkeit in laufenden Steuervorhaben, ASA 2015/2016, 51.
Matteotti/Roth, The OECD's Modified Nexus Approach for Patent Boxes - Is BEPS leading towards coherence or distortion in taxing income from intellectual property?, ASA 2014/2015, 755.
McLoughlin, Tax Havens May Need Resources To Satisfy OECD Substance Standard, TNI 2019, 1206.
Monsenego, The Substance Requirement in the OECD Transfer Pricing Guidelines: What Is the Substance of the Substance Requirement?, ITPJ 2014, 9.
Monteith, Steuergestaltung mit Lizenzboxen: Mögliche Gegenmaßnahmen des deutschen Gesetzgebers, StuB 2014, 883.
Morse, Value Creation: A Standard in Search of a Process, BIT 2018, 196.
Musselli, Intangible Revenues Assigned to the Developer and Not to the Funder Lacking 'Development Monitoring Staff': OECD Transfer Pricing Anti-Abuse Rule Clashes with Economics of Contracts, International Tax Journal 2017, 37.
Musselli, Anti-Abuse Notion of 'Control over Intangible- Related Functions' Is Beyond the Arm's Length Principle, ET 2018, 191.
Musselli/Musselli, Rise of a New Standard: Profit Location in Countries of Important Intangible Functions Managers, ITPJ 2017, 331.
Müller, Inputförderung: Forschung und Entwicklung im Ausland, Expert Focus 2016, 800.
Naumann/Groß, Verrechnungspreisaspekte immaterieller Werte - der OECD-Bericht zu Maßnahme 8 des BEPS Action Plan, IStR 2014, 906.
Navisotschnigg, Transfer Pricing Adjustments and Re-Characterization: Lessons Learned from the Canadian Tax Court Case Cameco, TPI 2019, 88.
Nikolakakis/Austry/Avery Jones/Baker/Blessing/Danon/Goradia/Hattingh/Inoue/Lüdicke /Maisto/Miyatake/Raad/Vann/Wiman, Some Reflections on the Proposed Revisions to the OECD Model and Commentaries, and on the Multilateral Instrument, with Respect to Fiscally Transparent Entities - Part 1, BIT 2017, 475.
Oliver/Libin/van Weeghel/du Toit, Beneficial Ownership, BIT 2000, 310.
Pamperl, Auswirkungen einer Verpflichtung zur Weiterleitung passiver Einkünfte auf eine DBA-rechtliche Quellensteuerreduktion, SWI 2013, 403.
Pankiv, Post-BEPS Application of the Arm's Length Principle to Intangibles Structures, ITPJ 2016, 463.
Peng/Lagarden, DEMPE Functions and the RACI Concept - More Clarity or Confusion Ahead?, ITPJ 2019, 3.
Penttilä/Isomaa-Myllymäki, Centralization of Intangibles and Transfer Pricing under BEPS and Finnish Tax Law, ET 2018, 82.

Petruzzi/Myzithra, Substance in Transfer Pricing in a Post-BEPS World and Beyond..., ITPJ 2020, 430.
Pijl, The Definition of 'Beneficial Owner' under Dutch Law, BIT 2000, 256.
Pijl, Beneficial Ownership and Second Tier Beneficial Owners in Tax Treaties of the Netherlands, Intertax 2003, 353.
Pinkernell, Ein Musterfall zur Internationalen Steuerminimierung durch US-Konzerne, StuW 2012, 369.
Pinkernell, OECD-Aktionsplan gegen internationale Gewinnverlagerung und Aushöhlung der Bemessungsgrundlagen (BEPS-Projekt), FR 2013, 737.
Poiret, Beneficial Ownership: Concept, History and Perspective, ET 2016, 274.
Polivanova-Rosenauer, Das Konzept des Nutzungsberechtigten aus abkommensrechtlicher Sicht, SWI 2001, 257.
Polonska, Cost Contribution Arrangements and Funding Activities, ITPJ 2018, 92.
Pross/Radmanesh, Seminar A: 'Patentboxen', IStR 2015, 579.
Puls/Heravi, DEMPE-Funktionen und wirtschaftliches Eigentum an immateriellen Werten - Plädoyer für eine differenzierte Betrachtung, IStR 2018, 721.
Raab, Patent-, Lizenz- und IP-Boxen - Übersicht und aktuelle Entwicklungen, SWI 2018, 125.
Rasch, Sperrwirkung reloaded, TPI 2019, 201.
Raschle/Borriello/Hämmerle, Substanz in internationalen Unternehmensstrukturen: Auswirkungen internationaler Entwicklungen auf Verrechnungspreispraxis und Steuerstrategie, ST 2013, 861.
Robertson, Time to Revisit the U.K. Patent Box?, TNI 2019, 843.
Roeder/Fellner, Base Erosion and Profit Shifting: Immaterielle Vermögenswerte und die OECD - Zusammenfassung des Arbeitsstands des Kapitels VI und erste Analyse aus deutscher Sicht, ISR 2014, 428.
Rouenhoff, Erste Analyse des OECD-Diskussionspapiers zur Berücksichtigung von Intangibles bei der Festlegung von Verrechnungspreisen, IStR 2012, 654.
Saint-Amans/Russo, The BEPS Package: Promise Kept, BIT 2016, 236.
Schmidtke, Maßnahme 8 des BEPS-Aktionsplans - Der Fremdvergleichsgrundsatz und BEPS, IStR 2015, 120.
Schmidtke/Tillmann, Der 2. OECD Diskussionsentwurf immaterielle Wirtschaftsgüter, IWB 2013, 709.
L. Schoueri, Arm' s Length: Beyond the Guidelines of the OECD, BIT 2015, 690 (714f).
P. Schoueri, The OECD's Approach to IP-Boxes as a Norm: Hard, Soft or Half-Baked?, BTR 2017, 438.
Schön, International Taxation of Risk, BIT 2014, 280.
Schwarz, Rationale, design and effectiveness of R&D tax measures, ASA 2014/2015, 711.
Screpante, Rethinking the Arm's Length Principle and Its Impact on the IP Licence Model after OECD/G20 BEPS Actions 8-10: Nothing Changed But the Change?, WTJ 2019, 425.
Shapiro/Mitra/Henshall/Sierra, The OECD Discussion Draft on Intangibles, TNI 2012, 1245.

Shi, IP Boxes in Light of the BEPS Project and EU Law - Part I, ET 2016, 334.

Shi, IP Boxes in Light of the BEPS Project and EU Law - Part II, ET 2016, 371.

Sim/Rigo/Agrawal, Treatment of Funding Risk and Capital - Financial Services versus Non-Financial Services: Never the Twain Shall Meet?, ITPJ 2020, 229.

Stein/Schwarz/Holinski, Funktionales Eigentum und Wertschöpfungsbeitragsanalysen: Steuerliche Erfolgsermittlung bei immateriellen Werten mithilfe betriebswirtschaftlicher Konzepte, DStR 2017, 118.

Stocker/Schmid, Entschädigung immaterieller Vermögenswerte: Auswirkungen des Updates 2017 der OECD Verrechnungspreisleitlinien, TPI 2018, 92.

Tasalov, Identifying Conduit Companies: A Russian Perspective on the Beneficial Ownership Concept, ET 2020, 536.

Tavares/Owens, Human Capital in Value Creation and Post-BEPS Tax Policy: An Outlook, BIT 2015, 590.

Theophilou, Patent Boxes: The Rise, the Change or the Fall?, BIT 2019, 286.

Vallat, Application of the DEMPE Concept in the Pharmaceutical Industry, ITPJ 2020, 168.

Van Weeghel, A Deconstruction of the Principal Purposes Test, WTJ 2019, 1.

Verdoner/Offermanns/Huibregtse, A Cross-Country Perspective on Beneficial Ownership - Part 1, ET 2010, 419.

Verdoner/Offermanns/Huibregtse, A Cross-Country Perspective on Beneficial Ownership - Part 2, ET 2010 465.

Verlinden/Ledure/Dessy, The Risky Side of Transfer Pricing: The OECD Base Erosion and Profit Shifting Reports Sharpen the Rules on Risk Allocation under the Arm' s Length Standard, ITPJ 2016, 109.

Vetter, Zur rechtlichen Bedeutung der OECD Verrechnungspreisgrundsätze, SWI 1997, 547.

Vukovic/Mermet, An Overview of the Future Luxembourg Intellectual Property Tax Regime, ITPJ 2018, 39.

Wardzynski, The 2014 Update to the OECD Commentary: A Targeted Hybrid Approach to Beneficial Ownership, Intertax 2015, 179.

Wheeler, The Attribution of Income to a Person for Tax Treaty Purposes, BIT 2005, 477.

Wheeler, The Missing Keystone of Income Tax Treaties, WTJ 2011, 274.

Wilkie, Substance in International Taxation, ITPJ 2014, 362.

Wittendorff, 'Shadowlands': The OECD on Intangibles, TNI 2012, 935.

Wittendorff, OECD Revised Discussion Draft on Intangibles — A Step in the Right Direction, TNI 2013, 1325.

Wittendorff, More Black Smoke From the OECD's Chimney — Third Draft on Intangibles, TNI 2015, 167.

Wittendorff, BEPS Actions 8-10: Birth of a New Arm's-Length Principle, TNI 2016, 331.

Yoshimura, Clarifying the Meaning of 'Beneficial Owner' in Tax Treaties, Tax Analysts 2013, 761.

Zammit, Centralized Intellectual Property Business Models - Tax Implications of EU Patent Box Regimes, BIT 2015, 540.

Contributions in edited volumes

Andree/Liebchen, Structuring intangibles, in *Lang/Storck/Petruzzi/Risse* (Eds), Transfer Pricing and Intangibles: Current Developments, Relevant Issues and Possible Solutions (2019) 87.

Arnold, The Concept of Beneficial Ownership under Canadian Tax Treaties, in *Lang /Pistone/Schuch/Staringer/Storck* (Eds), Beneficial Ownership: Recent Trends (2013) 39.

Avery Jones, The Beneficial Ownership Concept Was Never Necessary in the Model, in *Lang/Pistone/Schuch/Staringer/Storck* (Eds), Beneficial Ownership: Recent Trends (2013) 333.

Baker, The Meaning of 'Beneficial Ownership' as Applied to Dividends under the OECD Model Tax Convention, in *Maisto* (Ed.), Taxation of Intercompany Dividends under Tax Treaties and EU Law (2012) 87.

Baker, United Kingdom: Indofood International Finance Ltd v. JP Morgan Chase Bank NA, in *Lang/Pistone/Schuch/Staringer/Storck* (Eds), Beneficial Ownership: Recent Trends (2013) 27.

Bakker/De Baets/Mazio/Szotek, Increasing Importance of IP Rights, in *Verlinden /Bakker* (Eds), Mastering the IP Life Cycle from a Legal, Tax and Accounting Perspective (2018) 3.

Becker/Hoeck, Aktionspunkt 5: Bekämpfung von schädlichem Steuerwettbewerb durch mehr Substanz und Transparenz, in *Kofler/Schnitger* (Eds), BEPS-Handbuch: Maßnahmen gegen Gewinnverlagerung und Gewinnverkürzung internationaler Konzerne (2019) 309.

Brauner, Beneficial Ownership in and outside US Tax Treaties, in *Lang/Pistone/Schuch /Staringer/Storck* (Eds), Beneficial Ownership: Recent Trends (2013) 143.

Brown, Fifty Years of Tax Uncertainty: The Problem of International Neutrality for Collective Investment Vehicles, in *Vermeulen* (Ed.), The Tax Treatment of CIVs and REITs (2014) 19.

Bundgaard, The Notion of Beneficial Ownership in Danish Tax Law: The Creation of a New Legal Order with Uncertainty as a Companion, in *Lang/Pistone/Schuch /Staringer/Storck* (Eds), Beneficial Ownership: Recent Trends (2013) 91.

Canete/Pamperl, Einkünftezurechnung und Beneficial Ownership, in *Lang/Schuch /Staringer* (Eds), Einkünftezurechnung im Internationalen Steuerrecht (2012) 73.

Canete/Staringer, Missbrauchserfassung im DBA-Recht durch Anwendung von Beneficial-ownership-Konzepten, in *Lang/Schuch/Staringer* (Eds), Die Grenzen der Gestaltungsmöglichkeiten im internationalen Steuerrecht (2009) 169.

Danon, General Report, in *IFA* (Ed.), Cahiers de droit fiscal international, Vol. 100a Tax Incentives on Research and Development (R&D) (2015) 17.

Danon, Intellectual Property (IP) Income and Tax Treaty Abuse: Relevance of BEPS Actions 5 and 8-10 for the Principal Purpose Test, in *Maisto* (Ed.), Taxation of Intellectual Property under Domestic Law, EU Law and Tax Treaties (2018) 17.

Danon, The Beneficial Ownership Limitation in Articles 10, 11 and 12 OECD Model and Conduit Companies in Pre- and Post-BEPS Tax Treaty Policy: Do We (Still) Need

It? in *Maisto* (Ed.), Current Tax Treaty Issues: 50th Anniversary of the International Tax Group (2020) 585.

De Baets/Gao, Recent Developments on Comparability Analysis in Transfer Pricing, in *Lang/Storck/Petruzzi* (Eds), Transfer Pricing Developments Around the World 2018 (2018) 159.

Duff, Beneficial Ownership: Recent Trends, in *Lang/Pistone/Schuch/Staringer/Storck* (Eds), Beneficial Ownership: Recent Trends (2013) 1.

Dziwiński/Peng, Introduction to the post-BEPS transfer-pricing aspects of intangibles, in *Lang/Storck/Petruzzi/Risse* (Eds), Transfer Pricing and Intangibles: Current Developments, Relevant Issues and Possible Solutions (2019) 3.

Felder/Giezendanner, Liechtenstein, in *IFA* (Ed.), Cahiers de droit fiscal international, Vol. 100a Tax Incentives on Research and Development (R&D) (2015) 425.

Gassner, Austria, in *IFA* (Ed.), Cahiers de droit fiscal international, Vol. 87a Form and substance in tax law (2002) 119.

Gassner/Lang, Treaty Shopping, in *Gassner/Lang/Lechner* (Eds), Aktuelle Entwicklungen im internationalen Steuerrecht: Das neue Musterabkommen der OECD (1994) 43.

Gutmann, Beneficial Ownership as Anti-Abuse Provision: The Bank of Scotland Case, in *Lang/Pistone/Schuch/Staringer/Storck* (Eds), Beneficial Ownership: Recent Trends (2013) 167.

Gutmann, The 2011 Discussion Draft on Beneficial Ownership: What Next for the OECD?, in *Lang/Pistone/Schuch/Staringer/Storck* (Eds), Beneficial Ownership: Recent Trends (2013) 341.

Haumer, Brennpunkt immaterielle Wirtschaftsgüter – die eigentliche 'Substanz' jedes Unternehmens, in *Macho/Steiner/Spensberger* (Eds), Verrechnungspreise kompakt (2017) 366.

Jiménez, Beneficial Ownership as a Broad Anti-Avoidance Provision: Decisions by Spanish Courts and the OECD's Discussion Draft, in *Lang/Pistone/Schuch/Staringer/Storck* (Eds), Beneficial Ownership: Recent Trends (2013) 127.

Jiménez, Beneficial Ownership as an Attribution-of-Income Rule in Spain: Source and Residence Country Perspectives, in *Lang/Pistone/Schuch/Staringer/Storck* (Eds), Beneficial Ownership: Recent Trends (2013) 199.

Jiménez, Tax Avoidance and Aggressive Tax Planning as an International Standard – BEPS and the 'New' Standards of (Legal and Illegal) Tax Avoidance, in *Dourado* (Ed.), Tax Avoidance Revisited in the EU BEPS Context (2017) 25.

Kroppen, Behandlung immaterieller Wirtschaftsgüter unter BEPS, in *Lüdicke/Schnitger/Spengel* (Eds), Besteuerung Internationaler Unternehmen – Festschrift für Dieter Endres (2016) 199.

Kulcsar, Transfer Pricing Aspects of Licensing Arrangements: The Increasingly Enhanced Engagement between Taxpayers and Tax Auditors, in *Verlinden/Bakker* (Eds), Mastering the IP Life Cycle from a Legal, Tax and Accounting Perspective (2018) 403.

Lagarden, Attribution of intangible-related returns - case study, in *Lang/Storck /Petruzzi/Risse* (Eds), Transfer Pricing and Intangibles: Current Developments, Relevant Issues and Possible Solutions (2019) 51.

Lang, Die Stiftung im internationalen Ertragsteuerrecht, in *Csoklich/Müller* (Eds), Die Stiftung als Unternehmer (1990) 185.

Lang, Austria, in *IFA* (Ed.), Cahiers de droit fiscal international, Vol. 78a Interpretation of double taxation conventions (1993) 197.

Lang, Die Bedeutung des Musterabkommens und des Kommentars des OECD-Steuerausschusses für die Auslegung von Doppelbesteuerungsabkommen, in *Gassner/Lang/Lechner* (Eds), Aktuelle Entwicklungen im internationalen Steuerrecht: Das neue Musterabkommen der OECD (1994) 11.

Lang, Die Bedeutung der 1995 erfolgten Änderungen des OECD-Musterabkommens und des Kommentars des OECD-Steuerausschusses für die Doppelbesteuerungsabkommen, in *Lang/Loukota /Lüthi* (Eds), Die Weiterentwicklung des OECD-Musterabkommens (1996) 39.

Lang, General Report, in *IFA* (Ed.), Cahiers de droit fiscal international, Vol. 89a Double non-taxation (2004) 73.

Lang, Interpretation of the Term 'Beneficial Ownership' The Prévost Case - Tax Court of Canada, in *The Chamber of Tax Consultants* (Eds), International Taxation - A Compendium: Volume 1 (2008) 592.

Miyatake, General Report, in *IFA* (Ed.), Cahiers de droit fiscal international, Vol. 92a Transfer Pricing and Intangibles (2007) 17.

Navisotschnigg, The Beneficial Ownership Test, in *Lang/Pistone/Rust/Schuch/Staringer* (Eds), Tax Treaty Entitlement (2019) 91.

Navisotschnigg, Attribution of intangible-related returns - panel discussion, in *Lang/Storck/Petruzzi/Risse* (Eds), Transfer Pricing and Intangibles: Current Developments, Relevant Issues and Possible Solutions (2019) 77.

Ng, The Concept of Beneficial Ownership, in *Ecker/Ressler* (Eds), History of Tax Treaties: The Relevance of the OECD Documents for the Interpretation of Tax Treaties (2011) 509.

Perdelwitz, International Tax Structuring for Holding Activities, in *Cotrut* (Ed.), International Tax Structures in the BEPS Era: An Analysis of Anti-Abuse Measures (2015) 281.

Petruzzi/Navisotschnigg, BEPS and EU requirements for Country-by-Country Reporting, in *Lang/Haunold* (Eds), Transparenz und Informationsaustausch: Der gläserne Steuerpflichtige (2016) 51.

Prasanna/Petruzzi, Accurate Delineation and Recognition of Actual Transactions: Comparability Analysis, in *Lang/Cottani/Petruzzi/Storck* (Eds), Fundamentals of Transfer Pricing: A Practical Guide (2018) 35.

Reimer, How To Conceptualize Beneficial Ownership, in *Lang/Pistone/Schuch /Staringer/Storck* (Eds), Beneficial Ownership: Recent Trends (2013) 253.

Stevens, The 2010 CIV-Report: A Comparison with the 1999 Partnership Report, in *Weber/van Weeghel* (Eds), The 2010 OECD Updates: Model Tax Convention and Transfer Pricing Guidelines - A Critical Review (2011) 101.

Storck/Stradinger, Das Poolkonzept im Bereich Forschung und Entwicklung, in *Bernegger/Rosar/Rosenberger* (Eds), Handbuch Verrechnungspreise (2012) 475.

Tavares/Owens, Asia: Global Tax Policy Post-BEPS and the Perils of the Silk Road, in *Lang/Owens* (Eds), Removing Tax Barriers to China's Belt and Road Initiative (2019) 285.

Tetlak, Poland: Beneficial Ownership of Interest in the Context of Cash Pooling, in *Kemmeren/Essers/Smit/Lang/Pistone/Schuch/Staringer/Storck/Owens/Rust* (Eds), Tax Treaty Case Law around the Globe 2016 (2017) 275.

Vallada, Beneficial Ownership under Articles 10, 11 and 12 of the 2014 OECD Model Convention, in *Lang/Pistone/Rust/Staringer/Storck/Schuch* (Eds), The OECD-Model-Convention and its Update 2014 (2015) 25.

Vann, Beneficial Ownership: What Does History (and Maybe Policy) Tell Us, in *Lang/Pistone/Schuch/Staringer/Storck* (Eds), Beneficial Ownership: Recent Trends (2013) 267.

Vlasceanu, Intellectual Property Structuring in the Context of the OECD BEPS Action Plan, in *Cotrut* (Ed.), International Tax Structures in the BEPS Era: An Analysis of Anti-Abuse Measures (2015) 220.

Voje, Models for Exploiting IP Rights, in *Verlinden/Bakker* (Eds), Mastering the IP Life Cycle from a Legal, Tax and Accounting Perspective (2018) 397.

Walser, The Concept of Beneficial Ownership in Tax Treaties, in *IFA* (Ed.), The OECD Model Convention - 1998 and Beyond: The Concept of Beneficial Ownership in Tax Treaties (2000) 15.

Wheeler, General Report, in *IFA* (Ed.), Cahiers de droit fiscal international, Vol. 92b Conflicts in the attribution of income to a person (2007) 17.

Wilkie, Transfer Pricing Aspects of Intangibles: The License Model, in *Lang/Storck/Petruzzi* (Eds), Transfer Pricing in a Post-BEPS World (2016) 61.

Zimmer, General Report, in *IFA* (Ed.), Cahiers de droit fiscal international, Vol. 87a Form and substance in tax law (2002) 19.

Commentaries

Jiménez, Article 12: Royalties, in Vann et al (Eds), Global Tax Treaty Commentaries.

Kofler in *Reimer/Rust*, Klaus Vogel on Double Taxation Conventions[4] (2015) Article 9.

Rasch/Maier/Wenzel in *Kroppen/Rasch*, Handbuch internationale Verrechnungspreise: Band III[33] (2021) OECD-Kap. VI.

Reimer in *Reimer/Rust*, Klaus Vogel on Double Taxation Conventions[4] (2015) Article 13.

Rust in *Reimer/Rust*, Klaus Vogel on Double Taxation Conventions[4] (2015) Article 1.

Tischbirek in *Vogel/Lehner*, Doppelbesteuerungsabkommen[6] (2015) Vor Articles 10-12.

Valta in *Reimer/Rust*, Klaus Vogel on Double Taxation Conventions[4] (2015) Article 12.

Vogel, Klaus Vogel on Double Taxation Conventions[3] (1997) Preface to Articles 10-12.

Monographs

Baumgartner, Das Konzept des beneficial owner im internationalen Steuerrecht der Schweiz: Unter besonderer Berücksichtigung der Weiterleitung von abkommensbegünstigten Dividenden- und Zinseinkünften in *Reich/Simonek* (Eds), Schriften zum Steuerrecht (2010).

Bullen, Arm's Length Transaction Structures: Recognizing and Restructuring Controlled Transactions in Transfer Pricing (2011).

Collier/Andrus, Transfer Pricing and the Arm's Length Principle After BEPS (2017).

Danon, Switzerland's Direct and International Taxation of Private Express Trusts: With Particular References to US, Canadian and New Zealand Trust Taxation, in *Oberson* (Ed.), Droit fiscal Suisse et international (2004).

De Broe, International Tax Planning and Prevention of Abuse (2008).

Du Toit, Beneficial Ownership of Royalties in Bilateral Tax Treaties (1999).

Geyer/Hanke/Littich/Nettekoven, Grundlagen der Finanzierung (2015).

Jain, Effectiveness of the Beneficial Ownership Test in Conduit Company Cases (2013).

Kaul, Der Nexus-Ansatz: Auswirkungen auf IP-Boxen und Alternativansätze (2018).

Koch, Schaffung und Nutzung immaterieller Vermögenswerte im multinationalen Unternehmen, in *Bischoff/Kellermann/Sieben/Herzig* (Eds), Steuer, Wirtschaft und Recht; 345 (2014).

Lang, The Application of the OECD Model Tax Convention to Partnerships: a critical analysis of the report prepared by the OECD Committee on Fiscal Affairs (2000).

Lang, Introduction to the Law of Double Taxation Conventions (2013).

Leukefeld, Das Konzept der Substanz im Steuerrecht: Nationale und multinationale Substanzvorschriften unter besonderer Berücksichtigung der BEPS-Initiativen von OECD und EU, in *Watrin* (Ed.), Münstersche Forschungsbeiträge zu Rechnungslegung und Unternehmensbesteuerung (2018).

Meindl-Ringler, Beneficial Ownership in International Tax Law (2016).

Meyer/Reher, Projektmanagement: Von der Definition über die Projektplanung zum erfolgreichen Abschluss (2016).

Monsenego, Introduction to Transfer Pricing (2015).

Pankiv, Contemporary application of the Arm's Length Principle in Transfer Pricing (2017).

Schaffer, Domestic Attribution of Income and Taxation of International Entertainers and Sportspersons: Theory and Practice of Art. 17 OECD Model Convention (2017).

P. Schoueri, Conflicts of International Legal Frameworks in the Area of Harmful Tax Competition: The Modified Nexus Approach (2019).

Schwarz Martínez, IP Box Regime im Europäischen Steuerrecht (2017).

Torvik, Transfer pricing and Intangibles: US and OECD Arm's Length Distribution of Operating Profits from IP Value Chains (2019).

Van Weeghel, The Improper Use of Tax Treaties: With Particular Reference to the Netherlands and the United States (1998).

Wittendorff, Transfer Pricing and the Arm's Length Principle in International Tax Law (2010).

Materials

OECD (1967), Observations of Member Countries on Difficulties Raised by the OECD Draft Convention on Income and Capital, TFD/FC/216.

OECD (1967), Consolidated List of Outstanding Points Concerning the OECD Draft Convention on Income and Capital, TFD/FC/218.

OECD (1968), Preliminary Report on suggested amendments to Articles 11 and 12 of the Draft Convention, relating to interest and royalties respectively, FC/WP27(68)1.

OECD (1969), Note on the Discussion of the first report of Working Party No. 27 of the Fiscal Committee on interest and royalties during the 31st session of the Fiscal Committee held from 10 to 13 June, DAF/FC/69.10.

OECD (1970), Report on suggested amendments to Articles 11 and 12 of the Draft Convention, relating to interest and royalties respectively, FC/WP27(70)1.

OECD (1986), Double Taxation Conventions and the Use of Conduit Companies.

OECD (1991), Resolution of the Council on the Historical Archives of the Organisation, C(91)132/FINAL.

OECD (1994), The 1995 Update to the Model Tax Convention, DAFFE/CFA/WP1(94)9.

OECD (1995), Working Party Proposals for Preparing for the 1995+ Update, DAFFE/CFA/WP1(95)5/REV3.

OECD (1997), Council Resolution on the Classification and Declassification of Information, C(97)64/FINAL.

OECD (1997), Next Update to the Model Convention, DAFFE/CFA/WP1(97)6.

OECD (1998), Harmful Tax Competition: An Emerging Global Issue.

OECD (1999), The Application of the OECD Model Tax Convention to Partnerships.

OECD (2001), The OECD's Project on Harmful Tax Practices: The 2001 Progress Report.

OECD (2002), Restricting the Entitlement to Treaty Benefits.

OECD (2003), 2002 Reports Related to the OECD Model Tax Convention.

OECD (2009), Report of the Informal Consultative Group on the Taxation of Collective Investment Vehicles and Procedures for Tax Relief for Cross-Border Investors on the Granting of Treaty Benefits with respect to the Income of Collective Investment Vehicles.

OECD (2009), The Granting of Treaty Benefits with Respect to the Income of Collective Investment Vehicles: Public Discussion Draft.

OECD (2010), The Granting of Treaty Benefits with Respect to the Income of Collective Investment Vehicles.

OECD (2010), The 2010 Update to the Model Tax Convention.

OECD (2010), 2010 Report on the Attribution of Profits to Permanent Establishments.

OECD (2010), OECD Transfer Pricing Guidelines for Multinational Enterprises and Tax Administrations 2010.

OECD (2011), Transfer Pricing and Intangibles: Scope of the OECD Project.

OECD (2011), Working Party No. 6's Special Session on the Transfer Pricing Aspects of Intangibles: Meeting with Business Representatives on the Transfer Pricing Aspects of Intangibles.

OECD (2011), Clarification of the Meaning of 'Beneficial Owner' in the OECD Model Tax Convention - Discussion Draft.
OECD (2012), Discussion Draft: Revision of the special considerations for intangibles in Chapter VI of the OECD Transfer Pricing Guidelines and related provisions.
OECD (2012), OECD Model Tax Convention: Revised Proposals Concerning the Meaning of 'Beneficial Owner' in Articles 10, 11 and 12.
OECD (2013), Addressing Base Erosion and Profit Shifting.
OECD (2013), Action Plan on Base Erosion and Profit Shifting.
OECD (2013), BEPS Frequently Asked Questions.
OECD (2013), Revised Discussion Draft on Transfer Pricing Aspects of Intangibles.
OECD (2014), 2014 Update to the OECD Model Tax Convention.
OECD (2014), Countering Harmful Tax Practices More Effectively, Taking into Account Transparency and Substance - Action 5: 2014 Deliverable.
OECD (2014), Guidance on Transfer Pricing Aspects of Intangibles - Action 8: 2014 Deliverable.
OECD (2014), BEPS Actions 8, 9 and 10: Discussion Draft on Revisions to Chapter I of the Transfer Pricing Guidelines (Including Risk, Recharacterisation, and Special Measures).
OECD (2014), BEPS Action 10: Discussion Draft on the use of Profit Splits in the Context of Global Value Chains.
OECD (2015), Action 5: Agreement on Modified Nexus Approach for IP Regimes.
OECD (2015), Explanatory Statement - 2015 Final Reports.
OECD (2015), Addressing the Tax Challenges of the Digital Economy - Action 1: 2015 Final Report.
OECD (2015), Countering Harmful Tax Practices More Effectively, Taking into Account Transparency and Substance - Action 5: 2015 Final Report.
OECD (2015), Preventing the Granting of Treaty Benefits in Inappropriate Circumstances - Action 6: 2015 Final Report.
OECD (2015), Preventing the Artificial Avoidance of Permanent Establishment Status - Action 7: 2015 Final Report.
OECD (2015), Aligning Transfer Pricing Outcomes with Value Creation - Actions 8-10: 2015 Final Reports.
OECD (2015), Measuring and Monitoring BEPS - Action 11: 2015 Final Report.
OECD (2015), Transfer Pricing Documentation and Country-by-Country Reporting - Action 13: 2015 Final Report.
OECD (2016), Wirksamere Bekämpfung schädlicher Steuerpraktiken unter Berücksichtigung von Transparenz und Substanz: Aktionspunkt 5 - Abschlussbericht 2015.
OECD (2017), OECD Transfer Pricing Guidelines for Multinational Enterprises and Tax Administrations 2017.
OECD (2017), Country-by-Country Reporting - Handbook on Effective Tax Risk Assessment.
OECD (2017), Harmful Tax Practices - 2017 Progress Report on Preferential Regimes.
OECD (2017), 2017 Update to the OECD Model Tax Convention.
OECD (2018), Tax Challenges Arising from Digitalisation - Interim Report 2018.

OECD (2018), Harmful Tax Practices – Peer Review Results on Preferential Regimes (available at http://www.oecd.org/tax/beps/update-harmful-tax-practices-2017-progress-report-on-preferential-regimes.pdf).

OECD (2018), Resumption of Application of Substantial Activities Factor to No or only Nominal Tax Jurisdictions.

OECD (2019), Addressing the Tax Challenges of the Digitalisation of the Economy – Policy Note.

OECD (2019), Harmful Tax Practices – 2018 Progress Report on Preferential Regimes.

OECD (2019), Addressing the Tax Challenges of the Digitalisation of the Economy.

OECD (2019), Programme of Work to Develop a Consensus Solution to the Tax Challenges Arising from the Digitalisation of the Economy.

OECD (2019), Secretariat Proposal for a 'Unified Approach' under Pillar One.

OECD (2019), Substantial Activities in No or Only Nominal Tax Jurisdictions: Guidance for the Spontaneous Exchange of Information.

OECD (2019), Global Anti-Base Erosion Proposal ('GloBE') – Pillar Two.

OECD (2020), Statement by the OECD/G20 Inclusive Framework on BEPS on the Two-Pillar Approach to Address the Tax Challenges Arising from the Digitalisation of the Economy.

OECD (2020), Transfer Pricing Guidance on Financial Transactions.

OECD (2020), Public consultation document: Review of Country-by-Country Reporting (BEPS Action 13).

OECD (2020), Tax Challenges Arising from Digitalisation – Report on Pillar One Blueprint.

OECD (2020), Tax Challenges Arising from Digitalisation – Report on Pillar Two Blueprint.

OECD (2020), Harmful Tax Practices – Peer Review Results (available at https://www.oecd.org/tax/beps/harmful-tax-practices-peer-review-results-on-preferential-regimes.pdf).

OECD/Eurostat (2018), Oslo Manual 2018 – Guidelines for Collecting, Reporting and Using Data on Innovation.

Other sources

Avery Jones/Vann/Wheeler (2011), Response to the 2011 OECD Discussion Draft 'Clarification of the Meaning of "Beneficial Owner" in the OECD Model Tax Convention' (available at http://www.oecd.org/tax/treaties/48420432.pdf).

Cayman Islands Tax Information Authority, Economic Substance for Geographically Mobile Activities – Guidance (2020) 10, available at http://www.tia.gov.ky/pdf/Economic_Substance_-_Guidance_-_v2.0.pdf.

Duhigg/Kocieniewski, How Apple Sidesteps Billions in Taxes, New York Times, April 28, 2012.

Evers/Miller/Spengel, Intellectual Property Box Regimes: Effective Tax Rates and Tax Policy Considerations, ZEW Discussion Paper No. 13-070 (2013) (available at http://ftp.zew.de/pub/zew-docs/dp/dp13070.pdf).

EC (2010), Europe 2020: A strategy for smart, sustainable and inclusive growth.

EC (2014), A Study on R&D Tax Incentives: Final Report.

Germany/UK (2014), Joint Statement: Proposals for New Rules for Preferential IP Regimes (available at https://assets.publishing.service.gov.uk/government/uploads/system/uploads/attachment_data/file/373135/GERMANY_UK_STATEMENT.pdf).

G20 (2012), Leaders Declaration, Los Cabos, Mexico.

Ocean Tomo (2015), Annual Study of Intangible Asset Market Value (available at *http://www.oceantomo.com/2015/03/04/2015-intangible-asset-market-value-study/*).

Sanz-Gómez (2015), The OECD's Nexus Approach to IP Boxes: A European Union Law Perspective, WU International Taxation Research Paper Series No. 2015 - 12 (available at https://papers.ssrn.com/sol3/Delivery.cfm/SSRN_ID2589065_code1908122.pdf?abstractid=2589065&mirid=1).

Schwarz (2015), Are legal rights irrelevant for transfer pricing after BEPS Actions 8, 9 and 10?, Kluwer International Tax Blog (available at *http://kluwertaxblog.com/2015/11/15/are-legal-rights-irrelevant-for-transfer-pricing-after-beps-actions-8-9-and-10/*).

United Nations Economic and Social Council, Note by the Coordinator of the Subcommittee on Improper Use of treaties: Proposed amendments - Addendum: Progress Report of Subcommittee on Improper Use of Tax Treaties: Beneficial Ownership, E/C.18/2008/CRP.2/Add.1 (2008) (available at https://www.un.org/esa/ffd/wp-content/uploads/2014/10/4STM_EC18_2008_CRP2_Add1.pdf).

Van Raad (2011), Report on Beneficial ownership under the OECD Model Convention and Commentaries (available at *http://ibdt.org.br/material/arquivos/Atas/jfb_20111020093958.pdf*).

Judgments

United States Tax Court, 5. 8. 1971, 56 TC 925, Aiken Industries, Inc. v. Commissioner of Internal Revenue.

England and Wales Court of Appeal, 2. 3. 2006, A3/2005/2497, Indofood International Finance Ltd. v. JPMorgan Chase Bank NA, London Branch.

French Supreme Administrative Court (Conseil d'État), 29. 12. 2006, No. 283314, Bank of Scotland v. Ministre de l'Economie, des Finances et de l'Industrie.

Spanish Central Economic-Administrative Court (Tribunal Económico Administrativo Central), 22. 9. 2000, RG 6294/1996.

Spanish National Court (Audiencia Nacional), 18. 7. 2006, 1110/2003, Real Madrid F.C. v. Oficina Nacional de Inspección.

Swiss Federal Supreme Court, 16. 12. 2019, 2C_209/2017, A. Sàrl v. Eidgenössische Steuerverwaltung.

Tax Court of Canada, 22. 4. 2008, 2008 TCC 231, Prévost Car Inc. v. Her Majesty the Queen.

Tax Court of Canada, 24. 2. 2012, 2012 TCC 57, Velcro Canada Inc. v. Her Majesty the Queen.

High Court of Eastern Denmark (Østre Landsret), 20. 12. 2011, B-2152-10, ISS A/S (DK HoldCo) v. Skat.

Index

S

T

U

V

SERIES ON INTERNATIONAL TAXATION

1. Alberto Xavier, *The Taxation of Foreign Investment in Brazil,* 1980 (ISBN 90-200-0582-0).
2. Hugh J. Ault & Albert J. Rädler, *The German Corporation Tax Law with 1980 Amendments,* 1981 (ISBN 90-200-0642-8).
3. Paul R. McDaniel & Hugh J. Ault, *Introduction to United States International Taxation,* 1981 (ISBN 90-6544-004-6).
4. Albert J. Rädler, *German Transfer Pricing/Prix de Transfer en Allemagne,* 1984 (ISBN 90-6544-143-3).
5. Paul R. McDaniel & Stanley S. Surrey, *International Aspects of Tax Expenditures: A Comparative Study,* 1985 (ISBN 90-654-4163-8).
6. Kees van Raad, *Nondiscrimination in International Tax Law,* 1986 (ISBN 90-6544-266-9).
7. Sijbren Cnossen (ed.), *Tax Coordination in the European Community,* 1987 (ISBN 90-6544-272-3).
8. Ben Terra, *Sales Taxation. The Case of Value Added Tax in the European Community,* 1989 (ISBN 90-6544-381-9).
9. Rutsel S.J. Martha, *The Jurisdiction to Tax in International Law: Theory and Practice of Legislative Fiscal Jurisdiction,* 1989 (ISBN 90-654-4416-5).
10. Paul R. McDaniel & Hugh J. Ault, *Introduction to United States International Taxation* (3rd revised edition), 1989 (ISBN 90-6544-423-8).
11. Manuel Pires, *International Juridicial Double Taxation of Income,* 1989 (ISBN 90-6544-426-2).
12. A.H.M. Daniels, *Issues in International Partnership Taxation,* 1991 (ISBN 90-654-4577-3).
13. Arvid A. Skaar, *Permanent Establishment: Erosion of a Tax Treaty Principle,* 1992 (ISBN 90-6544-594-3).
14. Cyrille David & Geerten M.M. Michielse (eds), *Tax Treatment of Financial Instruments,* 1996 (ISBN 90-654-4666-4).
15. Herbert H. Alpert & Kees van Raad (eds), *Essays on International Taxation,* 1993 (ISBN 90-654-4781-4).
16. Wolfgang Gassner, Michael Lang & Eduard Lechner (eds), *Tax Treaties and EC Law,* 1997 (ISBN 90-411-0680-4).
17. Glória Teixeira, *Taxing Corporate Profits in the EU,* 1997 (ISBN 90-411-0703-7).
18. Michael Lang et al. (eds), *Multilateral Tax Treaties,* 1998 (ISBN 90-411-0704-5).
19. Stef van Weeghel, *The Improper Use of Tax Treaties,* 1998 (ISBN 90-411-0737-1).

20. Klaus Vogel (ed.), *Interpretation of Tax Law and Treaties and Transfer Pricing in Japan and Germany*, 1998 (ISBN 90-411-9655-2).
21. Bertil Wiman (ed.), *International Studies in Taxation: Law and Economics; Liber Amicorum Leif Mutén*, 1999 (ISBN 90-411-9692-7).
22. Alfonso J. Martín Jiménez, *Towards Corporate Tax Harmonization in the European Community*, 1999 (ISBN 90-411-9690-0).
23. Ramon J. Jeffery, *The Impact of State Sovereignty on Global Trade and International Taxation*, 1999 (ISBN 90-411-9703-6).
24. A.J. Easson, *Taxation of Foreign Direct Investment*, 1999 (ISBN 90-411-9741-9).
25. Marjaana Helminen, *The Dividend Concept in International Tax Law: Dividend Payments Between Corporate Entities*, 1999 (ISBN 90-411-9765-6).
26. Paul Kirchhof, Moris Lehner, Kees van Raad, Arndt Raupach & Michael-Rodi (eds), *International and Comparative Taxation: Essays in Honour of Klaus Vogel*, 2002 (ISBN 90-411-9841-5).
27. Krister Andersson, Peter Melz & Christer Silfverberg (eds), *Liber Amicorum Sven-Olof Lodin*, 2001 (ISBN 90-411-9850-4).
28. Juan Martín Jovanovich, *Customs Valuation and Transfer Pricing: Is It Possible to Harmonize Customs and Tax Rules?*, Second Edition, 2018 (ISBN 978-90-411-6134-5).
29. Stefano Simontacchi, *Taxation of Capital Gains under the OECD Model Convention: With Special Regard to Immovable Property*, 2007 (ISBN 978-90-411-2549-1).
30. Michael Lang, Josef Schuch, & Claus Staringer (eds), *Tax Treaty Law and EC Law*, 2007 (ISBN 978-90-411-2629-0).
31. Duncan Bentley, *Taxpayers' Rights: Theory Origin and Implementation*, 2007 (ISBN 978-90-411-2650-4).
32. Sergio André Rocha, *Interpretation of Double Taxation Conventions: General Theory and Brazilian Perspective*, 2008 (ISBN 978-90-411-2822-5).
33. Robert F. van Brederode, *Systems of General Sales Taxation: Theory, Policy and Practice*, 2009 (ISBN 978-90-411-2832-4).
34. John G. Head & Richard Krever (eds), *Tax Reform in the 21st Century: A Volume in Memory of Richard Musgrave*, 2009 (ISBN 978-90-411-2829-4).
35. Jens Wittendorff, *Transfer Pricing and the Arm's Length Principle in International Tax Law*, 2010 (ISBN 978-90-411-3270-3).
36. Marjaana Helminen, *The International Tax Law Concept of Dividend*, Second Edition, 2017 (ISBN 978-90-411-8394-1).
37. Robert F. van Brederode (ed.), *Immovable Property under VAT: A Comparative Global Analysis*, 2011 (ISBN 978-90-411-3126-3).
38. Dennis Weber & Stef van Weeghel, *The 2010 OECD Updates: Model Tax Convention & Transfer Pricing Guidelines - A Critical Review*, 2011 (ISBN 978-90-411-3812-5).
39. Yariv Brauner & Martin James McMahon, Jr. (eds), *The Proper Tax Base: Structural Fairness from an International and Comparative Perspective— Essays in Honour of Paul McDaniel*, 2012 (ISBN 978-90-411-3286-4).
40. Robert F. van Brederode (ed.), *Science, Technology and Taxation*, 2012 (ISBN 978-90-411-3125-6).

41. Oskar Henkow, *The VAT/GST Treatment of Public Bodies*, 2013 (ISBN 978-90-411-4663-2).
42. Jean Schaffner, *How Fixed Is a Permanent Establishment?*, 2013 (ISBN 978-90-411-4662-5).
43. Miguel Correia, *Taxation of Corporate Groups*, 2013 (ISBN 978-90-411-4841-4).
44. Veronika Daurer, *Tax Treaties and Developing Countries*, 2014 (ISBN 978-90-411-4982-4).
45. Claire Micheau, *State Aid, Subsidy and Tax Incentives under EU and WTO Law*, 2014 (ISBN 978-90-411-4555-0).
46. Robert F. van Brederode & Richard Krever (eds), *Legal Interpretation of Tax Law*, 2014 (ISBN 978-90-411-4945-9).
47. Radhakishan Rawal, *Taxation of Cross-border Services*, 2014 (ISBN 978-90-411-4947-3).
48. João Dácio Rolim, *Proportionality and Fair Taxation*, 2014 (ISBN 978-90-411-5838-3).
49. Paulo Rosenblatt, *General Anti-avoidance Rules for Major Developing Countries*, 2015 (ISBN 978-90-411-5839-0).
50. Gaspar Lopes Dias V.S., *Tax Arbitrage through Cross-Border Financial Engineering*, 2015 (ISBN 978-90-411-5875-8).
51. Geerten M.M. Michielse & Victor Thuronyi (eds), *Tax Design Issues Worldwide*, 2015 (ISBN 978-90-411-5610-5).
52. Oktavia Weidmann, *Taxation of Derivatives*, 2015 (ISBN 978-90-411-5977-9).
53. Chris Evans, Richard Krever & Peter Mellor (eds), *Tax Simplification*, 2015 (ISBN 978-90-411-5976-2).
54. Reuven Avi-Yonah & Joel Slemrod (eds), *Taxation and Migration*, 2015 (ISBN 978-90-411-6136-9).
55. Alexander Bosman, *Other Income under Tax Treaties: An Analysis of Article 21 of the OECD Model Convention*, 2015 (ISBN 978-90-411-6610-4).
56. John Abrahamson, *International Taxation of Manufacturing and Distribution*, 2016 (ISBN 978-90-411-6664-7).
57. Frederik Boulogne, *Shortcomings in the EU Merger Directive*, 2016 (ISBN 978-90-411-6713-2).
58. Angelika Meindl-Ringler, *Beneficial Ownership in International Tax Law*, 2016 (ISBN 978-90-411-6833-7).
59. Andreas Waltrich, *Cross-Border Taxation of Permanent Establishments: An International Comparison*, 2016 (ISBN 978-90-411-6832-0).
60. Sergio André Rocha & Allison Christians (eds), *Tax Sovereignty in the BEPS Era*, 2017 (ISBN 978-90-411-6707-1).
61. Peter Antony Wilson, *BRICS and International Tax Law*, 2018 (ISBN 978-90-411-9435-0).
62. Louise Otis, Brigitte Alepin & Blanca Moreno-Dodson (eds), *Winning the Tax Wars: Tax Competition and Cooperation*, 2018 (ISBN 978-90-411-9460-2).
63. Marta Castelon, *International Taxation of Income from Services under Double Taxation Conventions: Development, Practice and Policy*, 2018 (ISBN 978-90-411-9594-4).

64. D.M. Broekhuijsen, *A Multilateral Tax Treaty: Designing an Instrument to Modernise International Tax Law*, 2018 (ISBN 978-90-411-9872-3).
65. John Abrahamson, *International Taxation of Energy Production and Distribution*, 2018 (ISBN 978-90-411-9101-4).
66. Leopoldo Parada, *Double Non-taxation and the Use of Hybrid Entities: An Alternative Approach in the New Era of BEPS*, 2018 (ISBN 978-90-411-9991-1).
67. Richard Snoeij, *International Tax Aspects of Sovereign Wealth Investors: A Source State Perspective*, 2018 (ISBN 978-90-411-9431-2).
68. Aleksandra Bal, *Taxation, Virtual Currency and Blockchain*, 2019 (ISBN 978-94-035-0103-1).
69. Werner Haslehner, Georg Kofler, Katerina Pantazatou & Alexander Rust (eds), *Tax and the Digital Economy: Challenges and Proposals for Reform*, 2019 (ISBN 978-94-035-0361-5).
70. Eva Escribano, *Jurisdiction to Tax Corporate Income Pursuant to the Presumptive Benefit Principle: A Critical Analysis of Structural Paradigms Underlying Corporate Income Taxation and Proposals for Reform*, 2019 (ISBN 978-94-035-0640-1).
71. Jérôme Monsenego & Jan Bjuvberg (eds), *International Taxation in a Changing Landscape: Liber Amicorum in Honour of Bertil Wiman*, 2019 (ISBN 978-90-411-9234-9).
72. Kasper Dziurdź, *Non-discrimination in Tax Treaty Law and World Trade Law: The Impact of Formal, Substantive and Subjective Approaches*, 2019 (ISBN 978-94-035-0904-4).
73. Félix Daniel Martínez Laguna, *Hybrid Financial Instruments, Double Nontaxation and Linking Rules*, 2019 (ISBN 978-94-035-1074-3).
74. Jan Gooijer, *Tax Treaty Residence of Entities*, 2019 (ISBN 978-94-035-1301-0).
75. John Abrahamson, *International Taxation of Banking*, 2020 (ISBN 978-94-035-1094-1).
76. Richard Krever & François Vaillancourt (eds), *The Allocation of Multinational Business Income: Reassessing the Formulary Apportionment Option*, 2020 (ISBN 978-94-035-0614-2).
77. Ajit Kumar Singh, *Exploring the Nexus Doctrine in International Tax Law*, 2021 (ISBN 978-94-035-3363-6).
78. Galya Savir, *Regulation and Tax in Space*, 2021 (ISBN 978-94-035-3393-3).
79. Rita Julien, *Credit Method Compatibility and Constraints under EU Law: An Analysis of the Case Law of the CJEU*, 2022 (ISBN 978-94-035-2363-7).
80. Sergio André Rocha & Allison Christians (eds), *A Multilateral Convention for Tax: From Theory to Implementation*, 2022 (ISBN 978-90-411-9428-2).
81. Brigitte Alepin, Lyne Latulippe & Louise Otis (eds), *Coordination and Cooperation: Tax Policy in the 21st Century*, 2022 (ISBN 978-94-035-3740-5).
82. Chunyang Zhang, *The Role of Tax Law in Mergers and Acquisitions: A Chinese Perspective*, 2022 (ISBN 978-94-035-3741-2).
83. Florian Navisotschnigg, *Substance in International Tax Law: DEMPE Approach, Substantial Activity Requirement and Beneficial Ownership*, 2022 (978-94-035-4895-1).

www.ingramcontent.com/pod-product-compliance
Ingram Content Group UK Ltd.
Pitfield, Milton Keynes, MK11 3LW, UK
UKHW020817290926
15470UKWH00003B/1211

9 789403 548951